DATE DUE

#47-0108 Peel Off Pressure Sensitive

DOUBLE LIFE

The 'official' MGM portrait, c. 1950

DOUBLE LIFE

The Autobiography of
Miklós Rózsa

Foreword by Antal Doráti

MIDAS BOOKS

HIPPOCRENE BOOKS

For Margaret, Juliet and Nicholas

RES SEVERA VERUM GAUDIUM

First published in U.K. in 1982 by
MIDAS BOOKS
12 Dene Way, Speldhurst, Tunbridge Wells,
Kent TN3 0NX

ISBN 0 85936 209 4 (U.K.)

Copyright © Miklós Rózsa 1982
Designed by David Morley-Clarke

Book production for the publisher by
Chambers Green Ltd., Tunbridge Wells, Kent

First published in U.S.A. in 1982 by
HIPPOCRENE BOOKS INC
171 Madison Avenue, New York, N.Y. 10016

ISBN 0 88256 688 X (U.S.)

Printed by Great Britain by
Camelot Press, Southampton

Contents

Acknowledgements

Thanks are due to the following organisations or individuals for supplying illustrations:

Brian Jewell, The British Film Institute, Maurice Zam, Nicholas and Juliet Rózsa, Paramount Pictures, MGM Pictures, Derek Elley, RCA Records, The George Arents Research Library (Syracuse University, N.Y.), John W. Waxman, David Meeker, Richard Combs, the Hulton Picture Library.

Foreword

by Antal Doráti

The author of this book and I are old and close friends. Our paths, following our lives' respective patterns, seldom converge, yet we stay and remain near each other — by correspondence. We write frequently, old-fashioned, long, copious letters — in longhand — touching upon a great variety of subjects: first and foremost music, but also politics, people, literature, the fine arts and so forth. This we do year in, year out, as our natural way of communication.

So, when asked to introduce this volume of his memoirs — a request which honours me and which I grant with the greatest of pleasure — it comes quite naturally for me to cast my introductory words into the form of a letter to my

Dear Miki,

A few minutes ago I finished reading the galley proofs of your book. I waited long enough, but it was worth waiting for. As I now begin to write, I am in that state of stimulation my reading has brought about; I feel personally, privately, addressed, as if I had read one of your letters. It is, indeed, a curious thought that, this time, I shall have to share your news with many thousands of 'others'.

The last few pages of the book yielded the greatest surprise: your staggering work-register. As a well-behaved reader I reached it, as was right and proper, at the end — and I was and remain 'Spellbound' (with a capital 'S', of course, in your particular case). I knew that you had composed a great amount of music, but even to me the true bulk of your *oeuvre* remained, until this minute, somehow undefined.

Accordingly, I must tell you that your chosen title — *Double Life* — is a misnomer. Come on, confess, Miki — how many other lives must you have had to write all that music?

I can see your half-amused, half-embarrassed smile as you try to formulate an answer that will effectively minimise your achievement, so I shall help you: in fact, you have lived only *one* life, but a completely dedicated one — dedicated to nothing else but music, music alone, in many — not only two — of its facets.

This is evident also in your book, which is — severely analysed and in its essential aspect — a tersely, but very entertainingly and illuminatingly, given account, not of yourself or your life but of — your music.

That it contains so much information concerning your environment — indeed a wide landscape, much of it new even to me, your friend and fellow-musician — is the book's very special merit; all of it nicely, undemonstratively and appetizingly served up as 'asides', or 'encores', if you will.

During the period of our youth, before we met — curiously we never knew each other in Hungary, where as children we were for a while in the same music school, in the same building, at the same time — your Uncle Lajos proudly brought one of your compositions to my father for his opinion. The two were colleagues in the Budapest Philharmonic Orchestra, both violinists.

I was, by chance, present at that meeting.

After careful perusal of the score, my father said: 'This is truly excellent . . .', adding, thoughtfully, after a grave moment of silence, '. . . but how will he make his living?'

Time proved that his worry was unnecessary.

And you could not have shown him how unnecessary it was more succinctly, more precisely and more modestly than you have in your *Double Life*.

May you go on to add many new chapters to the one or the other — or both.

        Affectionately,
          Yours
              Tóni

Prologue

In 1947 I wrote the music for a film entitled *A Double Life*; in it an actor playing Othello (Ronald Colman) becomes obsessed by the part to the point of murdering the woman he imagines to be Desdemona. In other words he allows two quite independent strands of his life to become enmeshed, and tragedy is the outcome. Now this is precisely what I have always been at pains to ensure did *not* happen in the case of my own professional life. My 'public' career as composer for films ran alongside my 'private' development as composer for myself, or at least for non-utilitarian purposes: two parallel lines, and in the interests of both my concern has always been to prevent them meeting. Of course some contact was unavoidable, but in the main I am convinced that, for me, it was best that they be kept apart. This has been the dominant theme of my creative career, and is therefore the theme of this book.

I dictated the bulk of these memoirs into cassettes — some thirty hours' worth — in my holiday retreat on the Italian Riviera over a period of several summers. But English is not my mother tongue, and though for all practical purposes I have been able to make myself understood in it for over forty years, I realised that writing my life story in it would be another matter. Now it is an open secret that the original French versions of Stravinsky's autobiography *Chronique de ma vie* and of his *Poetics of Music* (*Poétique musicale*) were not his own unaided work. Of course the thoughts and ideas were his, but in order to express them in lucid and elegant French he sought the help of his friend and loyal admirer Roland-Manuel. Yet the fact of this collaboration was nowhere acknowledged in print. For my own part I see no point in making a secret, open or otherwise, of my indebtedness to Christopher Palmer for taking upon himself the main editorial burden of this work, and for co-ordinating the efforts of his admirable team of co-workers: Dorothy Bloomfield, Michael Bradburn, Anthony Bremner, Jill Burrows, Derek Elley, Alan Hamer and Josephine Steward. Alan Hamer also compiled the complete list of works and collaborated with Frank DeWald on the discography. For many helpful comments and suggestions I have to thank Messrs Abraham Marcus, Hans J. Salter and members of my family; and I take due paternal pride in acknowledging the help of my son Nicholas in the preparation of the illustrations, and of my daughter Juliet who was responsible for the index.

Santa Margherita Ligure
Summer 1981 **M.R.**

c. 1915

1: *Childhood in Hungary*

We all carry within ourselves the individual influences of our two parents. I feel this particularly strongly in my own case, for my parents came from two distinct cultural backgrounds. My father, a successful land-owning industrialist, came from the country: he had been born in the small Hungarian town of Tamási, in the county of Tolna. But my mother was born in Budapest and her background was therefore urban, while my father's was rural.

My father was a good man, upright and honest. At the beginning of this century he was very concerned with socialist ideals and was influenced partly by Tolstoy and partly by the Fabianism of Bernard Shaw and the Webbs. He had high-minded ethical principles and felt deeply the poverty of the Hungarian peasants and the hopelessness of their situation. He lived among them, loved them and fought for them. I was born in Budapest (on 18 April 1907), and so it was only later that I got to know these people, but I am sure I owe my love of them — which led, in due course, to my discovery of their music — to my father.

Before I was born, my father wrote a book called *To Whom Does the Hungarian Soil Belong?*, in which he demonstrated that the Hungarian peasants, the very people who should own the land, had no legal rights to it whatsoever. He had taken up politics in order to remedy this. He stood for parliament, but was not elected — which remained a sore point with him all his life. I remember one occasion in the country when he sat in a forest clearing talking to twenty or thirty of his employees — peasants — about their way of life, our way of life, and about politics. It was like the Sermon on the Mount, and the people listened to him as though he were preaching. I was very young, but it made a strong impression on me, especially when one of the more intelligent peasants stood up and said, 'You ought to be in Parliament. You could do wonders for us there.' I can still see his wry smile. He tried, but to no avail.

My love of music I owe to my mother. She had wanted to become a pianist, and before she met my father had studied at the Budapest Academy with Aggh·zy and Thomán, both of whom had been pupils of Liszt. Bartók was two classes ahead of my mother, but Professor Thomán often asked him, his star pupil, to come and play for the younger students. My father attended the graduation concert at which my mother played the Mozart D minor Concerto. They were soon married and it was not long before I arrived. (My sister Edith was born seven years later.) That momentous event was more or less the end of my mother's projected career as a pianist.

Presumably the earliest surviving picture

My father had always loved music, but it was not until his marriage that he came to know anything of 'highbrow' music; he enjoyed Hungarian folksongs and often sang them, and probably these were the first musical sounds I was exposed to.

The preferred composer in our home when I was a boy was Liszt. As I have said, my mother's teachers were pupils of Liszt, and his more popular piano music — the *Hungarian Rhapsodies*, the *Liebesträume*, *Consolations* and the rest — was in her repertoire. To please my father she played operatic excerpts — Puccini was a great favourite — and contemporary ballet music, for instance *Die Puppenfee*, a ballet by Joseph Bayer, the Austrian ballet composer and conductor. When I was taken (aged five) to see this ballet I fell in love with the magnificent 'Puppenfee' (doll-fairy) and wanted to take her home.

The extraordinary thing was that throughout my youth I never heard my mother, who after all was an accomplished musician with a diploma from the Academy, play a Beethoven or a Mozart sonata, let alone anything by Bach. Brahms was known, but not much appreciated; he was thought grey, heavy and Germanic. In fact the flashy and superficial salon music of the Hubay school — Jenö Hubay was the director of the Academy — corruptly conditioned the entire musical taste of Budapest. Gypsy music was everywhere, then as now. Every single town and village had its gypsy bands, good, bad and indifferent, all playing the same repertoire. In 1974 I returned to Hungary for the first time in 43 years and every restaurant we entered still had its gypsy musicians. And what were they playing? Gershwin's 'Summertime', excerpts from Lehár and Kálmán operettas, and the kind of pseudo-traditional Hungarian music written by amateurs over a hundred years ago, the same music that provided the raw material for Liszt and Brahms to use in their Hungarian rhapsodies and dances. This is apparently the music that Hungarians returning from the West wish to hear.

I was five years old when I started to learn the violin. My great-uncle Lajos was going to Paris one summer and he asked me what he should bring back for me. I asked for a violin — not a toy one, a *real* one! And when he came back he did bring me a violin, small, perhaps quarter-size, but real, and I started to learn to play it right away. I don't think I ever had any ambitions to become a virtuoso performer, but simply making music was a great pleasure to me, and at that time it was an all-absorbing hobby. When I was about seven years old I appeared in public dressed as Mozart or Haydn; I played a piece by Mozart and led Haydn's Toy Symphony. I conducted the performance and also played first violin, so I felt tremendously important. I still have a photo taken of me in my silk jacket, the Beau Brummel of Budapest, the youngest arbiter of fashion.

When I entered my private elementary school at the age of six, I could read music but not words. My musical aspirations were already well-developed, and the hours I spent with my violin were much more interesting than those devoted to arithmetic or other school subjects. I was even more interested in the piano, but it was not until I entered the Leipzig Conservatory that I had any formal tuition on this instrument.

Eventually I began to play, to improvise — something I loved to do — and to

With my mother and father *c.* 1910

The Beau Brummel of Budapest

Budapest from the Danube around the time I was born (painting by Mednyánszky)

compose little pieces. I still have one composition I wrote at the age of seven, called 'Student March'. My next piece depicted the Amusement Park in Budapest, the Városliget. My family gave me no encouragement as they feared my school work would suffer. They looked on music as a pleasant pastime, not as a profession.

When I was ten my parents had to decide which kind of high school I should be sent to. I had no say in the matter. There were two kinds: the 'Gymnasium' which taught a classical curriculum, including Latin and Greek, and the 'Realgymnasium' where you could study modern languages such as German and French. It was generally thought advisable to go to the 'Gymnasium' if you wanted to be a doctor, lawyer or scientist because you would need Latin later. I showed no inclination towards medicine or the law, and my parents, being practical people, thought that modern languages would be of more use to me than Greek or Latin. So I went to the 'Realgymnasium'. I can see now that this was a fatal mistake. Certainly I was taught French and German, but so poorly that, although I could recite reams of poetry by Goethe or Corneille, when it came to visiting the country and speaking the language I couldn't string two words together.

For eight years I was completely and utterly bored. Then, in my fifteenth year, a music teacher called Peregrin Turry was appointed. He was an excellent musician who played oboe in the Philharmonic Orchestra and in the Opera, and taught at the Academy. Now throughout my twelve years at the school I was never taught music and the arts were never mentioned at all. I never heard the names Bach, Mozart, Beethoven, Leonardo, Michelangelo, Raphael or Rembrandt. In the 'Realgymnasium' the accent was on the 'real' and one learnt about realistic, practical

c. 1925, Budapest   Bartók as a student

things. I was, however, lucky enough to be a member of the school orchestra, and it was not long before I became the leader of the violin section and got to know Professor Turry better. He took an interest in me and discovered that I was not a bad musician and even had the makings of a good one.

At about the same time I became orchestral librarian. My job was to look after all the music, and I often came across works published by Breitkopf & Härtel. I had an intimation that one day I might write a work which would be published by Breitkopf & Härtel. I remember looking at the list of composers' names on the back of a score and printing my own name after Julius Röntgen's with the title of a piece I had just composed, hoping that some day my dream would come true. Well, it did, and sooner than I could ever have anticipated.

As President of the Franz Liszt Music Circle of our school I was required to make a speech at a concert of Hungarian music I organised and, as so often in later life, I put both feet in it at once. My speech was entitled 'The History of Hungarian Music', and I set out to give an account of Hungarian composers of the past, declaring them all mediocre. That, apparently, was an extremely unpatriotic viewpoint. I then drew to the conclusion that Hungarian music had produced only two composers of outstanding quality, Béla Bartók and Zoltán Kodály. In 1924 these were dangerous sentiments in a school where music by Bartók and Kodály was seldom played and certainly not understood.

But it was too late, the programmes were printed and the concert scheduled. Of course we had no virtuoso pianists or instrumentalists within the school and so we could not play the most difficult of these composers' works. We had chosen a

15

Endre Ady

number of little pieces from Bartók's *For Children*, basically folksongs in Bartók's own settings and harmonisations. Today they seem the most innocuous pieces imaginable, but at the time they were quite revolutionary.

The next day the Principal called me into his office. He told me he had great respect for my talent, but that the previous day's concert had been a fiasco and that Bartók and Kodály were not fit to be performed before such an august assembly. I tried to argue my case with him, but I soon saw that we were getting nowhere. We were talking in different languages, of different worlds. He said that on this occasion he would overlook the disrespect we had shown him, his staff and the public, but he warned me that such a thing must never happen again. I was dismissed.

My readers should remember that although Bartók had been researching Hungarian peasant music for some twenty years and had for some time been basing his own compositions on its assimilated essence, the resulting idiom was still too unfamiliar to win general acceptance. Earlier, composers like Erkel, Liszt and

Mosonyi had tried to invest their music with an authentic Hungarianism but had succeeded merely in masking its basic Western-European orientation with the tawdriness of the *Verbunkos*, a type of Hungarian functional dance of eighteenth-century origin which, when corrupted by gypsy and other extraneous influences, gave rise to the much-favoured pseudo-national style which Bartók renounced when he came to discover — and uncover — the *real* music of Hungary's peasants. This vast reservoir remained unknown to or ignored by nineteenth-century composers until Bartók and Kodály began their research. Before that, Liszt's declared attitude was typical: Magyar folksongs were regarded as perversions or distortions of gypsy instrumental prototypes. No doubt if Bartók had never chanced upon Magyar peasant music he would have continued the neo- or pseudo-Hungarian tradition of Liszt; and no doubt much the same thing would have happened to me.

All through those early years I was composing, wildly and badly, with no tuition of any kind. I continued my violin studies, but I knew that I could never become a professional violinist, first because I had insufficient talent and secondly because I was not interested in practice for its own sake. A piece of music would hold my interest until I knew it; but thenceforth memorising passages and learning fingerings and bowings seemed a complete waste of time. However, I played through all the standard repertoire, including the one concerto every violinist in Hungary had to play: Karl Goldmark's. It is a very nice piece, if greatly influenced by his friend Brahms. Goldmark was born in Hungary, but lived all his life in Vienna; and his *Queen of Sheba* was one of the best-known operas in the repertoire of the Vienna and Budapest Opera Houses, although not much performed elsewhere. He was as overrated in his lifetime as he is underrated now.

I was still having no coaching in music theory. When I said that I would like to have a tutor or even go to the conservatory full-time, my father always replied that my grades in school were so bad that I had no time to spare for anything but school work. One Christmas, however, when I was about sixteen, I asked him for copies of whatever textbooks on composition were in use at the Academy of Music. For years those books were the only ones I studied, and thereby gained a general idea of the rudiments of composition.

At that time I was setting poem after poem by the great Symbolist poet Endre Ady, who was probably the greatest influence on me in my early years; and in due course I had a song performed in one of our school concerts, the first time a work of mine was performed in public. It was a setting of a beautiful poem by Ady about solitude and the sea ('Alone with the Sea'). Later I discovered that it had also been set by Bartók (as one of his *Five Songs*, op. 16), though at the time I was unaware of the fact.

On one occasion our school's 'Franz Liszt Music Circle' held a competition for an original composition. I wrote a patriotic poem called *Hungarian Twilight* about the dismembering of our country after the First World War. Millions of Hungarians were forced to live in neighbouring countries, and my poem said more or less that one day all this would change, the twilight would pass and once again we would be the great and glorious Hungary of pre-war days. I won the competition with my setting of this poem. I still possess the manuscript with Professor Turry's report written on it: 'The composer of this small work shows a definite talent for composition'. It went on to say that as yet I had little idea of how to handle my material; but here was a testimonial from a professional musician to the effect that I was 'one of the rare breed who might become composers'. I was overjoyed. From that moment on I felt like a real composer. I had, after all, won a competition.

After this success Turry somehow regarded me as a professional colleague. Without his protection I don't think I would have completed my normal schooling, but he saw all my teachers and explained that music was to be my career, a career in which physics and algebra would not figure prominently. For once I wholeheartedly accepted the otherwise despised Hungarian *protekció*, which, roughly translated, means 'preferential treatment', 'influence', 'nepotism' or 'knowing the right people'.

The Academy was only about ten minutes' walk from where we lived, opposite the Opera, and I was able to go to most of the concerts there. I attended all the Philharmonic concerts conducted by Dohnányi, not a great conductor, but a great musician. Once when Erich Kleiber came to conduct the third Mahler Symphony I played truant all the week in order to attend the rehearsals. I had to be careful because Professor Turry played oboe in the Philharmonic and if he had seen me he would have asked me why I was not at school. Those Mahler rehearsals with Kleiber were a revelation. He was kind, understanding and ready to explain everything. He spoke German, a language the orchestra understood well. This was my first contact with a musician of this calibre.

I was also able to listen to much music by means of a fascinating machine we had in Hungary but does not seem to be known anywhere else in the world: the telephone newscaster. It had been invented by the Hungarian Tivadar Puskás and brought music and news into your home every hour, on the hour. You had to wear headphones and it worked more like a telephone than a wireless. Budapest was the only city to have it. Every evening an opera was relayed direct from the Opera House, where there were microphones on stage and in the pit, and as the year progressed you could hear the company's entire repertoire. I had a telephone newscaster fixed up in my room, and as a result I knew the operatic repertoire very well by the time I was sixteen or seventeen.

Establishment musical life in Hungary was very conservative. Hubay's second-rate lyrical operas all had to be put on. Dohnányi, of course, was much the better composer, but he too was conservative and German-oriented. His attitudes and his music were firmly rooted in the tradition of Schumann and Brahms, with a dash of Richard Strauss thrown in for modernity's sake; very musical, very agreeable and, as Stravinsky would have put it, 'very unnecessary'.

Bartók had great difficulties in getting his dramatic works staged. The trouble was that his libretti were written by people who were politically out of favour at the time. In Budapest there was a strong division of feeling for and against Bartók and Kodály, the older generation being totally opposed to them. The same people were firmly against new developments in literature and against Ady who was labelled as decadent and incomprehensible, because what he was writing was something fresh and different. The younger generation found Ady's poetry as relevant and exciting

Our country home in Nagylócz, 1922

as they found the music of Bartók and Kodály. Every time Bartók or Kodály had a premiere all we young men went to the concert to give the piece an ovation.

I was an ardent patriot. I loved my country and its people, particularly the peasants. I shall never forget the time I spent on our estate, where it made no difference that I was the future owner of a thousand acres, with all the houses and animals that went with it. I was on first-name terms with all the boys of the so-called intelligentsia in the village and with some of the peasant boys too. There were no barriers of social status or class between us; we were just boys, young Hungarians who loved our country, language and music dearly. I was always impatient to get out of the city (which I disliked) and when the time came and the exams were over I would be off.

Our family estate lay north of Budapest in a village called Nagylócz in the county of Nógrád, at the foot of the Mátra mountains. The whole area was inhabited by the Palóc, an indigenous Magyar people with their own dialect, customs and costumes (on Sundays the girls wore up to ten layers of skirts!). It was the music of the Palóc that I heard during those summers I spent on the estate and that intrigued me from my earliest childhood, although of course it wasn't until later that I realised what a vital shaping force it was proving on my own musical personality. The music was all around me; I would hear it in the fields when the people were at work, in the village as I lay awake at night; and the time came when I felt I had to try to put it down on paper and perpetuate it.

I travelled round the Palóc region. The people there were not Slovaks, and their songs show no Slovakian influences. They were strange songs, very powerful, strong in emotion and fascinating rhythmically, and I took them down. The market place was not far from our house; sometimes on Sunday evenings I would hear the peasants singing and dancing there, and I would try to transcribe what I heard. Later I would ask our employees or friends or the daughter of our next-door neighbour to sing for me, and I jotted down the melodies in a kind of delirium. I studied these songs closely and later created my own music in their image.

I was never a methodical folksong collector like Kodály or Bartók; I was interested only in the music, not in its ethnographical connotations. I had no Edison phonograph like Bartók; I just went around with a small black notebook and wrote down what I heard as best I could. I never bothered with the text, which interested me not at all. In other words as a *bona fide* folklorist I was an amateur. I sometimes played violin with the gypsies for fun, and we might join together to serenade a certain village beauty (whose name I still remember) under her window, troubadour or knight-errant style. Of course all this could happen only when my parents were away and I, as the 'young master', could engage a handful of gypsy musicians to accompany (with wrong harmonies) my fanciful improvisations. It must have sounded like nothing on earth, but the young lady in question seemed to like it, and that was the main thing. My folksong collection (now lost, alas) also included tunes from the nearby villages of Rimócz, Hollókö and others which were also inhabited by the Palóc, so their music was similar. (Incidentally the word 'Palóc' sounds in English very much like 'palowtz'. Little did I know that one day I should write my own 'Polovtzian Dances'). I incorporated songs from my collection in various early works — the *Variations on a Hungarian Peasant Song* and *North Hungarian Peasant Songs and Dances* — and in my ballet *Hungaria*. By this time the folkmusic of this area of Hungary had become an integral part of my musical language, and I found my own melodic style evolving quite spontaneously out of it. I felt this constant urge to express myself musically in the language of my patrimony and of my origins; it was a living source of inspiration. That was where my music began, and where it almost certainly will end. I have no choice in the matter and never have had. However much I may modify my style in order to write effectively for films, the music of Hungary is stamped indelibly one way or other on virtually every bar I have ever put on paper.

2: *Leipzig*

I finished school in 1925. I took my Matura degree and could now go on to higher education. My father was in the fortunate financial position of being able to send me wherever I wanted, and he suggested that I go to the University of Budapest and take chemistry. The problem was not that I was not interested in chemistry, but that I was, of course, far more interested in music. My father and I discussed it at great length and he cited many cases to show how impossible it was to make a living out of composing music. In a way he was right. But at eighteen I was desperate to be a composer and full of ideas, and it was difficult for me to see his point of view. Moreover, I did not like the people of Budapest and had wanted to break away from it for a long time. It was a town full of tension and hatred and petty jealousy. There was very little privacy and everyone seemed to want to know everyone else's affairs, and whether the other person was more successful — in business, in love or whatever — than he was himself. Professional jealousy I can understand — I have seen enough of that in Hollywood — but ill-feelings were much more intense in Budapest, and even at the age of eighteen it was enough to make me wish to leave.

Great talents have been born in Hungary — Nobel prize-winners, playwrights, film-makers, painters, composers — but many have found it necessary to live elsewhere to gain the recognition they deserve, or sometimes simply to make a living. I often think of the great play by Imre Madách, the nineteenth-century Hungarian poet and dramatist, *The Tragedy of Man*. It is based on the Faust legend and starts with Adam and Eve and finishes with the end of the world. The world gradually shrinks until finally life is possible only at the North Pole, and in a scene with Eskimos one asks the other why life is so difficult. The answer is 'There are too many Eskimos and not enough seals'. It has gone into the language as a catch-phrase and sums up life in Budapest at that time very well: in other words, too many talents and not enough opportunities. I sensed that I needed a wider framework in which to develop and that I would never be happy so long as I was forced to remain in Budapest. Eventually my father and I compromised: I would go to Leipzig, to take chemistry as my main subject at the University, and musicology (not, alas, composition) as a subsidiary study.

Later my father compromised further. I would study chemistry at the University and music at the Conservatory simultaneously.

After Budapest, Leipzig seemed a small town, and of course, compared with the major German cities like Berlin or Munich, it *is* small, and quite dominated by the University and the Conservatory. Academics and musicians were everywhere and in abundance. The big publishing houses for both literature and music, including Breitkopf & Härtel, were situated in Leipzig. It was an enchanting sleepy little town, but because there were so few old buildings left it was not very beautiful. Yet Goethe liked it and called it his 'small Paris': 'My Leipzig calls for praise; it is a small Paris and moulds and shapes its people.' There were two fine large parks, and in summer they smelt strangely of garlic. Legend had it that a failed composer who had studied at the Conservatory a hundred years before had taken his revenge on the town by planting garlic in the public parks. It wasn't *me*, because the parks already smelt of garlic before I arrived there!

The University was one of the oldest and largest in Germany; the Conservatory had been founded by Mendelssohn, who had taught there himself, as had Schumann, Moscheles, Ferdinand David and all the major figures in music in mid-nineteenth-century Germany. The Gewandhaus was world-famous, even before Mendelssohn's time. It had a beautiful bronze statue of Mendelssohn at the entrance which the Nazis later removed. On the building there was a Latin legend: RES SEVERA VERUM GAUDIUM which became the motto of my life. There were also many old churches, among them Bach's Thomaskirche. Life revolved round these monuments and was extraordinarily pleasant. But a 'small Paris' the town was not.

Twice a year Leipzig completely changed its outward aspect when something like the big Carnival festivals in Munich or the Rhineland took place which was called the 'Messe', the Leipzig Fair. Businessmen came not just from Germany but from all over the world to see the latest industrial inventions. They would stay no longer than a week, many in private houses because there was not enough hotel accommodation. Apart from ordering cars and radios and other merchandise, they were determined to have a good time and were nicknamed 'Mess'-Onkel' ('Fair-Uncles'). The grossly overweight Germans who came for the fair were known as Bierbäuche ('Beer-bellies'), and the young, or not so young, vulgarly-dressed ladies of easy virtue who arrived at the same time were called 'Mess'-Püppchen' ('Fair-dolls'). These good ladies would parade up and down the town's two main streets, past the University, the Post Office, the Museum, the Opera and the brand new fourteen-storey skyscraper. Leipzig was extremely proud of its skyscraper, although it wouldn't look so impressive now and never scraped the sky. Its motto was: 'Omnia vincit labor'. Mind you, 'labor', not 'amor'!

I kept my word to my father and worked hard at chemistry as well as at musicology. The chemistry laboratory was in the Liebigstrasse, named after the great German scientist, Liebig. To get there I took a tram; the route took me past the imposing Breitkopf & Härtel building on the Nürnbergerstrasse and every time I went by my heart beat faster. I was much more interested in that building than in the chemistry laboratory. To some extent I took my chemistry seriously, or at least tried to. But I got much too reliant on my older Hungarian friend for help in analysis, until finally he refused point-blank to bail me out of any more of my difficulties. He told me I had to make my choice between chemistry and music; I couldn't do both. I was furious, but he explained that it was in my own best interests that he was refusing to help me, and of course he was right. Perhaps fortunately I was not at that time aware of the fact that Borodin had been no less celebrated a chemist than a composer.

Most evenings I went to musicological lectures at the University; I could not go during the day because I had to be at the laboratory. The music lectures were much more interesting, even if they were not exactly what I wanted. I took a harmony course, the first opportunity I had to study the subject. There I was, eighteen years old, wanting to be a composer, and until that point I had never been allowed to study harmony! Professor Brandes taught an elementary harmony course, and when I had enrolled I remember coming out into the Augustusplatz on a lovely evening early in October after my first lesson and jumping up and down like a happy idiot because at long last I was doing something I wanted to do.

There were many other interesting courses. One of my professors was Theodor Kroyer, a famous German musicologist, who seemed to live in the twelfth or thirteenth century. He once referred to Bach as 'a modern composer', since for him the eighteenth century was already dangerously modern. The University gave me a grounding in musicology which was to stand me in good stead later.

The greatest musical assets of life in Leipzig were the Friday evening and Saturday afternoon motets and the Sunday morning cantatas at the Thomaskirche. The Thomanerchor sang under the direction of Karl Straube, who worked as diligently with those children as had his predecessor J. S. Bach two hundred years before, and they sang like angels. Not only were all Bach's choral works performed, but so was the pre-Bach literature of Schütz, Buxtehude, Pachelbel and some of the less important composers and forerunners of Bach. Günther Ramin was the organist, and his Bach and Max Reger interpretations were unsurpassed. He was a pupil of Straube and later became his successor as Thomaskantor. Here was where the Leipzig intelligentsia met: judges from the Reichgericht (the highest German court), lawyers, doctors, painters, sculptors and, of course, the whole musical fraternity. From the music each Saturday they apparently derived enough spiritual sustenance to last them through the coming week.

During the course of that first year it became apparent to my father that my heart was only in music, and he reluctantly agreed to my abandoning chemistry; so when I returned to Leipzig in September 1926, I entered the Conservatory. Of the various composition professors, the best-known was Sigfrid Karg-Elert whose organ works are still played in England. Another was Hermann Grabner, who asked me what I had composed so far. I took out a piano trio I had written and played it through for him, and he accepted me on the spot. He said that in the future he would see to it that I stopped composing in the style of Mendelssohn. It is natural enough to have a model when one is starting to compose and since I used to play the Mendelssohn D minor Trio my piece was very much influenced by that and was highly romantic. I had gained confidence by the last movement, and some of the Hungarian folksongs I had learned from the peasant women on our estate put in an early and tentative appearance.

My studies with Grabner naturally led me towards the music of Reger, which I did not greatly like. I admired his immense contrapuntal facility but found the music uninspired, dry and too Germanic. Grabner did not expect me to imitate

Interior view of the Leipzig Conservatory

Reger's style, but he did want me to study it and benefit from its contrapuntal mastery. After a couple of months or so, when I was quite well advanced in harmony but had not yet actually started on counterpoint, Grabner asked me to compose a Sonatina for piano. I did so; he liked it and suggested I tackle something bigger, a sonata for violin and piano. I lost no time complying. I worked very fast in those days, and I know exactly what Rossini meant when he said: 'Until I was thirty, the melodies were chasing me. After thirty, I was chasing the melodies.' At nineteen I was still being chased by many melodies.

When I had finished the sonata, Grabner brought his violin along (he played violin and viola) and we played it through together. He called it a fine work, although of course he had criticisms to make and altered things. From here we proceeded to the study of counterpoint; since Grabner had been schooled by Reger this was probably his 'forte' as a teacher. I still have workbooks with pages of fugal exercises which were the fruit of Grabner's counterpoint lessons, and people have noticed that frequently when I have had chases to write for scenes in motion pictures I have tended to do them in fugal style (in Latin 'fuga' means 'flight').

Twice a week Grabner held a class in which the composition students could hear each other's work. If they were not pianists, he would help them to play their efforts on the piano. It was very instructive to listen to what my fellow-composers were doing. They all composed in more or less the same style — dry, contrapuntal and institutional. When in later life I was teaching at the University of Southern California, I came across an entirely different type of music, but despite the contemporary mode of expression it was essentially the same: arid, academic and uninspired — typical conservatory or university music.

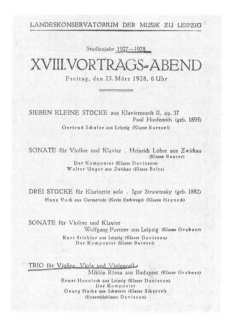

Hermann Grabner   First performance of my String Trio

Grabner had considerable patience, something I later discovered I did not possess myself. He judged each work on its merits and did not try to mould the student or make him into a carbon copy of his teacher. Grabner himself wrote a good deal: an opera, several oratorios, symphonic works and much chamber and organ music. There was nothing distinctive about his compositions, however; he had no special style of his own and could scarcely expect his students to imitate something that was non-existent. This was a blessing for them. All Schoenberg's pupils in Berlin ended up copying him. Schoenberg insisted on discipline and a thorough study of classical music and harmony. His harmony textbook is excellent and he must have been a very good teacher, but sooner or later all his pupils became pale imitations of him, just as Kodály in Budapest tried to make miniature Kodálys out of all his pupils. The opposite was true of Grabner. It made no difference to him whether a student composed in the style of Hindemith or of Grieg; he criticised the work purely from the standpoint of its technical components, its form, harmony, counterpoint and rhythm. For that, if for nothing else, he was an ideal teacher.

Every Thursday before the 'Hauptprobe', the general rehearsal for the Gewandhaus concerts (to which students could gain access for only one mark) Grabner gave a lecture on the programme. This is something that is now often done in America before concerts for the general public, but in Leipzig only Conservatory students attended Grabner's lectures. We would analyse together symphonies by Beethoven and Mahler and Strauss's symphonic poems; after the lecture and rehearsal we would go to the concert and our appreciation would naturally be that much keener. Little did I know then that Grabner would soon ask me to give these pre-concert talks. Between a hundred and two hundred students would be there, and I might have to talk about a Handel oratorio or Bach's B minor Mass. That was after I became his assistant and it made me feel very uneasy. I always expected the students to laugh at my German, but they never did. I had a pianist to play the music examples, and in the end I learned far more by explaining points to other people than by just reading them up for myself.

Much of my juvenilia is lost or destroyed, but my Opus 1, a String Trio, was one of the works written at Grabner's request. When it was given at the Conservatory I myself played the viola part. I also played the viola in the student orchestra, which I did not want to join, but Grabner insisted, saying that it was the only way to get to know it thoroughly.

The Conservatory orchestra was conducted by Professor Walter Davisson. He was a great violin teacher and later became director of the Conservatory. He was not a great violinist, but often great teachers are not great players, and it is rare to find a man who is both. Davisson considered himself something of an expert on French music, which was unusual because the music we were expected to study and perform was all German. I do not know whether there were political reasons for not playing French music in Germany at that time, or whether it stemmed from a kind of chauvinistic assumption that German music was far superior to French which, particularly since Debussy and the Impressionists, was considered decadent and unwholesome. This was in 1927, when Debussy had been dead for ten years and his stature was supposed to be recognised all over the world. Davisson told me about the time he played the Debussy String Quartet in Frankfurt, before the First World War. It was greeted by stony silence. Eventually the players left the platform, but after they had returned and played a classical work, a quartet by Mozart or Beethoven, the audience gave them a standing ovation to show that it was not that they disapproved of the quartet's performance, but that they objected to Debussy's 'outlandish' music. This was typical of the German attitude to foreign music, particularly French. We were in Germany and we would be trained to be German musicians.

The String Trio was my first great success, and is now available on record in a revised and abbreviated form. It originally played for three-quarters of an hour, which is rather long for a string trio; but my fellow students at the Conservatory gave me an ovation notwithstanding, and I became something of a celebrity. It was at about this time that my father wrote to Grabner and asked him what chance I stood of becoming a composer. Grabner wrote him a wonderful letter saying that if anyone had the right to be a composer, I had. That put an end to the differences between my father and me, and chemistry finally became a thing of the past.

Moreover the String Trio was the first work Grabner said he would show to Karl Straube. This was the greatest good fortune that any young composer could wish for, since Straube, close friend and champion of Reger and Kantor at the Thomaskirche, was held in universal veneration and esteem in Germany. He was largely responsible for rescuing Bach's organ works from the neglect into which they had fallen by the end of the nineteenth century, but at the time I crossed his path his main preoccupation was the promoting of the works of Reger. He was a brilliant organist and one of the greatest living authorities on the music of the

Lutheran church. He was also known for his exceptional kindness and for the great personal interest he took in his students. It was said that if Straube accepted you as a pupil your future was assured, and this was quite true; within a year or so of graduation you could count on a post somewhere as organist and choirmaster. This was the man to whom Grabner was promising to show my String Trio. I had no idea of his intention in so doing, although I knew that Straube had great influence with Breitkopf & Härtel, as he had everywhere.

Meanwhile my next large work was a quintet for piano and strings: its first performance took place in the Great Hall of the Conservatory. It was an even greater success than the Trio. All my friends and fellow-students were on their feet cheering, and I had to come forward to acknowledge the applause. Grabner said that in all his years as a teacher, in all the different institutions he had taught, he had never known a pupil of his to have such a triumph. A few days later I learned that Professor Straube wanted to hear the piece; apparently Grabner had told him about the reception the work had had. Straube still had my String Trio and I did not know whether he had looked at it or not. We gave him a private performance of the Quintet and he was very kind about it. He told me to telephone him in three days' time. I asked Grabner what he meant by this and he said, 'Can't you guess? He's going to talk to Breitkopf & Härtel about it.' For three days I was in torment. At the appointed time I rang him and he said, very matter-of-factly, 'Would you go along to Breitkopf & Härtel? You know where it is?' Yes, I did know where it was. I did not tell him that I used to pass the building and look at it longingly every day on my way to the chemistry laboratory. He told me to ask for a Herr Theodor Biebrich, who would be expecting me. I didn't know what to say apart from 'Thank you'. Later I discovered that gratitude embarrassed him more than anything, so perhaps it was as well that I didn't say any more.

I went along to Breitkopf & Härtel with my heart beating as if it was about to explode and presented myself to Herr Biebrich. He told me that Professor Straube had talked to the head of the firm, Dr Hellmuth von Hase of the Härtel family, about my work, and they had decided to publish it. Here was I, a young man of twenty-one, talking to important representatives of the greatest and probably the oldest publishing house in Germany. Biebrich told me that a contract for the first two pieces had already been drawn up. They were going to take on both the String Trio and the Piano Quintet. My hand shook as I signed the contract. It was the hundredth anniversary of the death of Schubert, and Biebrich said: 'The good spirit of dear Schubert should be watching over us as we sign this contract.'

I was paid 100 marks for the Trio and 250 marks for the Quintet. This seemed rather on the low side to me, but of course I would have let Breitkopf & Härtel have them for nothing. The satisfaction of having an income from music was the greatest joy I have ever experienced. After we had signed the contract and Biebrich had given me an envelope with the money in it, he introduced me to Dr von Hase, with whom I maintained a close relationship until his death in 1979. Breitkopf & Härtel still publish nearly all my music, and our friendship continues with Dr von Hase's successor in the firm, his daughter Lieselotte.

Grabner now thought that I ought to write a work for orchestra, and I produced

27

Dr von Hase and his daughter Lieselotte   Karl Straube

three scherzi. I have no idea why three; sometimes one scherzo is more than enough. They were meant to sound witty and sardonic. Grabner liked them and showed them to Heinrich Laber, the conductor of the Gera (Saxony) Opera House and Orchestra, who also conducted the second local orchestra, the Leipzig Symphony. Apparently he liked them too and accepted them for performance. Grabner encouraged me to write a violin concerto. I cast it in one movement; why I'm not sure. It was long (well over half an hour) and its structure was badly flawed. However, it was well-written as far as the violin was concerned; Grabner thought it far better than the scherzi and persuaded Laber to substitute the former for the latter, to be played by a fellow-student of mine, Ruth Meister.

The concert took place shortly before my graduation at about the same time that my String Trio was published. The music had the same familiar Breitkopf & Härtel cover I had first come across when I was orchestral librarian at my school in Budapest: there were the lovely baroque angels with *my* name in the middle and 'Opus 1' underneath. I put the score on the music stand beside my bed and I woke up many times that first night just to look at it. My dream had come true.

Then came the first performance of the Concerto. I went to the rehearsal with Grabner; we sat together with the score, and Walter Davisson was there with Ruth Meister, his prize pupil. I was so excited that I hardly took in a single note until the second rehearsal. It was a good concert and the Concerto was very well received. At the end I had to appear on the podium and take bow after bow with conductor and soloist.

We had a big celebration after the concert. Grabner had written a long poem in honour of my success and we all enjoyed ourselves enormously. Champagne was

28

served: we had ordered Mumm which was probably the dearest of all and cost the equivalent of two weeks' living expenses, but it was well worth it. This was the first time I had had a work performed in public, apart from the Conservatory concerts, which were really private events.

I was still far from satisfied with the structure of the Concerto and had long discussions with Grabner about whether or not to publish it. At that time all I needed to do was take it to Breitkopf & Härtel and they would have accepted it, but we finally came to the conclusion that it was better to leave it unpublished. So it has remained, and so I hope it always will remain.

I took my finals at the Conservatory, and they were far from easy. I was required to compose a number of pieces, sit a viva and undergo a practical piano examination. The works I had to write were a string sextet; a motet to a given text; a Benedictus; and an operatic scena, recitative and aria, again to a given text. Of the written examinations the most important was the fugue on a given theme, to write which the candidates were given a room and four hours. I finished mine in an hour, but that made no difference to the marks. We also had to write an essay on 'impressionism in music', but in our own time and not as a set examination. In the practical examination, one of the tests was to modulate melodically from one given key to another in only eight bars in front of all the professors, including the head, Siegfrid Karg-Elert, who gave me the near-impossible C major to B sharp major. Luckily I was well prepared and solved the problem to the jury's satisfaction. Karg-Elert, a funny-looking little man, congratulated me. He also complimented me on the motet and the sextet, both of which he liked, and I got my diploma in composition 'cum laude'. The diploma was something nice to have, but what practical purpose did it serve?

Grabner called me to his office to say how pleased he was, and to ask me what I was going to do for a living. When I replied that I wanted to compose he repeated the question. Suddenly I realised, as I had actually known all the time, that nobody made a living from composing alone. Hindemith, Schoenberg and many others were all teachers. Teaching was part of a composer's life, but somehow I revolted against the idea. I told Grabner that I wouldn't mind teaching as long as I had talented pupils. He was kind enough to say that if I expected pupils as talented as myself I was going to starve.

Grabner taught me all I knew, but he was much more than a teacher to me, he was like a father. I owe him an immense debt of gratitude for the interest he took in me. I came to him with nothing except, perhaps, a latent talent, and in three years he moulded me into a composer. Years later I was touched and honoured to find that he had quoted a passage from my 1953 Violin Concerto in the seventh edition of his well-known *Allgemeine Musiklehre*, the very same book from which I had earlier studied samples of Scriabin, Debussy and Schoenberg.

My music began to be played and reviewed in Germany. Many of the reviews were very favourable, and appeared in old-established magazines read by all musicians and music lovers. Before I even graduated my picture appeared in Breitkopf & Härtel's quarterly magazine. I have always been rather on the shy side and could no more 'push' my music then than I can now. It was entirely due to the

Early 1930s

efforts of Grabner that, at the age of twenty-two, my name was not entirely unknown to the German public.

After graduating I stayed in Leipzig to continue my musicological studies. Grabner found me pupils, and I was allowed to deputise for him at the Conservatory in his absences. During the summer I returned to my family in Hungary and went off to our country estate with my little black book to gather more folksongs. This had become a passion. But back in Leipzig Grabner took me to task for composing nothing during the vacation. He told me that a composer's creativity should be like the sacred flame of the vestal virgins, never extinguished. I have since found this to be very true. When for some reason I have been obliged to stop composing for a period, I have found it impossible to take up where I left off; I have had to start again practically from the beginning. Just as an apple tree goes through its natural cycle every year, so the creative man, be he composer, painter or writer, must be constantly creating. I have preached this dogma to all my students. There was a time when Sibelius promised the world a new symphony; he never fulfilled his promise because he waited too long. One must go on — good, bad, indifferent, it doesn't matter — what does matter is keeping the fire alight.

Breitkopf were eager to publish more of my music. In the Gewandhaus Orchestra was a fine cellist called Münch-Holland, and for him I wrote the Rhapsody op. 3. Stylistically it is a transitional piece, still much influenced by Germanic prototypes. But the more contemporary German music I heard, the more I became aware that it wasn't for me. I wanted to go back to my origins, to Hungarian folksong, and this is exactly what I did in my next two works — the *Variations on a Hungarian Peasant Song* op. 4 and the *North Hungarian Peasant Songs and Dances* op. 5, which is a collection of folk tunes from our village. Both these works were immediately published, and the op. 5 in particular was taken up by many concertising violinists.

Let me pause to survey the contemporary musical scene in Leipzig. The Gewandhaus Orchestra performed little modern music apart from Hindemith. Kodály's *Psalmus Hungaricus* was given, and Honegger's *King David*, both conducted by Straube. It was emphasised that Honegger was Swiss, because no one would have performed a 'decadent' French work in the Gewandhaus. Furtwängler was the chief conductor, and his interest in French music was practically non-existent. Of Debussy I heard only two of the orchestral *Nocturnes*. I once heard Bruno Walter conduct *The Sorcerer's Apprentice*, and the Franck Symphony was acceptable because Franck was Belgian. A Saint-Saëns Violin Concerto received terrible reviews. English music was unknown. Stravinsky came once and played his *Capriccio* for piano and orchestra. Again, everyone was outraged; Leipzig was a conservative city. The tradition was German, and had to be upheld. Schoenberg was a kind of myth. His name was known, and one read about him in music magazines, but one never heard his music. The same went for his two pupils Berg and Webern. However, Scherchen gave Honegger's *Pacific 231*, Kodály's *Háry János Suite* and a typically Soviet work called *Iron Foundry* by Mossolov. The first performance of Bartók's *Miraculous Mandarin* as a pantomime was given in Cologne directed by Eugene Szenkár, a friend of Bartók's. During the performance there was an unbelievable fracas, not unlike the famous premiere of *The Rite of Spring*. The Nazis threw stink-bombs, people shouted, the music couldn't be heard. The next day the Mayor of Cologne demanded Szenkár's resignation on the grounds that he had perpetrated an outrage on the largely Catholic Cologne public. But after the performance Bartók came round to Szenkár's dressing-room and said: 'Eugene, on page thirty-four the second clarinet is marked *mezzo forte*. I couldn't hear it. Would you please make it *forte*?' Bartók had been unaware of anything but his music, like a saint who is unaffected by worldly matters. A few years later Scherchen gave the Leipzig premiere of a suite from the ballet and during the performance somebody started to whistle. The whistling and shouting grew until the noise in the auditorium was much louder than any the musicians could make. Scherchen downed tools and walked out. Oddly enough, some years later in Paris I attended a performance, again conducted by Scherchen, hoping to hear the end of the piece, but at the same point which had inflamed the Leipzig audience whistling and shouting broke out again. I did not hear how the work ended until after Bartók's death, when Fritz Reiner conducted it on the radio in America.

I heard no Stravinsky and no Sibelius at this time. I bought myself the score of *The Rite of Spring*, which astounded me, but I didn't actually hear it until some years later in Paris; and this is music which has to be heard, not merely read. The reigning master of contemporary music was Paul Hindemith, a brilliant viola player who wrote two concertos for the instrument, which he himself performed all over the country. His operas, chamber music and orchestral works were played everywhere, and his influence on young composers was enormous. They all imitated his style but none achieved his brilliance.

These then were the musical influences that surrounded me in those early years.

Again, admirable though some of them were, none greatly affected me; I longed for the crystal clarity of Hungarian folksong as a basis for my music.

Grabner thought it time that I compose a larger work for performance in the Gewandhaus, and had Straube talk to me about a motet I had written. Straube said that although musically it was very interesting, from a practical point of view it was completely unsingable. He sat down with me and corrected everything that was difficult for the voices and then insisted that I join his choir. After a year, he told me, I would know just what a choir could and could not sing. I am still grateful to Straube for all I learnt about writing for choirs from his rehearsals. He took every voice separately, and then in different combinations, finally putting them all together. I will never forget his patience, for most of the singers were amateurs. Every note, every word, was studied carefully; and as a result the performances were exemplary. Once a week I attended these rehearsals. On one occasion we were preparing a Requiem by my friend and contemporary Günter Raphael, a very large work. Straube made a number of changes during the rehearsals, and afterwards would take Raphael and myself back to his home to mark the changes in the choir parts. Straube would slump into his easy chair exhausted, and offer us wine. When he had recovered somewhat he would explain exactly why he had made the changes, always stressing that 'modern' music was impossible for a choir. We would work late on the alterations; sometimes he went to bed and left us to it. We were happy to work for him.

Because of Straube's strictures I had decided that my 'larger work' would have to be a symphony. He often asked how it was coming along, but wanted to wait until it was finished before hearing it. At last it *was* finished, and I played it through to him on the piano. He was very pleased with it and suggested that we approach Furtwängler. A week later he told me that the great conductor was expecting me the following Sunday in Berlin after his concert with the Philharmonic. My embarrassment must have shown on my face; it was the end of the month and I was short of money. He promptly pushed a hundred-mark note into my hand, saying 'This will help.' I am still touched by his generosity. I was not his pupil, and yet he was opening doors for me which otherwise might have taken years to open of their own accord.

I went to Berlin. When I met Furtwängler he was very kind, but hadn't a moment to spare before he went off on a week's tour with the orchestra. With Straube's hundred-mark note in my pocket I decided I could stay a week in Berlin, and I spent a wonderful time going to museums and concerts. At the end of the week I went to see Furtwängler again. This time he told me he had to leave at once for Zurich and asked if I could go with him. Sadly I had to decline. Later I heard that Paul Kletzki had a similar experience with Furtwängler, as a young composer. Furtwängler suggested Kletzki meet him in New York, five days' journey away.

I returned to Leipzig with my unplayed symphony, and to Straube, who was somewhat annoyed. He suggested that if I'd been a beautiful young girl, things would have been different. However, a week or so later he made an appointment for me to see Bruno Walter at the Gewandhaus. I met Walter in the Artists' Room after the rehearsal. He was sitting exhausted, listening to a young lady from the

Siegfried Wagner's funeral, Bayreuth 1930; all the pall-bearers were renowned Wagnerian artists.

Conservatory singing a Mozart aria. She had no voice and was distressed when Walter had to tell her that no career lay ahead of her. I was nervous as I started to play my symphony to him, but he listened patiently from beginning to end. When I finished he told me that I was very talented but that the symphony was too long; he wouldn't be able to get the necessary rehearsal time. Seeing my disappointment, he promised that if I wrote him a shorter work he would play it; and he kept his word.

All I wanted then was to hear my symphony, so I decided to approach Dohnányi when I went home at Christmas. At that time he was Director of the Academy of Music, Musical Director of the Philharmonic Society and also the Radio's Musical Director. He and his wife were very kind to me when I took my symphony along. His reaction was the same as that of Walter, however, and he too promised that he would play a shorter work. I know now that it was a symphony to end all symphonies in length, but alas not in invention or originality.

The following summer, 1930, some French music-loving friends invited me to the Wagner Festival at Bayreuth. I arrived on the day of the funeral of Wagner's son Siegfried, whom I had met years before in Leipzig. The memorial concert that evening in the Festspielhaus was one of the most memorable and moving experiences of my life. The orchestra, normally hidden in the pit, occupied the stage. The concert began with the *Siegfried Idyll*, conducted by Toscanini, the piece which was written by Wagner for his wife Cosima to celebrate the birth of the man whose funeral had just taken place. Then Karl Elmendorff, the conductor of the *Ring*, conducted a work by Siegfried Wagner himself, and the concert closed with

Siegfried's Funeral March conducted by Karl Muck. When it was over the whole audience was weeping. There was of course no applause, and Muck slowly and theatrically left the stage.

It was customary in Bayreuth to go to the Festspielhaus restaurant after each act, particularly after the last act to applaud the singers as they came in. Last of all, the conductor enters to receive his tributes. This getting-together after the performance became the climax of the evening. After this memorial concert my friends and I went to our table in the restaurant, which was full as usual. There was no rejoicing. However, I found it strange that the whole Wagner family, including Siegfried's widow, Winifred, was there. The children were dressed in black but behaving like children, running from table to table greeting the singers and the well-known Bayreuth personalities. This kind of wake seemed barbaric to me. The only one not there was Toscanini, who said that on the night he had buried his best friend he wasn't going to a restaurant to celebrate.

Bayreuth in 1930 was a strange place. Your reaction depended entirely upon your preconceptions. If you had gone there, as Stravinsky did, prejudiced against it, your reaction would undoubtedly have been as negative as his. On the other hand, if you acknowledged the genius of Wagner and loved his music dramas, Bayreuth was unique. The orchestra comprised the best musicians of Germany, under the baton of Toscanini or Muck. The greatest singers in the world performed to perfection. Everything revolved around the Festspielhaus (Wagner didn't use the town theatre, of course — he had to build his own) and Villa Wahnfried, where he and Cosima lived. Cosima's godfather, Liszt, is buried in the cemetery, interestingly enough in a mausoleum designed by Siegfried Wagner, who was trained as an architect. There is a Wagner museum too, of course, although all Wagner's manuscripts are in the archives. For Hitler's fiftieth birthday the Rheinland industrialists bought the original score of *The Mastersingers* and presented it to him. It went up in flames in the bunker in Berlin when he died.

This 1930 visit of mine to Bayreuth had an important influence on my future, because of a group of French people I met there. Madame Gaston Fournier became my beloved *tante-Aimée*, and through her niece, Hilda Gélis-Didot, I was introduced to some of the literary and musical society of Paris. The great organist Marcel Dupré was in their party. He was really the first Frenchman I had ever met and epitomised what I later came to admire in so many of the French — intelligence, awareness, fine culture, exquisite manners. He was kindness itself. He spent hours looking over my compositions, including the unpublished and unperformed symphony, and in the end he urged me to try Paris. I had too much talent for Leipzig, he told me; Paris was where I should be, and he would do all he could to help me gain a footing if I came. I needed little convincing and immediately set about planning a visit there.

3: Paris

I arrived in Paris in the spring of 1931 and stayed in the Hotel Vernet in the rue Vernet, off the Champs Elysées. I was twenty-four, but no matter how old you are, your first impressions of Paris — the incredible panorama as you look up the Champs Elysées from the Place de la Concorde, the bustle of the *grands boulevards*, the uniqueness of the Tuileries, the Louvre — these are overwhelming. Even the peculiar odour of the Metro is intoxicating. The beauty of the women, the well-dressed men, the Opéra, the Folies-Bergères — these are all experiences which become quite commonplace as time goes by, but the first time round they are exhilarating.

Dupré kept his word; through him I met all sorts of fascinating and talented people. His organ playing was exceptional, quite different from the German style, in which the performer tries to impose and overwhelm. Dupré was of the French school — all clarity, colour and delicacy. His Bach playing was impeccable and his improvisational skill unique. He could go on for hours, with new ideas and new contrapuntal combinations popping up from nowhere. He and his wife lived at Meudon, not far from Paris (Wagner had once stayed there), and Dupré often gave concerts in his splendid organ room on an instrument built specially by Cavaillé-Col for the great organist Guilmant. *Le tout Paris* ('everybody who was anybody') would come to these wonderful evenings, which he always ended with his brilliant improvisations. Dupré was a modest man who never spoke of his career or his successes. It is characteristic that he makes no mention in his 'Recollections' of an incident which I once witnessed — his receiving of the Légion d'Honneur, the highest award in French culture. The ceremony took place at a celebratory dinner given by Hilda Gélis-Didot, where I was fortunate enough to be included among the guests. The minister of Cultural Affairs made a stirring speech in which he compared the Duprés, father and son, with the Bachs. After dinner another guest arrived. It was Charles-Marie Widor,* Secretary of the Académie, teacher of Dupré, and now over ninety. The old man had begged to be excused from attending the whole evening, and from wearing a dinner jacket. Honegger kissed his hand and led him to Dupré where, with tears in his eyes, Widor pressed the coveted rosette into the buttonhole of his famous pupil. Then, amid a cheering ovation, Honegger led him gently out again. Dupré *père* remarked to me: 'Moments like these make life worth living.'

---

*Composer of the famous *Toccata* so popular at weddings.

c. 1929, Leipzig   Marcel Dupré

After the war Dupré and his wife came to Hollywood. From the organist of the church where he was performing he learnt of the existence of my first motet ('To Everything there is a Season') and asked me to play him the recording. When I did so, the final 'Alleluia' interested him so much that he asked my permission to improvise on it at the end of his next recital. Of course I consented, and at the concert I was astounded by his skill. My modest theme grew to major symphonic proportions, appearing in a variety of harmonic and contrapuntal guises until the climax was reached in a strict four-part fugue crowned by a chorale. I wished I had composed it like that!

We paid a visit to the MGM studios and the Duprés were amazed by their size in comparison with the French ones. I introduced André Previn who showed them round the sound stages and, at Dupré's request, played the piano for them. On our way home Dupré remarked that it was a pity that such a talented young man should be wasting his time in a film studio. A pity he didn't live long enough to see the success that 'this talented young man' made of his life.

Oddly enough, I owe much of my own success to organists. Without the help of Karl Straube I should never have come to Breitkopf & Härtel, or have met Bruno Walter. Without Dupré I would never have met his fellow-pupil Honegger. And even my Hungarian memoirs (*Stories from my Life*)* are the outcome of interviews with the Hungarian organist Iános Sebestyén. Yet, ungrateful as I am, this is one instrument I have completely neglected so far in my composing.

---

*Published in 1980

The highlight of that first trip to Paris was meeting over lunch at Hilda Gélis-Didot's Pierre Monteux, the famous conductor who, in addition to all his other achievements, had presided over the first scandalous performance of *The Rite Of Spring* with Diaghilev's company. The reason for our meeting was that he should listen to my symphony. I thundered through the piece on the Bechstein, and his complaint was the same as was everyone else's — it was too long and would need too many rehearsals. But he offered to do the scherzo movement alone, if I were willing. I was disappointed, and asked for time to think about whether or not I should take out the 'plum', as he called it, and discard the rest. It never came to a performance, as I never sent it to him. Though he later did another work of mine, the Cello Rhapsody, I realised that the symphony was not striking people as the sensation of the decade, and I gradually began to forget about it. It is put away now, nicely packed, and as it represents my first major disappointment I don't have the courage to look at it. Maybe I should.

A concert of my chamber music was arranged for the following spring at the Ecole Normale de Musique, and this was to be my Paris début. Then I returned to Leipzig, finished my *Serenade* for small orchestra, and in Budapest Dohnányi kept his word about performing a shorter piece than my gigantic symphony. The *Serenade* had five movements; the first and last were the same — a march — except that whereas at the beginning it started very quietly and grew louder, as though the serenaders were approaching, at the end it died away into the distance.

Widor and Dupré   Dohnányi

Dohnányi asked me whether I wanted audience success or good reviews — it was impossible to have both with the order of the movements as it stood. He proposed to rearrange them, playing the march at the beginning as it was, but ending with the lively 'Danza'. I agreed, of course, and on the night of the concert at the Opera I was sitting in a box with my parents.

Dohnányi conducted a bit lackadaisically, with his left hand permanently in his pocket; but nevertheless it was a nice, musicianly performance. At the end there was polite applause, nothing more. I was an unknown quantity to the Budapest public. Then suddenly a wonderful thing happened. Richard Strauss was in the audience, having come to Budapest for some performances of his opera *The Egyptian Helena*, and was sitting with Mrs Dohnányi in a box. Whether he liked my piece or not I don't know, but he must have felt that the future of a young man was in his hands. Every eye was on him and he began to applaud furiously. He was like a cheerleader. If the great Strauss was enthusiastic, the piece must be good! And the half-hearted applause, which was just beginning to die away, was transformed into a thunderous ovation. I was led down to the stage, which was quite a long way, but when I arrived in the wings the applause was still continuing. Instructions were whispered to me that my first bows should be to the Regent, Admiral Horthy, and to Archduke Joseph, the Hungarian Hapsburg. I came out, but all I was aware of was the beautiful head of Strauss and his applause. It was to Strauss that I made a deep bow, and this brought on a new wave of applause. After that the Regent and the Archduke got their turn.

When I met Strauss after the concert I was almost speechless with admiration. It was like meeting Beethoven. He asked me what, at the time, I thought a very curious question. Why did I use only one horn? I replied that this was the idea of the piece: one flute, one oboe, one clarinet and so on. Yes, said Strauss, but more horns were available and I should have used them. It was only later, in discussion with the player himself, that I understood what Strauss had meant. Horn players specialise as 'high' and 'low' players, because the instrument has such a big range. In orchestras the first and third horns play the higher parts, the second and fourth the lower. In my piece the single horn had to do both, which was very difficult for him. Strauss, of course, was a master of orchestration, and his father had been a superb horn player, so he certainly knew what he was talking about. I have since revised the piece, and it is published as *Hungarian Serenade*.

The following spring I made my Paris début as a composer. The chamber concert comprised the premiere of the Variations for Piano op. 9, the two duos (one for violin and piano, one for cello and piano) and the Piano Quintet. My friend the pianist, Clara Haskil, took part, incomparably, and everybody played well. The concert was well attended, and the public was more than enthusiastic. Students from the Hungarian Academy came as cheerleaders, which was heartwarming. Two Paris-based Hungarian composers, Teodore Szántó and Tibor Harsányi, came as well.

I had vowed that if the concert were a success I would set up house in Paris. It *was* a success. The newspapers wrote columns; all — more or less — heralded a new star on the horizon. Arthur Honegger was kind enough to praise my music and express the wish to know me better. His publisher, Maurice Sénart, asked what unpublished works I had, and at the time there was only the Variations for Piano which had been rejected by Breitkopf. Clara Haskil played it for them, and they accepted it immediately.

I went home to settle my affairs, and at last on a beautiful September morning arrived in Paris to begin my life as a Parisian composer. Somehow I forgot or disregarded the words of Grabner when he asked me how I wanted to make a living. After all, my concert had been a success, the reviews had been enthusiastic and somehow I was going to make a career as a composer! This stubborn part of my character has never changed. I wanted to compose music, and that is what I have always done, as there is nothing else I can do.

Sitting in a café at seven in the morning drinking a café-crème, I considered where to make my home. Somehow Montparnasse and the Boulevard St. Michel area did not appeal to me, although it was popular as a student quarter and lodgings would be cheap. I found an attractive-looking hotel on the rue du Faubourg St. Honoré. The price was acceptable, and with an incredulous shrug the management agreed to my intention of bringing in a piano. The room seemed rather dirty, but I was very tired and lay down fully dressed to sleep. When I woke I saw that the room was *very* dirty, and later throughout the whole night I was disturbed by the sound of people coming and going. By the morning I realised what sort of hotel it was and why they were surprised when I said I wanted to bring in a piano. I paid my bill and went to look for something less specialised.

The Hotel de Périgord on the rue de Gramont was just off the Boulevard des Italiens. It had been the town house of a noble family, built in the sixteenth century: now, as a hotel, it was run by an elderly couple from Milan. They gave me a room on the ground floor so that the piano would not disturb anyone but those in the restaurant, and I spent three happy years there. My room looked on to the rue St. Augustin. Directly opposite, at No. 13, was a place called 'Dinah' which my hosts told me was 'un dansing'. Men and young ladies arrived at early afternoon and night for the 'dansing', welcomed by a trim maid in uniform at the door. I was such an innocent in those days. It wasn't until months later when, feeling very Parisian, I was recognised on the street as a foreigner and offered the delights of a famous place called 'Dinah', that I knew it for what it was. After that I frequently saw the man who had approached me on that occasion arriving at 'Dinah' with clients for the ladies within. It was all very Parisian and so different from small, puritanical Leipzig.

I was absorbing Paris, its beauty, its strangeness, its newness to me. I spent hours in the Louvre. But I had to make my living, and decided that the first thing to do was to have concerts of my music, to get my name and music known. I had often played on the radio in Germany, Hungary, Belgium and Holland, either the piano part of my chamber works or easier pieces for solo piano. There had always been a fee, not much, but a fee just the same. Clara Haskil arranged a broadcast on the Paris Radio, but no fee materialised. At last I asked her what had happened, to which she replied that in Paris you do this for the publicity. Well, publicity is fine, but it is difficult to buy groceries with it.

In the rue Vaugirard was a 'Hungarian House' — a meeting place for all the Hungarians in Paris. The President was a painter, and he arranged for me to present my music in another chamber concert. Many people came, a speech was made about me, everybody liked the music — but again no fee. Again *la gloire* was the only reward.

Monteux gave my Cello Rhapsody with the Orchestre Symphonique de Paris, and with the radio broadcasts, the Budapest concert and this orchestral performance, I was on my way. But still it brought me no income.

I had met Honegger several times, at Madame Fournier's or at Hilda Gélis-Didot's, and I decided to discuss my financial problems with him. Of course, anyone who has read his book *Je Suis Compositeur* knows what he thought about making a living by music, but at that time the book wasn't written. Honegger told me what I knew already: it is impossible at the outset to earn much money as a composer. It is probably the only profession for which you have to study for years, for which you have to have great talent, and yet from which so little income derives, even when you are quite well-known and successful. Over the years many efforts to remedy this rather dire situation have been made, some in a modest way by me. I was still a student of Grabner when my first works started to be performed in public, and he it was who explained to me that a composer's greatest assets are his performing rights — royalties due to him after each performance. It was necessary, of course, to belong to a Performing Right Society, and I was enrolled with the German society GEMA on Grabner's recommendation. For a while the royalties came in, but then I began to strike difficulties. Shortly after I settled in Paris the new German currency regulations made it impossible for any money to reach me, while at the same time the French society SACEM would not accept me as a member because I was a foreigner. By the time I got to England the regular newsletters from GEMA (now changed to STAGMA) were crammed with chauvinistic Nazi propaganda. I well remember the issue which contained an open letter to Hitler from STAGMA's President Paul Graener, a minor composer but apparently a major Nazi. 'Mein Führer,' it began, 'I greet you as the first artist of the German Reich.' First *artist*, when Richard Strauss, Thomas Mann, Gerhardt Hauptmann and countless others were alive? The fact that this outrageous salute emanated from the President of the society of which I was a member was too much for me and I wrote an angry letter of resignation. I applied for membership with the British Performing Rights Society and in 1937, when Bartók, Kodály and Dohnányi also found a haven with the PRS, I was accepted. This was the wisest move of my life as the PRS is a most excellent and efficient organisation, through which I have never had the slightest difficulty in receiving royalties. When I got to the United States I was surprised to learn that American film composers (unless they were songwriters) were not accepted by the American Society of Composers and Publishers (ASCAP), and that despite ASCAP's enormous receipts from films the composers got nothing. Something had to be done, for everywhere else in the world a composer automatically received a royalty for a public performance of *anything* of his (even 'background music', as ASCAP insisted on calling our contribution); and so the Screen Composers' Association (SCA) was founded to

Arthur Honegger, composer of *Pacific 231*

fight for proper royalties for all. The fight was long and tough. In the ten years from 1955, when I held the Presidency, I visited the British, French, German, Austrian, Italian and Swiss societies to enlist their aid in remedying the miserable situation in America. To describe this crusade step by step would fill another book, but I am happy to report that today the American composer is at last relatively well protected — only in the United States itself does he receive nothing for a screening of one of his films, a sad and unjust situation still to be remedied.

But to return to Honegger in the Paris of the 1930s: he went on to ask if I had any talent for 'lighter music', and at his suggestion I went to see his friend Roland-Manuel. Roland-Manuel had been a pupil of Ravel and later wrote a biography of the composer. But as a composer himself, once a close associate of Les Six, he had never quite made it. Now he was the Artistic Director of a publishing firm called

Editions Echo, close to the Ile de la Cité on the Quai des Orfèvres. Editions Echo was the publishing firm associated with the Pathé-Nathan film company. What Roland-Manuel proposed was this: in every one of the seven hundred Pathé cinemas in the country records were played during the intermission, and these records were supplied by Pathé in order to collect the performing rights. In other words, the records were of compositions commissioned by Pathé themselves. Any music would do, he told me, provided that it was entertaining and light. It shouldn't be a double fugue, but on the other hand it didn't need to be 'Le Jazz Hot' either. He told me to write something and come back and play it for him.

I returned with all sorts of silly things — 'Humoresque', 'Gypsy Fantasy', 'Scherzo' — light trash of the kind I had so despised in Budapest and Leipzig. Roland-Manuel chose four, and sent me off to discuss financial terms with the Business Manager. I learnt that I would receive one sixth of the 'author's rights', but nothing in advance. A sixth didn't sound very good, but beggars can't be choosers and I signed.

This turned out to be an association of several years' standing. I supplied my silly little pieces and they were all recorded. Later I discovered why it was I received only a sixth. No matter what I wrote — even a piece crammed with rapid notes — somebody wrote nonsensical lyrics to it. One of the employees chose words at random from Larousse — a two-syllable word, a three-syllable word, whatever he needed, and immediately became the author. It was a crooked business, but quite normal in Paris at that time. As there were several 'lyricists' they all went down as co-authors and received their share, so did the publishers and a fictitious co-composer. All I had to do was deliver a piano score into the hands of the arrangers. Sometimes I went to the recording sessions, sometimes not, it didn't matter. I consoled myself with the knowledge that Wagner, living in Paris a hundred years before me, had had to make piano arrangements of Donizetti operas, and later Bizet did the same.

Sometimes I stood outside a cinema on the boulevard at intermission time and heard my music being played, hoping that I would never be found out. Some of the tunes were quite catchy, and one was considered worthy of being recorded by a singer. The lyric went: 'Je suis d'humeur charmante, tout me plaît et m'enchante, dog-a-dig-a-doo, dog-a-dig-a-doo, doo!' Most of the lyrics conformed to this high level of poetic inspiration. But Roland-Manuel told me that my tunes were so good I should have a permanent collaborator as my lyricist. He found me a man who called himself Jean Solar — nobody used their real name — and through working with him alone my sixth became a quarter. Solar also had a radio show — he was a singer too — and every Sunday we performed our latest potential hits, he singing, I at the piano. One of our songs became quite popular. It was called 'Bobby Chéri', and was a rumba. My first attempt at a rumba for Pathé had been met with scorn by a composer called Jean Wiener who had moved to jazz from a classical background. It was he who told me the secret of rumba-writing: 'The right hand is adagio, the left hand is allegro'. This is well put. Listen to 'The Peanut Vendor', for example. The bass bounces along with the rhythm, but on top there sails a slow tune. Well, 'Bobby Chéri' was published and recorded and became something of a success.

Péchés de jeunesse

Roland-Manuel told me that I needed a pseudonym. I shouldn't jeopardise my reputation by linking my real name with what the French call *musique alimentaire*. So I became Nic Tomay. Tomay was the name of a family I knew at home, and Nic was short for Nicholas, of course, which in Hungarian is Miklós. So my Double Life began, after a fashion, there and then in Paris.

Concert life in Paris was, of course, much more cosmopolitan than in Leipzig. The greatest soloists and conductors appeared. Of the five orchestras, four performed on Sunday afternoon, which was ridiculous. There were plenty of people to fill every concert on any night of the week, but not enough for four simultaneous concerts on one day. When I asked why this was the case I was told, 'C'est la tradition'. Only the Conservatoire Orchestra gave its concerts on Thursday; this also was 'la tradition'.

I had a subscription to Monteux's concerts in the Salle Pleyel. The orchestra rehearsed for six days and performed on the Sunday. The musicians did not receive a salary, only a share of the profits, which were practically non-existent. The cellist who had played my rhapsody told me he made between ten and twenty pounds a year. Monteux got all sorts of gifts of money from rich friends for many years, but at last the friends tired of their generosity, and that was the end of the orchestra. Around this time my finances had sunk to a very low ebb, and I frequently had to make my way to the State Pawnshop, the Mont de Piété, where my Swiss gold watch could always be pawned for 500 francs. As I was entering the large courtyard of the seventeenth-century building, I saw a familiar face coming towards me,

Pierre Monteux

carrying in both hands a pair of silver candelabra. It was the great Maestro himself. He recognised me, turned his head immediately the other way, and I did the same. We passed each other like two ships on the ocean. A few weeks later we met at a concert, where my Cello Duo was being performed. He paid me compliments and the embarrassing circumstances of our previous encounter were not mentioned. My readers will be relieved to know that my watch was later redeemed and I am still carrying it in my pocket. I hope the silver candelabra also made a good end.

At this time more and more Germans were arriving as refugees from Hitler's Germany. The French have never been known for their love of the Germans and, refugees though these people were, the loud German voices in the cafés irritated the Parisians. At a concert in the Salle Pleyel, Maurice Abravanel (later conductor of the Salt Lake City Symphony) conducted something jazzy by Kurt Weill. Weill's music was not known at that time in Paris, and at the end a gaunt, bearded man ran down to the front and shouted: 'À bas les juifs allemands!' 'Vive Hitler! Vive Hitler!' There was pandemonium; some were for him, some against — mostly against — and the man was thrown out. Weill was sitting next to my box and I can still see his face turning white. He had been expelled from Germany because of his origins; here he was in the land of 'liberté, égalité, fraternité'; yet still the nightmare pursued him. The man who shouted was Florent Schmitt, a famous composer and a critic for a daily paper.

Another unpleasant incident occurred when Harriet Cohen, the English pianist, played a Bach concerto with the orchestra. Not only was the Bach not to the taste of the public — they wanted the old war-horses, Liszt, Grieg, Tchaikovsky, Rachmaninov — but her name was Jewish. I don't think they knew she was English, they probably supposed her to be another German refugee. After she finished, someone yelled, 'Come on now, Pierre! How much did you get from the Jewess?' A riot started, people shouted and hit one another, and Harriet Cohen bowed graciously to those who were applauding. When she turned to bow deeply to the orchestra we all saw her (very lovely) derrière, and more pandemonium broke out.

Something always happened at these concerts, or anywhere where something controversial was given. Ida Rubinstein commissioned many new stage-works like Debussy's *Le Martyre de Saint Sébastien*, Ravel's *Boléro* and Honegger's *Jeanne d'Arc au Bûcher*. Stravinsky's *Perséphone* was another of her commissions and in this she appeared as the reciter of Gide's text. Rubinstein, the former Diaghilev dancer, was no longer young, and she preferred to recite rather than dance. When she got to the line 'comme ceci' her Russian accent made it sound like 'comme Cécile' and someone called down from the gallery 'comme Cécile Sorel!' Cécile Sorel was a famous old actress who had recently been obliged to retire from the Comédie Française on account of her age. Her name had been prominently in the newspapers just then, and everybody laughed. This was at the Opéra, where good behaviour was *la tradition*, but you could see whole rows silently shaking. When it was over Stravinsky put down his baton and said to the orchestra, 'Eh voilà!' That was all. The public loved to participate in every performance pro or contra, and artistic life was never dull in Paris.

I have always felt inhibited at the idea of approaching conductors. They are all besieged by letters, telephone calls and visits from importunate composers. They are sent a vast number of scores every year, very few of which are really good. Besides, very few conductors are interested in new music; most stay with the established repertoire for their entire lives. I have never felt able to approach a conductor and ask him to perform one of my works. The only time I did try was with the Symphony when I was very young, and even then it was always through somebody else's introduction or at a meeting arranged by a third party. As I explained, it was never accepted, and perhaps that is why I stopped trying. If I did meet a conductor, I would be so embarrassed that I would talk about the weather or politics or any subject, as long as it was not music, especially my own.

I had known Charles Münch well in Leipzig, but now he had resigned from his posts as second leader of the Gewandhaus Orchestra and Professor at the Conservatory and had gone to Paris. He had married a wealthy woman and set himself up as a conductor, even though he was over forty and had never conducted a concert in his life. His publicity made mention of all the conducting he was supposed to have done in the Gewandhaus, but the only time he had ever conducted the Gewandhaus Orchestra was during a carnival when they all dressed up in the wigs and costumes of Mozart's time; their regular leader, who would of course be expected to conduct (as was the practice in Mozart's day), refused to have anything to do with it. Münch had jumped at the chance to take over, but of course that could hardly be called conducting. Whenever there was a call for a violin solo it would be Münch who played; he played all the big obbligatos in the Bach Passions and the B minor Mass under Straube, but he could not be described as a conductor by any stretch of the imagination.

I was not in Paris at the time of his first concert, but I heard that Strauss's *Don Juan* broke down completely. Then on the recommendation of Furtwängler, a close personal friend of his, he started to study with two conductors. He gave a series of concerts with Cortot, who himself had ambitions to conduct just as Furtwängler had ambitions to compose. Cortot was a great pianist and a fine musician, but had little talent as a conductor. In his youth he had gone to Bayreuth and become a voice coach in order to learn the Wagner operas that he hoped he would soon be conducting. In Paris he was naturally always in demand as a soloist, but nobody ever asked him to conduct. Then Münch came along. He was a totally unknown name, but he had the money to put on concerts. Together they mounted a series of subscription concerts and called them the Cortot-Münch concerts. Cortot also played the piano, sometimes in his own concerts and sometimes for Münch. Cortot's name had great magic and brought in the audiences, and so Münch began to make a name for himself.

While I was living in Paris I would often see Münch's name on concert posters, but I never plucked up the courage to telephone him because I was afraid he would think I wanted something. But one day I came face to face with him on the Boulevard des Italiens. He was very pleased to see me, and we sat in a café talking for hours. He was very friendly, told me the details of his concert plans and said that his one consuming ambition was to be a great conductor (which he later achieved). He asked me if I had anything for him. I had to admit that at that time I hadn't, but that I was just starting work on a piece that might prove suitable, and if it did we could discuss it when it was finished.

I now decided to write what every conductor had asked me to write, and that was a medium-sized symphonic work. The initial idea for the *Theme, Variations and Finale* came to me on the boat as I was leaving Budapest to come and settle in Paris. My mother, father, sister and a friend of mine had travelled with me as far as Visegrád, a medieval town on the Danube. From there I would travel to Vienna, and thence by train to Paris. I was sure I would never see Budapest again. That I did not mind, but I was sorry to be parting from my family. It was the last time I saw my father. A melancholy Hungarian oboe theme floated into my head. I jotted it down and later in Paris kept looking at it, until I began to feel a set of variations growing up around it.

The theme sounded as if it might have been a folk tune, but it wasn't; it just arose out of my feelings of nostalgia for the village where I had felt at home. Instead of writing a set of variations I tried to express in each variation an inherent aspect of

Charles Münch

this so-called folk tune, thinking that the way in which a folk melody often develops and changes naturally could be applied equally well to symphonic music. This was at the time when there were no important Hungarian variations on Hungarian themes in existence. Dohnányi's *Variations on a Nursery Song* was far removed from any Hungarian feeling. Kodály did write a set of variations on a genuine Hungarian folk-song, *The Peacock*, but that was much later. I do not know whether he heard Charles Münch conduct my piece in Budapest in 1934 or not. Münch told me that he was present, so perhaps my piece gave him the idea for his own. Again, I can never know for sure, but it would be difficult to find two works solving the same basic problem in such different ways.

I wrote the *Theme, Variations and Finale* very quickly and when I had finished the orchestration I showed my work to the two men in Paris I respected the most, Arthur Honegger and Marcel Dupré. I went first to Dupré and played it through to him in his wonderful concert-hall at Meudon. All he had to say was that he liked it, it was the kind of music he had been expecting from me, that he would telephone a number of conductors who were friends of his, he was sure I would be able to get the piece performed in Paris, and he wished me luck with it.

Then I went to see Honegger, whose charming wife, Andrée Vaurabourg, was a fine pianist and later a teacher of counterpoint and composition. Honegger was unable to work at home, perhaps because he was disturbed by his wife playing the piano, and he had his own studio at the top of a modern block of flats. It was there that I went to play him my *Variations*. He had a large piano covered with hundreds of scores, manuscript paper and all sorts of different-coloured pens and pencils. The only thing in perfect order was his collection of pipes which were displayed around the walls, at a rough guess at least a hundred. Every imaginable design was represented. He would go to his pipe rack and consider first one and then another, as if trying to resolve a problem of counterpoint. Eventually he would take one from the rack, and that would be the pipe for the day. On this occasion he chose one and came and sat down beside me at the piano, saying, 'Let's see then.' It was quite different from playing for Dupré. Dupré behaved like an audience, Honegger more like a colleague. He liked the piece but thought one of the variations superfluous. I am always stubborn in matters of this kind and I refused to take it out; but after the first performance I could see that he was right and I eliminated it. Honegger also made some very helpful comments about the orchestration. For instance, in one variation the whole orchestra plays an abrupt staccato figure and for some reason I had a timpani roll going on at the same time. Honegger explained that the timpani would completely obliterate the staccato passage. He suggested regular drum beats in time with the staccato in the rest of the orchestra. Whenever I reach this point in the piece, whether I am actually conducting or just listening, I remember Honegger with warmth and gratitude.

Before I had the chance to show the score to Charles Münch, I received a letter from Otto Volkmann, the conductor of the Duisburg Symphony Orchestra. He had heard my Piano Quintet back in 1929 and now, four years later, he still remembered me. At the time, we had met briefly and he had told me to let him see any future compositions. After his letter I took this to be a definite offer and so I sent him my score. Within two weeks I had an answer from Volkmann, giving me the date of the first performance of my *Variations*. This meant I could go to Münch without needing to ask him to do me any favours. I could tell him that a first performance was already arranged and if he wanted the second performance then he could have it.

I played the score for Münch. He liked it, including the variation that Honegger had wanted me to discard, and made plans to take it on tour to Prague, Vienna, Budapest, perhaps even to Berlin. He was of course meeting the expenses of these concerts himself; it was all part of his plan to become accepted and gain recognition and experience as a conductor. He asked if he could keep the score, but when I explained that the fair copy was in Duisburg for the first performance there the following week, he said that he might even be able to come. I thought he was just being polite, but the first rehearsal in Duisburg, there indeed, was Charles Münch. He attended most of the rehearsals and pored over my score. The performance was a great success; the piece sounded exactly as I hoped it would, and Honegger's little improvements made a big difference. There was a celebration banquet afterwards to which Münch came, and the following week he conducted the work in Budapest. My parents sent me a telegram saying, 'Great reviews'.

It was through Münch that I later had my first and only 'meeting' with Ravel.

During one of my trips between London and Paris in the mid-1930s Münch was giving a Ravel concert with the Conservatoire Orchestra in the old Conservatoire building, and he invited me to one of the rehearsals. I was sitting in one of the back rows when two men came in: the one small, white-haired and daintily-dressed, the other tall and husky-looking. The first was Ravel, who came over to me, shook my hand and said: 'Bonjour Monsieur, n'est-ce pas que je vous connais?' ('Don't I know you?'). Before I had a chance to reply the other man was at his side, took him by the arm and led him away. This other man was, I later discovered, a kind of nurse-companion-guardian, for the composer was by this time too severely incapacitated by the mysterious brain disease which was to kill him in 1937 to be allowed out on his own. The two made their way to the front; Münch stopped the rehearsal, the musicians stood up and Ravel made a vague movement with his hand in acknowledgement of the tribute. Occasionally Münch would refer to him over tempi, but he never had any comment to make; everything seemed to be to his liking. At the end his man led him gently out. It was pathetic to hear this glorious music and at the same time see its creator sitting there, prematurely aged and enfeebled and scarcely aware of what was going on around him.

Even before their first performance I had set about trying to get the *Variations* published. I wrote to Breitkopf, but the response was that they were fully occupied with my *Serenade* which had had ten or fifteen performances and that, as it was not possible to work on two pieces of music by the same composer at the same time, they would forgo the *Variations*.

I was familiar with the little yellow pocket scores that the Leipzig publisher Eulenburg brought out. They did not publish many new works, but seemed to have the entire established repertoire in study score form. They had recently brought out new works by one or two contemporary German composers, however, so the name was fresh in my mind. I wrote to Dr Kurt Eulenburg and told him about the forthcoming Duisburg performance of the *Variations* and said that, as I would be in Bayreuth in the summer, if he wished to contact me he should do so immediately as I was on the point of leaving France. I received an extremely courteous answer in which he expressed interest in my work and told me he would try to meet me in Bayreuth.

The summer of 1934 was not the best moment to visit Germany, but I had been invited again to Bayreuth, I was about to meet a new publisher and the following autumn would see the premiere of my most recent and most ambitious work so far. So I went. Just before I left, the newspapers were full of Hitler's murder of Ernst Roehm in Munich. Roehm was one of Hitler's earliest friends and supporters; he had organised the Nazi S.A. (the Stormtroopers) without whom Hitler would never have come to power. According to the French newspapers, about 'sixty or seventy' people were killed in one night allegedly because they had been plotting to take control of the Party.

The day I arrived in Duisburg to meet Volkmann to discuss the *Variations*, the radio announced that the Fuehrer was going to make a public speech that night. Germany came to a standstill; everyone was awaiting the Chancellor's speech. As usual, he shouted and barked in his gutteral Austrian accent and then told the world that nearly two hundred people had been put to death in Munich. They had been discovered committing the most repulsive homosexual acts and were conspiring against him. Everyone knew that Roehm was homosexual, but apparently it was news to Hitler, such an innocent was he in these matters. The reaction in Germany was more or less that if Hitler had done it, he must have had good reason. Roehm and his crew were homosexuals and they were out to get Hitler, so they had it coming. The Fuehrer was always right. I didn't hear a single person express shock or horror. I was concerned more with art than with politics, so I kept my opinions to myself and travelled on to Bayreuth.

In the four years since I had last been there, the town had changed completely. The old Bayreuth of Toscanini had gone and had become the Bavarian arsenal for the National Socialists. The S.A. and the S.S. paraded up and down in their uniforms. As far as I could see they didn't harm anybody, but I found their militarism repugnant and threatening.

When the Festival opened it was totally unlike my memories of four years earlier. Gone was the cosmopolitan audience, the international stars. Toscanini refused to conduct, and the performances were second-rate. Previously dinner jackets had been *de rigueur*, even though the performances started at three or four o'clock in the afternoon. It showed respect for what Wagner's Bayreuth stood for. Now nearly everyone in the audience was in Nazi uniform and had been sent there because they were school-teachers or Party members. You would still find the odd isolated dinner jacket worn by a Wagner aficionado, who would make the pilgrimage to Bayreuth whatever the political situation, come Kaiser, Republic or Hitler. But even the Kaiser's youngest son, August Wilhelm (known as Auwi) was running round in a Stormtrooper uniform.

The first performance was *Die Meistersinger*. The printed programmes included the line 'The Fuehrer requests you to refrain from all demonstrations'. Wagner had built a box in the middle of the Festspielhaus for the crowned heads of Europe. At the opening in 1876 Ludwig II of Bavaria, the Prussian Emperor, Wilhelm I and all the minor princes of Germany had been present. Bayreuth became a playground for Germany's aristocracy, though how much of Wagner's music they understood is another matter. Now it was Hitler and his entourage sitting in the box instead — Goebbels and Goering and their wives, the whole Nazi gang and of course Winifred Wagner. It seemed that the new German regime must care very deeply for Wagner's art and that they were all there to pay him homage. The first act came to an end. Usually there were tremendous ovations for the singers and conductor, and four years earlier I had sat in an audience totally captivated by Wagner's music. The conclusion of the first act is theatrically very effective, but on this occasion there was hardly any applause; one or two people clapped, myself among them. Suddenly the entire audience turned to face Hitler's box and raised their arms in the 'Heil Hitler' salute. The Fuehrer sat there and lifted his hand a few inches in his own inimitable way to acknowledge the crowd.

In the interval a great crowd gathered outside the Festspielhaus. Hundreds were dressed in *Lederhosen* just as you would expect in Bavaria in the summer. I asked someone who they all were. I was told they were just ordinary people from Bayreuth

Hitler at Bayreuth; in the background two of Wagner's grandchildren, Friedelind and Wieland

who had come to see the Fuehrer. Hitler could be seen through a window, just as Wagner and later Cosima once used to be seen in the intervals, and dancing attendance on the Fuehrer and his henchmen was Wagner's daughter-in-law Winifred. To her dying day Winifred Wagner never renounced her passion for Hitler and his ideas. Even when her husband Siegfried was alive she and the whole Wagner family were very friendly with Hitler and he used to come and stay with them at Wahnfried. It is said that when he was in prison in the early twenties the paper on which he wrote *Mein Kampf* was sent to him by Winifred Wagner. *Mein Kampf* ('My Struggle') became the Bible of the German nation, a Bible of hate and war and pestilence, and there sat its Wagner-loving author during the interval with all these people gazing up at him adoringly; of course the moment he looked in their direction their hands would fly up in the 'Heil Hitler' salute. It was the same at the end of each act: polite applause for the performance and silent ecstatic adulation for the Fuehrer, despite the note from the great man himself requesting people to control their feelings. Obviously this wasn't an audience who, of their own choice, would have come to Bayreuth to see Wagnerian opera. They had been sent by their schools or by whatever party organisation they belonged to and were there for political reasons.

At the end of the opera it was customary to have supper at the Festspielhaus restaurant. My friends had had their own table there for years. Madame Fournier had first gone there as a young woman because her father had been an early Wagnerian enthusiast and had given money to help to build the Festspielhaus. He had never missed a performance at Bayreuth and attendance there had become a family tradition. When we reached our table, reserved as always for Madame Fournier's party, we found it surrounded by men in S.A. uniform, like a Roman phalanx. Sitting at our table were three or four German ladies and a man in uniform. I was the only one who could speak fluent German, and so I explained to the waiter that the table was already reserved. He told me in his Bavarian accent that he appreciated that, but there was nothing he could do about it. The ladies, all in their seventies, had been there since the early afternoon and refused to move until they had seen the Fuehrer, who was expected to take supper at the restaurant. Our party consisted of Madame Fournier, Hilda Gélis-Didot, Jane Bathori the great singer and a few other Frenchwomen — and French, of course, was not a popular language in Bayreuth at this time. Suddenly a cordon of young men in uniform formed itself around us: the chief guest and his entourage had arrived. It was all very cleverly arranged, with Hitler's table in front of a balustrade. He was surrounded on all sides and above by high-ranking officers, and the tables were set out in such a way as to make it possible for them to protect him against any eventuality. On his right was Winifred Wagner, beaming with pleasure at the honour of sitting with her beloved Fuehrer in public, and on his left sat Frau Goebbels. The rest of the large table was occupied by people from the army and the government.

I shudder to remember what happened next. The elderly German ladies were stuttering with the excitement of seeing their Fuehrer. They could scarcely believe that they were sitting within twenty feet of Adolf Hitler, the Saviour of the World. They were saying how beautiful his eyes were, and when I looked at him, all I could see were the ruthless eyes of a man who had just murdered his best friend, the friend who had helped him to the Chancellorship. But that had happened all of two weeks earlier and was completely forgotten now. The old ladies continued to extol the Fuehrer's beauty. Then one of them suddenly exclaimed, 'Oh! How great is love!' To this day I'm not quite sure what she meant; probably she was so carried away by the emotion of the moment that all she wanted was somehow to express the intensity of feeling that this man stirred within her.

The cordon was close around us. A man in S.A. uniform with a boy of about eight wearing a Hitler Youth outfit came up to speak to one of the men in it. He was explaining how much it would mean to the little boy if he were allowed to go up to Hitler and salute him. The S.A. man let him through. The man turned to his son and said: 'My son, you must understand that this is the greatest moment of your life. Go up to the Fuehrer, salute him and say, "Heil, mein Fuehrer". You will remember this moment as long as you live.' The little boy burst into tears and said he didn't want to go. The man tried to tell him that he was too young to understand, but that he would never again have another chance like this and that he should go and do what he was told. But the child was frightened by now and said no, he didn't want to. The man became furious, his face turned bright red and he was so angry that his son had dishonoured him in public that he slapped the boy's face twice and dragged him away.

At this time there was a big move to unite all the German-speaking peoples and those of German origin. Already people were clamouring for the annexation of Austria. Next, it would be all racially-related Teutonic countries, Switzerland, Holland, Norway and so on. There was a piece in my newspaper I bought after the performance about Dollfuss, the Austrian Chancellor, being held in the Chancellery, while outside in the streets there were demonstrations calling for Hitler to move into Austria and make the country a part of the German Reich. It was much later that we discovered the truth: that Dollfuss was shot by two Austrian Nazis and imprisoned in the Chancellery, that he wasn't allowed a doctor and that he bled to death. My French friends asked me to translate, the headline in huge type being 'Ein Volk Steht Auf' ('A nation rises'). Just as I was starting to read it a Stormtrooper came up to me and asked me to turn my newspaper round as the Fuehrer was looking at it. I turned and looked. He was only one table away. I had no real choice, so I turned the paper round for him. He nodded but didn't give me his famous salute. I nodded back and didn't salute him either, and thus ended our short acquaintanceship. He was still drinking milk, while everyone around him was quaffing beer. He made a big point of being a vegetarian and of not drinking alcohol or smoking. He was the perfect German, an example to everyone, a paragon of every conceivable virtue. So he ostentatiously drank milk and ate salad.

I don't know what these criminal fanatics were saying to each other, but it later transpired that the whole thing had been a well-planned charade. They were there, not for the music, but because Bayreuth is near the border, and from there they could most easily direct operations toward Austria. The world would think that Hitler had nothing to do with it, that the Austrians had killed Dollfuss, that the Austrians wanted the Anschluss and not Hitler. Hitler had been spending all his time in the opera house, absorbed by the music of Richard Wagner and not thinking about politics at all. I looked round at the murderous young faces of the S.A. men, and it struck me that they were probably the very ones who had massacred two hundred of Hitler's friends and supporters in Munich only two weeks earlier.

It was a remarkable evening, but soon over. The great man rose to his feet and kissed the hands of Frau Wagner and Frau Goebbels in a display of diplomatic courtesy designed to show how civilised he was. They left and suddenly all the uniforms were gone as well, and we could stay for another hour without being watched all the time by police. That night I was kept awake by the rumble of the tanks and cars and lorries driving through Bayreuth towards Austria: Hitler was directing operations from the Villa Wahnfried where he was staying. He would have overrun the entire country there and then if Mussolini had not had an alliance with Dollfuss and had not sent his troops to the Brenner. This was a problem, and for the time being he held his fire.

The following day was very peaceful. Hitler and his cabinet had gone, and the only uniforms we saw were worn by local officials. The performances went on as usual and some semblance of normality returned to Bayreuth. I saw Eva Wagner, the daughter of Richard and Cosima Wagner. She was the widow of Huston Stewart Chamberlain, the renegade Englishman who became more German than the Germans. He was an ardent Nietzschean and the first to propound the theory of racial purity for the producing of the German superman, a theory then expanded and developed by Rosenberg, the so-called philosopher of the Party. Frau Chamberlain walked around in a drab black dress and I understand she was *persona non grata* at Villa Wahnfried. When you look into the history of the Wagner family you find the same situations arising again and again. The fight over the Rhinegold, the power-struggles, the hates and passions of *The Ring* were all played out within Wagner's own family.

I received a telegram from Kurt Eulenburg, to whom I had offered the *Theme, Variations and Finale* for publication, to say that he was arriving in Bayreuth the

Administration de Concerts A. & R. FÉLIX, 33, av. de Suffren, Paris 7ᵉ, Tél. Suff. 04-87

8, RUE DARU – SALLE DEBUSSY – 8, RUE DARU
87ᵐᵉ CONCERT MAURICE SERVAIS
Propagande pour la Musique Vivante (5ᵉ année)

Le Samedi 22 Décembre 1934, à 16 h. 30

Œuvres de :

Arthur HONEGGER
et Miklos ROZSA

avec le concours de :

Mesdemoiselles Marianne COMPOSTINO, Clara et Jeanne HASKIL ;
MM. Charles BARTSCH, Maurice SERVAIS.

Participation aux frais : 7 *frs.* 12 *frs.* 15 *frs.* - 1/2 *tarif aux Étudiants*
Abonnements : 35 frs (six places utilisables en une ou plusieurs fois)

ENSEIGNEMENT MUSICAL PSYCHOLOGIQUE MAURICE SERVAIS
29, av. de Suffren, PARIS (VIIᵉ) Tél. : Ségur 27-73
Programme au verso

IMP. FERREY, PARIS XIVᵉ

The concert of chamber music by Honegger and me

next day. We went to the famous restaurant, 'Die Eule', where all the Wagner conductors used to go. There were plaques over their regular seats and the place had a marvellous atmosphere. A small gentleman arrived and asked for me; it was Dr Eulenburg. I took an immediate liking to this vivacious middle-aged gentleman, who told me he had had his eye on me for a long time, but knowing of my association with Breitkopf had assumed that he had little chance of acquiring anything of mine himself. But now he had a contract with him, if I would care to sign it. I signed and we shook hands. He said that he would be in Duisburg for the first performance of my *Variations* and he hoped that we would have a long and happy association. This was the start of a warm and lifelong friendship between us. After the success of the *Variations* he wrote me a letter giving me news of other performances. He went in person to see Bruno Walter in Vienna — who wasn't allowed to conduct in Germany any more — and showed him the score. Karl Böhm conducted it in Dresden, Swarowsky in Vienna and Walter in Amsterdam, and countless more performances took place. Suddenly I was well-known in central Europe, and everywhere the reviews were excellent, the public's reaction enthusiastic.

When I had heard all the operas in Bayreuth that season I suddenly felt homesick for Leipzig and all my old friends. The performances were not up to the old standard, and *The Ring* bored me as never before. I said goodbye to Bayreuth and never returned.

I took the train to Leipzig and stopped for about an hour in Munich. I got out and saw the newspaper headlines announcing the death of Hindenburg. Up to that point Hindenburg had been the elected President of Germany, with Hitler as his Chancellor. I bought a paper and was just about to start reading when I heard the click of heels and found two young S.A. men standing in front of me, giving me the fascist salute. I was speechless. One of them said, 'Are you Miklós Rózsa?' That sounded ominous. I said yes, I was. Then he said, 'Were you a student at the Leipzig Conservatory in 1928?' Again yes. I was about to give myself up when the two stern S.A. men started to smile; the one who had been asking the questions threw his arms around me and said how nice it was to see me again. It seemed that he had been in the same class, studying piano. I didn't remember him at all, but I smiled faintly and said that of course I remembered him and how was he? All three of us shook hands like long-lost friends. The train whistle went and I had to get back in and say goodbye to my 'old friend' from the Conservatory who now found it necessary to be a Nazi stormtrooper.

August wasn't the best time of the year to try to see my friends because they were all away on holiday. I walked through the town, thinking back to the time when I had first arrived there with such high hopes. Now it was full of men in uniform. I reached the town centre, the Augustusplatz, where the University, the Opera, the Museum and the main Post Office stood. It was a part I knew well, and I used to visit the Museum every Sunday. In front of it now were three large, strange, menacing objects. They were bombs, with placards describing their chemical components and their strategic use. One, dropped from a height of a thousand feet, would destroy so many buildings; another, dropped from a height of five thousand feet, would destroy a whole block. As people went past, some walked straight on, some stopped and read the notices, shrugged and went on their way. I couldn't understand what was happening, what all this was intended to achieve. In Paris there had been no talk of bombs or of war, everybody was leading a very pleasant life. Yet here were uniforms everywhere, display bombs designed to make people familiar with the idea of war — and all this in 1934, five years before the war actually started! Leipzig wouldn't be the only city where bombs were being exhibited in the streets. They must be on display in every German city. Weren't the Allies aware of all this preparation? Many years later, after war broke out, I asked my great friend Vansittart the same question and he smiled and said yes, he had known, but nobody would believe him.

It was good to be back in Paris where there was peace. There were no bombs on view in the Champs Elysées or the Place de la Concorde. Nobody talked about war. Of course Hitler and National Socialism were always in the news, but somehow nobody took it very seriously. I certainly didn't. Much more important for me was a message from Honegger proposing a joint recital with me in the Salle Debussy, a small chamber music hall in the Salle Pleyel. This was extremely kind of him. He didn't need my music, merely wanted to help me. He suggested what he called a 'parallel' concert of works by us both for the same forces.

Meanwhile Roland-Manuel got in touch again and offered me a way to make money with music, although there would be no artistic value in the exercise. He was involved with the famous Pathé-Journal whose newsreel appeared in over 700 cinemas. They were desperately short of good fanfares: they didn't like what was already available and wanted some specially written music of their own for occasions of pomp and ceremony. He said that they should be in all sorts of different styles, 'oriental', 'patriotic', 'mourning' and so on, and all different lengths. They needed about fifty.

The work took me several days, as I wrote nearly a hundred, and then I went back to Roland-Manuel and played them on the piano. He was delighted, accepted fifty of them, and said that they would be recorded the following week. He sent me off to their business manager who offered me a hundred francs for each of the fanfares I had written. I enquired about a contract. 'A contract between friends?' he said incredulously. I blushed with shame. There was I, an uncivilised boor, coming to one of the most highly civilised countries in the world and asking about a contract between friends! So I said that of course his word was good enough for me. We shook hands and I delivered the fanfares. Two weeks later I was hearing my own music in the cinema for the first time, and I wondered when I was going to be paid. It was difficult to ask, but I had to ask because there were bills to pay. The general manager explained that they were short of money and I would have to wait until they received their next payment from the French Performing Rights Society, in about three months' time. There was nothing I could do because they already had my music. I was obliged to agree.

The concert in the Salle Debussy shared by Honegger and myself was a sell-out. The hall held only about 400 people, and of course they had been attracted by Honegger's name, not mine. The concert went well, and afterwards Honegger and I went out for dinner. I decided to ask him about something that was troubling me. It wasn't an easy question to put. The income the two of us had received from the proceeds of the concert had been just enough to meet the cost of our very modest dinner and a bottle of red wine. I said to him that I knew it was his name that had attracted the audience, but even so we hadn't made any money out of it. 'How,' I asked him, 'are we composers expected to make a living?'

He laughed and said that surely I realised there was no money in composing serious music. So I pressed him further. He had a wife and child to support, and had a studio as well as the family home. He didn't teach. How did he manage to live? 'Film music,' he said. 'What?' I asked incredulously. He explained that he wrote music for films. I was unable to believe that Arthur Honegger, the composer of *King David, Judith* and other great symphonic frescos, of symphonic poems and chamber music, could write music for films. I was thinking of the musicals I had seen in Germany and of films like *The Blue Angel,* so I asked him if he meant fox-trots and popular songs. He laughed again. 'Nothing like that,' he said, 'I write serious music.' I had no idea what he was talking about, so he recommended that I go to see *Les Misérables* the next day and pay close attention to the music he had written specially for it.

The next morning I went along to the cinema to see *Les Misérables*. The film itself was very good and so was Honegger's music. It was dramatic and lyrical, and so much in his individual style that you would have known who the composer was even without seeing his name in the titles. I was amazed and rang him straightaway to congratulate him, to tell him I had learned something new and to apologise for asking him if he wrote fox-trots. I told him that he should make a suite from the *Misérables* music, that it was as good as anything else he had written and worthy to stand on its own. (Later he did so.) I also said that the idea of film music excited me very much and that I thought I could do it myself, even though at that time I had not written anything dramatic. I asked Honegger how to set about getting a job for the films. He said it was a difficult field to break into, but if he was offered a film he couldn't take on, he would recommend me. Whether someone who had never done a film before would be accepted was another matter; it was rather like getting your first work published. I had been very lucky in being taken up by a big publishing house so early in my career. Normally you would be asked what you had published already, and of course at the very start of your career you would have to say nothing. Then the publisher would tell you to come back when you had something published and he would consider your next work. It was exactly the same in the film world. No one unknown would stand a chance unless he came with a personal recommendation from someone who knew his music well and was a friend of the producer. This sounded like being in the country of the notorious *protekció* again.

The only man I knew who worked in the cinema was Jacques Feyder. I met him from time to time at dinner parties with his famous actress wife, Françoise Rosay. One day he invited me to tea saying that he would like to hear some of my music. I went to their lovely flat in the rue de l'Université and after tea I played all the music I had written that could be performed on the piano. He asked me if I had something more dramatic, more suitable for a film. I asked him to suggest a scene and said I would try to improvise something around it. He described a city in uproar, with people running all over the place. So I improvised some 'uproar music' for some minutes. He enjoyed it and said, 'That tells me everything.' He didn't say anything else and I didn't know why he had asked me to play, but I had a hunch that he had something in mind. He certainly did, as I was to find out later.

I tried once more to get my fee for the fanfares. Back I went to the gentleman who had been so shocked at the suggestion of a contract between friends. I said the three months were up and could I please have my money. He replied that the company was in great difficulties, but that if I gave them another three months, I would be paid. Again I had no choice, but I was beginning to get disillusioned about the Parisian way of doing business. When the three months were up and I was asked to give them another six, I realised my case was hopeless. So much for the 'contract between friends'.

Somehow I had to start earning a living. I met an Hungarian called Ákos Tolnay who worked in films as a scriptwriter. He suggested I came to London where he was going to work on a film called *Sanders of the River*. He thought I would stand a better chance of making headway there than in Paris. Then it looked for a moment as if the chance to write music for a French film was coming my way; but the whole thing fell through when it became clear that the production manager was expecting to be paid a fee for himself before he would commission me. After this the lure of London grew stronger. Eventually my mind was made up: I would try my luck. There was however a problem. I could afford the time and money for just ten lessons in English at the Berlitz School, which taught me enough to make myself understood, but not enough to understand what was said to me. Thus equipped for survival, I embarked on my first cross-Channel journey.

4: London (Part I)

I knew practically no one in London so I paid a visit to the Hungarian Embassy, a lovely building in Eaton Place. I had an interview with the Cultural Attaché and explained to him who I was and why I had come to London. He told me that by an amazing coincidence he had just had a visit from a lady who was going to choreograph a ballet for the Markova-Dolin Company and needed a Hungarian composer for it. The lady's name was Derra de Moroda, and the attaché made an appointment for me to meet her. She told me that she was planning a Hungarian folk ballet called *Hungaria* which needed a score based on Hungarian folk material. This, of course, was right in my line; I still had my little black book full of the tunes I had collected on our country estate. Miss Moroda seemed pleased with me and arranged for me to go and see the business manager of the company, Vivian Van Damm. Our meeting got off to a difficult start since my English was practically non-existent and he knew no other language. When I did manage to understand him, I tried to answer in French. He seemed to be asking how many pages the score would amount to. In Paris, I was used to being paid for orchestrations by the page; this was to be a full-length ballet and so I said it would run to five or six hundred pages. I had no idea what rate to suggest, but I thought that if Mr Van Damm offered me £100 it would seem like a fortune. I had £16 in my pocket when I had arrived in England, and with a fee of £100 for the ballet score I would be well set up. When Mr Van Damm offered me £600 in all, my command of the English language vastly improved and I became instantly fluent. 'Yes!' I said. He gave me an advance of £100, told me to expect the rest when I delivered the score and promised me the usual royalty agreement. I signed the contract and tumbled out of the Windmill Theatre into Shaftesbury Avenue with my head spinning. For the first time in my life I had £100 in my pocket.

Somehow I had had a premonition that it was going to happen. I was crossing Portland Place when a horse pulling a delivery cart lost its horse-shoe. There it was lying in front of me. I pretend not to be superstitious, but I picked it up anyway and, lo and behold, my luck changed for the better the next day. I still have it; it crowns the top of one of the bookcases in my music room.

I went back to Miss Moroda to discuss the scenario. She said she wanted as much folk material as possible, which was fine by me. We were not under pressure of time, so I took the opportunity to make a short trip to Paris to collect my things and to attempt yet again to get my fee for the fanfares. I rang the same gentleman at Editions Echo and he said, 'I'm delighted to be able to tell you that we now have the money and can pay you.' I rushed to his office and he said, 'We're very grateful for your patience and forbearance. Here is your money. You gave us fifty fanfares, didn't you? Fifty times fifty francs. . . .' 'Excuse me,' I interrupted, 'but we agreed it was to be a hundred francs for each fanfare.' 'That was a year ago,' said the gentleman who had poured scorn on the idea of a contract between friends, 'and everything is different now. Business is very bad at the moment and we can't afford those prices any more. All we can offer is fifty francs.' I had to accept, and thought what a fool I had been not to insist on a contract. I took the money and hoped never to set eyes on the gentleman again, and I never did. I picked up my things and returned to London.

I went back to working with Miss Moroda. I made a piano score first so that she could start work on her choreography while I went ahead with the orchestration. I delivered the score on time, and the ballet eventually opened in Glasgow. It was exciting and colourful to look at and the authentic costumes were beautiful. It was well received. The bottle dance, in which I used four village tunes, was very popular; English audiences had seen Russian dances before but not Hungarian ones, and they found them new and exotic. The ballet remained in the company's repertoire for two years and I was sent my royalties every week, so for the first time in my life I didn't have to worry about money.

I missed the incomparable beauty of Paris, if not its inhabitants' methods of conducting business, but every three months I had to return to get my visitor's visa renewed. On my fourth return to London I decided to stay for good; but when it came to renewing my visa for the fourth time the authorities grew suspicious and asked me how I was going to support myself in London. I told them I had a bank account, and had to supply them with a letter from my bank. Apparently everything was satisfactory and they granted me the visa. Even so I thought it advisable to consult the Hungarian Embassy's legal expert and he suggested I become a student. It didn't matter what subject I was studying; as long as I was an accredited student I would automatically get permission to stay for a year or two years, which could then be easily extended. So I took up choral conducting and became a pupil of Charles Kennedy Scott of the Trinity College of Music.

Kennedy Scott had exactly the right kind of temperament for a chorus director. He was patient and kindly, a first-class musician and a very charming man. I attended many of his rehearsals of the great Bach and Handel choral works at St. Margaret's, Westminster. I was his only pupil at that time, and he told me he would much rather I went to him at home instead of to the College; this I did for a whole year. We worked our way through the choral repertoire; I conducted while he played the piano and watched my beat. This was the first formal tuition in conducting I ever received. It had never entered my head to think of conducting; but that one year with Kennedy Scott opened my eyes and I realised that this was something I could do, and do well.

After a year Kennedy Scott said that there was nothing more he could teach me, so I went to John Fry, the conductor of the College orchestra, for further tuition in conducting. I was his pupil for four years, and he gave me an extremely thorough training. After the first year he allowed me to start conducting the college orchestra;

THE MAGAZINE PROGRAMME

DUKE OF YORK'S THEATRE
ST. MARTIN'S LANE, W.C.2

Proprietors ... ... MELNOTTE LIMITED
Directors ... ... A. P. MOORE, JOSEPH GREEN, F.C.A and J. WYATT
Licensed by the Lord Chamberlain to ... A. P. MOORE

VIVIAN VAN DAMM PRODUCTIONS, LTD.

present

THE
MARKOVA DOLIN
BALLET

with

MARKOVA

and

ANTON DOLIN

Supported by full Corps-de-Ballet

Full Symphony Orchestra
under the direction of
ARTHUR HAMMOND

The Magazine Programme may be obtained from Westby & Co., Ltd., 63/5, Piccadilly, W.1.

THE MAGAZINE PROGRAMME

THURSDAY and SATURDAY EVENINGS
December 26th and 28th

HUNGARIA

First Performance in London

A BALLET IN ONE ACT
Founded by Derra de Moroda on traditional Hungarian customs
Music selected from Hungarian Folk tunes orchestrated and arranged
by MIKLOS ROZSA
Choreography by DERRA DE MORODA
Decor by HEDLEY BRIGGS
Costumes by "SANDOR"

Aranka (a Peasant Woman)	...	JOAN BURNETT
Mariska } (her Daughters)	...	KATHLEEN CROFTON
Rozsika }	...	WENDY TOYE
Anuska } (their Friends)	...	PHYLLIS STICKLAND
Vilma }	...	EILEEN BAKER
Zorka (a Gipsy)	...	MOLLY LAKE
Janos (betrothed to Mariska)	...	FREDERIC FRANKLIN
Arpad (his Friend)	...	GUY MASSEY
Gyula (a Peasant)	...	ALGERANOFF

Peasants ... MOLLY RADCLIFFE, NATASHA GREGOROVA, CHRISTINE ROSSLYN, VERA LAVROVA, JOAN VAN WART, CECILY GRAYE, ANNA MARITA, DEIRDRE FAHY, MOLLY BERGMAYR, JOAN INNES, BERYL RIGBY, JOAN KENT, ELLA BENNETT, DAPHNE CHARLTON, BERNARD DE GAUTIER, TEDDY HASKELL, JOHN CRANSTON, JOHN REGAN, ROBERT DORNING, NORMAN WALLER, JOHN THORPE, PETER MICHAEL, TONI REPETTO

INTERVAL

The Magazine Programme may be obtained from Westby & Co., Ltd., 63/5, Piccadilly, W.1.

The Markova-Dolin *Hungaria*

---

he suggested that the best thing to start with was one of my own works, and I chose the *Variations*. It was the first time I had conducted a work of my own with a large orchestra. I found it a thrilling and fascinating experience, and the best possible way to learn.

I was still conducting the College orchestra each week when war broke out. Fry asked me if I would like to conduct the Civil Service Orchestra, made up of elderly gentlemen who had retired for one reason or another from professional orchestras, but who had joined together now to take music into army camps to entertain the troops. At the first rehearsal a trombone player came up to me and said, 'Sir, I have not touched this instrument for thirty years. But now it is my duty to play it again with you.' I rather wished he wouldn't touch it for another thirty years when I heard the sounds he was producing. I conducted the Civil Service Orchestra right up to the time when I left England for America. It mightn't have been the best in the world, but its members were marvellously dedicated and enthusiastic. But all this is to look ahead.

At the time of my arrival, in 1935, there was much talk about Hitler and the rearmament of Germany. Reports of Hitler's constant attacks on the Treaty of Versailles caused general anxiety about Germany's belligerence. Nobody, however, seemed unduly concerned, or to think that war was imminent. On my very first night in London I went to Piccadilly Circus, then the heart of the British Empire, the place every visitor must see. It wasn't exactly the Place de la Concorde or the

Jacques Feyder   Françoise Rosay

Etoile, but it had a certain excitement about it. Suddenly I saw the newspaper placards, 'England in Danger!' I felt frightened. I had only just arrived in this foreign country, and if war did break out Hungary would inevitably come in on Germany's side. It was too close geographically and too vulnerable to German influence to avoid doing so. I thought I would be classed as an enemy alien and probably interned. I bought a paper and searched through it for the article about Germany, but all I could find was a piece on the back page about England being in a weak position in the test match against South Africa. That was why England was in danger. I sighed with relief and thought what a happy country England must be.

All this time I was receiving letters from Kurt Eulenburg in Leipzig about further performances of my *Variations*. It appeared to be the most often-performed contemporary work on the continent. He had asked me for a new piece, and although I was considering one I had other things on my mind. For instance, I was spending a lot of time with my friend Tolnay who by now had his own film company, Atlantic Films. Whenever I saw him I heard the same story. The company was set up, a film was about to be made, I was to write the music, but there were problems with the script. He had to explain to me that the script was what I thought of as the libretto. Then Tolnay went off to Hollywood for a month or so. He wanted Edward G. Robinson for the main part but had to negotiate with Warner Brothers who had him under contract.

Meanwhile the ballet kept me going, and I was beginning to think about the piece for Eulenburg. Then one day I read in the paper that Jacques Feyder, my friend from Paris who had liked my music, was in London. I had recently seen his film *La*

Kermesse Héroique, and thought it a masterpiece. I decided to ring him up and tell him how much I admired his film. When he came to the telephone he asked me to come over to his hotel right away as he was in trouble.

When I got there I discovered that the 'trouble' was that he could speak very little English — despite having directed a film with Greta Garbo in Hollywood — and he could not make anybody understand him. He wanted his laundry done and a suit pressed, and would I please explain that to the hotel staff on his behalf. I had been in England for a year by this time and my English was up to dealing with the problem. Once his laundry had been taken away he wanted to take me out to dinner.

Now this was the first evening that my ballet was back in London after being out on tour, and I thought I ought to go and see what kind of shape it was in. Feyder asked if he could come with me, and we took a taxi to Streatham where the show then was before opening again in the West End. Neither of us had the least idea where Streatham was and we were both rather surprised when it took an hour to get there. Feyder enjoyed the ballet and thought it very colourful, tuneful and Hungarian. On the return journey we discussed it in detail, and for a film director he was very knowledgeable and intelligent about music. When we got back to town he took me out to a nightclub for supper and ordered champagne. I am teetotal so I just took the occasional sip, but Feyder enjoyed a drink; soon he had polished off the first bottle more or less on his own and immediately ordered a second. With every mouthful that went down his opinion of me as a composer went up. At one point he called me the greatest composer in the world. I smiled politely. Who was I to disagree? Then he told me I was going to write the music for his next film. I said that I had never written film music, an objection which Feyder summarily over-ruled. He still remembered my dramatic improvisations in his Paris flat. We were to discuss the whole thing the next day over lunch. His wife Françoise would have arrived by then from Paris and she would join us. By this time he was in no state to walk home unaided, so I helped him back to his hotel and assumed that by the next morning he would have forgotten the whole thing.

At ten the next morning the phone rang. It was Feyder to say his wife had arrived. I put on the only decent suit I possessed and went to the hotel for lunch. Françoise was as charming as ever, and we were joined by a Belgian gentleman, a costume designer. From time to time Françoise would say something like 'She's late,' but I didn't know who 'she' was and dared not ask. Eventually sherry was served and at about half past two the door opened and an extremely elegant lady in an extremely elegant hat came in, accompanied by a gentleman. They were introduced as Mr and Mrs Sieber; both had pronounced German accents and I had no idea who they were. We were now the only party in the restaurant. I sat between Mrs Sieber and Feyder and noticed that the waiters kept nudging each other and looking in our direction. I hardly thought that the fame of my ballet at the Streatham Theatre merited such attention, but every time a waiter passed us he would turn and stare. Suddenly Mrs Sieber turned to me and asked if her song was ready. I hadn't the slightest idea what she was talking about and so I said, 'What song?' Apparently Feyder had told her that I was writing the music for their picture and that she was going to have a song in it. At this point Feyder dug me in the ribs

Alexander Korda and Merle Oberon

with his elbow, none too gently, so I stammered out something about its not being quite ready but that I was working on it. She said that she was looking forward to hearing it, and turned to speak to the person on her right. I asked Feyder in a whisper who she was. 'Idiot! It's Marlene Dietrich,' he whispered back. I stole another glance at her. I had seen *The Blue Angel* only about three years earlier, but I wouldn't have recognised her. She looked completely different in real life, and besides, if you are introduced to a 'Mrs Sieber', Marlene Dietrich is the last person you expect her to be.

When the Siebers had left, Feyder rubbed his hands together with glee and said how pleased he was with the way the lunch had gone. It seemed that Dietrich had liked me, so now we could go and see Alexander Korda at Denham Studios. The film Feyder was about to make was for Korda's company, London Films, and we were going to have tea with Korda's brother, Vincent, who was an art director. I didn't know what an art director was, and Feyder, sighing heavily, had to explain that he designed the sets for the film. So we went out to Denham Studios to which, at that time, the finishing touches were just being put. I was introduced to Vincent Korda, who had piercing dark eyes that seemed to look straight through you. I felt very uncomfortable because I knew he was studying me closely, but he didn't address a single word to me.

We sat drinking tea for a good half hour and then, just as Feyder was standing up to go to keep his appointment with Alexander Korda, Vincent turned to me and asked, in Hungarian, if I was Hungarian. I said I was, and that was the full extent of our conversation. Feyder left me in an office off the main corridor to wait for him while he was with Alexander Korda. When he came out he was smiling and he embraced me. He had told Korda that he wished to discuss the composer he wanted for the film. Korda asked who it was, and when Feyder told him it was me he said, 'Rózsa? Never heard of him. Who is he?' Feyder had once been an actor, and now he pulled out all the stops. 'You mean you don't know Miklós Rózsa? One of the greatest talents of the age? Why, only the other night I went to his ballet for the Markova-Dolin Company. It's a masterpiece. A Hungarian masterpiece. Here we are doing a Russian picture and he could do the same thing for us. He'd give us exactly what we want.'

Korda said he had someone else in mind, a composer who had already worked for him. Feyder replied that he hated his music and he wanted me. Korda hesitated for a moment. Naturally he was anxious to please his new director (an old Hollywood friend), so he said he would think it over. Feyder said: 'You don't have to think it over. Just ask Vincent. He and Rózsa are old friends and practically lived in each other's pockets on the Montparnasse.' It was true that Vincent had lived in Paris for many years, but that was before my time there. I had never met him, I had never even heard of him; but this was the Feyder touch. In the end Korda realised he was getting nowhere. He didn't want to antagonise Feyder and he trusted his judgement, so he said, 'All right, you can have Rózsa.'

It would have been the easiest thing in the world for Korda to get on the phone to his brother Vincent and find out whether we really had 'lived in each other's pockets in Paris', and what he thought of my work. He would have discovered that we had met for the first time only half an hour before. Luckily for us this didn't happen, and Korda kept his word. Feyder was overjoyed and thought we would have a great time working together. And that was how it all started. That was how I became a film composer. That was how I began to live a musical Double Life.

5: London (Part II)

Tolnay came back from Hollywood, and I told him I had been engaged by London Films to do the music for *Knight Without Armour* with Marlene Dietrich and Robert Donat. He was pleased, and said he wanted me to do his film as well, and gave me a letter to that effect. So here was I, about to write the music for two different films, without any idea of how to set about it. How I envy the training available to young composers nowadays, with its wealth of technical advice! I became a regular visitor at the Gaumont Palace and the Chelsea Classic, where I saw some terrible films and heard some equally terrible scores. For me, film music meant Honegger's score for *Les Misérables*; that was what I wanted to hear and what I hoped to achieve myself. I managed to find one or two books on film music and film-making in a bookshop in the Charing Cross Road, one by Kurt London and another translated from the Russian. I learnt all I could glean from these books, which explained the vocabulary of film-making, but gave me very little idea of what was actually required of the composer. Consequently it was with some apprehension that, having received my contract for *Knight Without Armour*, I started work for Feyder.

All this time I kept one eye on what was happening with Tolnay's film, *Thunder in the City*, starring Edward G. Robinson. Tolnay invited me to sit in on a screen test; this was the first time I had set foot on a film set. The girl who was being tested was well-known in provincial repertory theatre; she had to read her lines with someone feeding her her cues in a monotone, off-camera. She was very beautiful, with flaming red hair. I was convinced she would get the part, the film would go into immediate production and I would soon be getting my first pay-cheque. It took two days for the test to be processed, and when I rang Tolnay to find out the result he told me that the girl didn't look good on the screen, she wasn't photogenic. The girl was Greer Garson; she was soon working for MGM and became a star within a year. When I finally came to do the music for *Thunder in the City* I made any number of novice's 'howlers'. In one scene an English family was taking tea outside on the lawn, all talking animatedly. This I underscored with an energetic scherzo for full orchestra. The director patiently explained to me that in order to allow the dialogue to be heard the music would need to be dubbed at such a low level that all we would hear would be a vague irritation of upper frequencies, principally the piccolo. So far from enhancing the scene the music would merely distract the audience. A pastoral oboe solo over a few strings or something of the sort was all that was needed. Well, I soon learned.

Knight Without Armour was a much bigger proposition than *Thunder in the City*, and first of all I had to write the song for Marlene Dietrich. She was playing a Russian princess and they wanted her to sing a Russian song. Feyder had in mind the sort of gypsy song that was sung in the Shéhérazade Night Club in Paris. I had never been there and I didn't know any Russian gypsy songs myself, so I scoured the London music shops and bought up all the Russian gypsy music I could lay my hands on. These songs weren't unlike Hungarian gypsy music, nearly all in the minor key and drenched in the same sickening melancholia and sentimentality. After I had played through the first hundred I decided I was ready to write the hundred-and-first myself. When I played it to Feyder he liked the main tune, but wanted a passionate, stormy middle section. He ranted and raved to demonstrate what he wanted and to get me in the mood. Finally I came up with something he liked.

We now needed a lyric for it and approached Arthur Wimperis, who had worked for Korda ever since he had co-written the script for *Henry VIII*. I played him the tune and a day or two later he brought me his lyric, which started with 'I love you, Petrushka'. I said we could never use that because Petrushka was the title of Stravinsky's ballet and everyone would laugh. Wimpy said it didn't matter because 'Petrushka' was simply the diminutive of 'Piotr', and so the song was about 'little Peter'.

We were now ready to present the song to Miss Dietrich. She liked the tune and hummed it through. I had to transpose it down a fourth; I had known she had a deep voice, but I hadn't expected it to be that low. Then we gave her the words and she started to laugh. 'This is ridiculous,' she said; 'I can't sing a song about Stravinsky's ballet!' Poor Arthur Wimperis had another try, but Dietrich still didn't like it. Two or three other lyric writers tried to put words to my song, but none of them met with her approval. We were still looking round for someone to write a suitably melancholy lyric when we were informed that the scene in which it was to be featured had been cut out.

The film was set during the Russian Revolution in October 1917 and needed a lot of 'on-scene' music — soldiers' choruses, military marches and the rest. A Russian expert was specially brought over from France to advise on the film, and from him I learnt about the Revolutionary song 'Yablochka' ('Little Apple') which I used during the titles. I didn't know about the copyright situation, but I thought if the song was really so well-known and popular during the Revolution it ought to be heard in the film. Later I found out that Glière uses the same tune in his ballet *The Red Poppy*.

There was one scene in which all the officers were gathered around the piano singing; when Princess Alexandra, the character played by Dietrich, came into the room they all stood up. The day this scene was due to be shot I arrived to find consternation at the studio because the pianist hadn't turned up. Feyder told me to get into the uniform myself. I was horrified, and protested that I didn't know the first thing about acting. He told me I didn't have to act, merely play the piano. Half an hour later I was back on the set dressed as a Russian officer and ready to make my debut in motion pictures. I can't say I stole the scene; I was no threat to Clark

Marlene Dietrich and Robert Donat in *Knight without Armour*

Gable or even Robert Donat. But it went well and a week later I was surprised to receive an actor's salary in addition to my usual pay-cheque. This was England, not France.

Unfortunately, that kind of opportunity didn't often arise and I had to wait thirty years for my next appearance in front of the cameras, in Billy Wilder's *The Private Life of Sherlock Holmes*. Wilder needed someone to conduct *Swan Lake* in one scene and I agreed to do it. I was kitted out in a genuine Victorian set of tails, but all that appears on the screen is my dramatic downbeat. That is the sum-total of my acting experience in films.*

Feyder helped me greatly with the music for *Knight Without Armour*. He kept impressing on me that he did not want 'polite' music, but something violent and strong. He said, 'This is a revolution. You can be as sweepingly dramatic as you like, as symphonically passionate and tempestuous as possible, and when it comes to the love scenes you can be really poetic and warm. There were two love scenes, one in the forest and one in the railway station. What Feyder said was a marvellous

---

*My back view can briefly be glimpsed in *The Story of Three Loves*, again conducting a ballet — Rachmaninov's this time.

guide, because I needed to be told how far I could go, what kind of orchestral colours I could employ. He came along to all the music recordings and we dubbed the film together. When it was finished I was finally introduced to Alexander Korda, who congratulated me and expressed his approval of the music. That was the beginning of a long friendship that was eventually to take me to America.

The first, and most difficult, film technique for a 'serious' composer to learn is how to write music with a stopwatch. It isn't enough to write music for a particular dramatic situation, it has to be for a given duration as well. This was a completely new technique as far as I was concerned. Even when a composer is bound by words, whether an operatic libretto or a sacred text, he is still ultimately his own master. Bach can make a single sentence in the B minor Mass last for a quarter of an hour. With a ballet, the choreography will be designed to synchronise with the music and not the other way round. But the timing of an action in a film is immutable. All the skills a composer has acquired in order to build a climax or create a satisfying musical shape and structure are useless to him in a film studio. Many good composers are simply unable to work back-to-front in the way that is necessary for films. During the mid-fifties I was asked to write music for *Green Mansions*, an MGM film set in the Brazilian jungle. I didn't like the script, and recommended Villa-Lobos for it. To my great surprise they engaged him. I met him when he arrived in Hollywood, asked him whether he had yet seen the film, and how much time they were allowing him to write the music. He was going to see the picture tomorrow, he said, and the music was already completed. They had sent him a script, he told me, translated into Portuguese, and he had followed that, just as if he had been writing a ballet or an opera. I was dumbfounded; apparently nobody had bothered to explain the basic techniques to him. 'But Maestro,' I said, 'what will happen if your music doesn't match the picture exactly?' Villa-Lobos was obviously talking to a complete idiot. 'In that case, of course, they will adjust the picture,' he replied. Well, they didn't. They paid him his fee and sent him back to Brazil. Bronislau Kaper, an experienced MGM staff composer, fitted his music to the picture as best he could.

The musical director for London Films was a young Scot called Muir Mathieson. After my contract came through I was told to report to him and introduce myself. He was a likeable man and our friendship lasted for many years. He was kind and helpful to me when I was first learning the job, although he didn't, I think, particularly like my music and never forgave me for not being British. He used to make fun of my poor English, and in return I would tease him about his Scottish accent. He had studied under Malcolm Sargent at the Royal College of Music and had therefore received a thorough musical training. He was very experienced at synchronising music and action and was a competent and serious musician, which is more than can be said for a good many conductors, used to conducting variety or vaudeville music, who drifted into films at this period.

My third film in London was *The Divorce of Lady X*, a charming picture with Merle Oberon, Laurence Olivier and Ralph Richardson. It was a comedy, and actually a remake of an earlier cheap version which Korda had made when he first came to England, *Counsel's Opinion*. For the first time I faced the challenge of writing 'comic' music, and I avoided the jazz overtones which were in vogue at that time, principally because I knew nothing about jazz. I provided a jolly little tune on the bassoon for Ralph Richardson, who was a Baron Ochs-like figure, and a lilting waltz-theme for Merle Oberon. I was rather pleased with my music and approached Chappell's, the official pubishers of London Films, to see whether they would consider publishing some of it. Their reason for refusing was that 'divorce' was such a non-commercial, malodorous word that nobody would buy the music. I mentioned that I considered my music far more original than another certain film score they had just brought out. 'Originality is not a quality we look for in the music business,' was their reply. My score earned the further distinction of being described in a review by Ernest Newman, doyen of English music critics, as 'largely unnecessary.' Encouraging words for a young composer.

It was the easiest thing in the world to be a Hungarian at the Denham studios. The three Korda brothers were Hungarian; so were Lajos Biro, the head of the script department, and Stephen Pallos, the head of the sales department. Alexander Korda was, I know, inundated with letters from Hungarians demanding work. It was said that he had a sign on his desk saying, 'It is not enough to be Hungarian. You have to be talented as well.' I used to think he had got it the wrong way round, and that it was not enough to be talented, you had to be Hungarian as well! There was an underlying resentful feeling against this Hungarian invasion of the British film industry, and a popular joke was that the three Union Jacks flying over the Denham Studios were one for each of the Englishmen working there. I hadn't come by my job at Denham through knowing any of the Hungarians there, but through the Frenchman Feyder. But, regardless of that, I was still looked on with suspicion, particularly in the music department.

I am not one to make friends easily and it was many years before I could say that I knew the Korda brothers well. My friendship with Zoltan was the first to blossom. He was always friendly and we often sat together in the studio canteen. He invited me home and I got to know his charming wife, the film actress Joan Gardner. Apparently he liked my music and we would discuss the future together. He used to say, 'What you need is a big, important picture,' and I would wholeheartedly agree with him. Finally the day came when he could say, 'I'm going to make a big, important picture. Would you like to do the music for it? I was overjoyed. The picture was *The Four Feathers*, a famous Victorian novel which had already been made into a film three times, but this was to be the first time in technicolour. This was a big step forward for me because, knowing nothing of the Englishry of Parry or Elgar, here was I being given this most English of films, against the will of the very chauvinistic musical director.

Much of the film was made on location in the Sudan and the crew was gone a long time, leaving me free, and without any financial worries, to write a suite in four movements. In the end it turned into a suite in three movements, because I cut out the first and later used it as the opening Allegro of my Concerto for Strings. I always work better for a change of scene, and so I went back to compose in my old room in Paris. When I returned to London the piece was finished.

I now had to set to work researching for *The Four Feathers*. Naturally the syllabus

70

Zoltan Korda

at Leipzig hadn't included Arabic or Sudanese music, and I studied indigenous music in the British Museum Reading Room in order to create the atmosphere.

Zoltan Korda came back from location a sick man. He had contracted malaria, and the tuberculosis he had suffered during the First World War on the Italian Front had flared up again. He went to Switzerland to convalesce, but he was still not properly fit on his return. Many interior scenes remained to be shot and he struggled on in the studio day after day. He was often to be seen with a thermometer sticking out of his mouth. Some people thought this an affectation, but he was really very ill all this time.

The film was marvellous. Zoltan was a high-principled man who had a great feeling for the under-dog; he was always fighting injustices on behalf of people not able to protect themselves. *The Four Feathers* had brought out the best in him.

We all knew it was a great picture. When it was finished Zoltan and Alexander had a private showing of it; I met Zoltan immediately afterwards and asked him

Ralph Richardson (right) in *The Four Feathers*

what the verdict was. Alex had said that the film should do great business. I felt as though a bucket of cold water had been thrown over me, but after forty-four years in films I realised that that was intended as high praise indeed. Pictures are made to make money and it was only my naïveté that made me see Alexander's comment as a gross insult to all the creative minds involved in the making of the film. There had been the long trip to the Sudan, every conceivable effort had been made in the cause of authenticity, and all Alexander Korda could find to say was that it should do great business. Well, it did, and that didn't hurt anybody.

Now we were ready to discuss the music. Zoltan Korda, like his brothers, was no musician, but he had an acute musical instinct and was well able to express exactly what he wanted from the music dramatically. There were two particularly important dramatic scenes. In one, Ralph Richardson is blinded by sunstroke and stumbles down the mountainside. The other was a beautifully staged scene with the barges being pulled up the Nile. I had an image in mind of the boatmen calling to each other in a kind of antiphony. I wanted to use a traditional boatman's song, in Arabic, and have the two groups on either side of the river answering each other. Zoltan was very keen on the idea, and in the end we used two choruses of male singers singing a primitive Sudanese melody I had discovered during my researches in the British Museum, accompanied by percussive African rhythms. This was before the days of stereo — it would have made a wonderful stereophonic impact — but we had the two choruses in opposite corners of the recording studio with the Arabic texts notated phonetically on their parts.

The day of the recording happened to be the day arranged for Queen Mary to visit the studio. She arrived with her lady-in-waiting and Alexander Korda just as we were about to start recording. Muir and I were introduced and she asked about the music. I explained to her that the Arabic words had been transcribed into phonetic English for the choir's benefit. She followed the music closely while Muir Mathieson conducted, and after several takes everybody was satisfied. Alex then took her to see a few scenes from the film. William Hornbeck, Korda's editor, had already edited three of the best — the blinding of Richardson, the battle of Omdurman and the scene with the barges. Zoltan himself wasn't there for the Queen's visit. He was an extremely shy man, and as I got to know him better I realised that being presented to Her Majesty would have been an intolerable embarrassment for him. Alex, on the other hand, was in his element. It was said that he had worn a dinner jacket for his first evening in England and hadn't taken it off since. He was instantly at home and made welcome in English society. Queen Mary was given tea in a little room next to the recording studios, and she seemed greatly interested in everything that went into the making of a film. She was a very gracious lady.

I witnessed another interesting encounter at about this time. I was walking down the long central corridor at Denham, with the studios on one side and the offices on the other, and coming towards me was a very tall man with long snow-white hair, walking a little stiffly. I recognised him immediately as Ignaz Paderewski, who was there working on the film *Moonlight Sonata*. Suddenly another man came round the corner into the corridor, a stocky little fellow who bellowed 'Paderewski!' Paderewski turned and saw him and exclaimed, 'Churchill!' They shook hands and stood there smiling at each other. As I passed them I thought it might be the first time they had met since the Versailles Conference, at which Churchill represented Britain and Paderewski was there in his capacity as the first President of the newly-constituted Poland. I thought to myself, 'How are the mighty fallen!'* One was at Denham acting in a film called *Moonlight Sonata*, even if he did also play the piano in it, and the other was there as a scriptwriter, working on a proposed film for Korda about his ancestor, the First Duke of Marlborough.

The Four Feathers, probably the first technicolour film shot on location, was premiered at the Odeon, Leicester Square, on 20th April 1937, and was a tremendous success. This premiere was a great occasion with all the men in tails and the ladies in long dresses. The author, A. E. W. Mason, made a speech and there was a feeling of celebration in the air. Not only did the picture do great business, as Alexander Korda had prophesied, it was also an artistic triumph for British filmmaking.

About this time I received a telegram from Budapest to say that I had been awarded the Franz Joseph Prize. The memory of Franz Joseph is frowned on these days in Hungary, but at the turn of the century he had set up a Foundation to award prizes in the arts — for architecture, painting, sculpture, music and literature. The

---

*When Clemenceau learned that Paderewski had accepted the Polish premiership, his reaction also was 'quelle chute!'

prize was a considerable sum and was given in recognition of past work; it was awarded one year and then renewed for another if the artist merited it. I was twenty-nine when I entered for it. Considering that I hadn't been resident in Hungary since my eighteenth year, had no important patrons there and no 'protekció', I was surprised to win. The prize was awarded to me again the following year, 1938.

My name appeared in the newspapers and one day I received a phone call from BBC Television who wanted to interview me. I would be taken to a lady's private house where she would discuss the content of the interview and prepare a script. Then we would go on to Alexandra Palace for the actual telecast. This was all very exciting, particularly as television was still in its experimental stage and very few people had access to a set. I was very nervous when I arrived at the lady's house because although I could make myself understood, my grammar was still very imperfect. We wrote a script for the interview and agreed that at the end I would play some of my own music on the piano. On the bus to Alexandra Palace my lady suggested that it might be wise for me to study my script. I was getting more and more stage-frightened, but managed to memorise my answers to the prepared questions. When we arrived I was introduced to Leslie Mitchell, the famous inter-viewer of the thirties, and the run-through went well enough. I was then made up, another new experience for me. I seized a few free moments to check my script for the last time, pacing up and down and trying to assume an English accent to outdo all English accents. At last the time came and Leslie Mitchell and I sat down, without our scripts, at a table, ready to go. I answered his first question quite brilliantly and likewise his second. Then came the third. I had noticed Leslie Mitchell looking slightly uneasy, and the question he came out with wasn't the third in the script I had memorised. I realised that my third answer didn't fit his third question, so I just mumbled something incoherently. Likewise the fourth question bore no relation at all to anything we had discussed earlier, and so of course, my fourth answer had nothing whatsoever to do with it. So I muttered and mumbled and all the people behind the cameras were trying to get me to smile at the camera. But how could anyone smile in such a desperate situation? Eventually I did manage a wan smile, but no words would come, because whatever I thought of saying would have been quite wrong in the circumstances. Eventually Leslie Mitchell saved the day by saying, 'Perhaps you would now play some of your music for us?' Nobody has ever moved to a piano faster than I did then. I played some of my piano *Bagatelles*. Afterwards everybody was smiling; Leslie Mitchell shook my hand and said what a great interview it had been. I decided, however, that as a television personality my prospects were poor.

One day when I was visiting a friend at the Hungarian Embassy in Eaton Place, he introduced me to Gabriel Pascal. I had read quite a lot about Pascal in the papers at this time because he was about to make a film of Shaw's *Pygmalion*. He knew I was working for Korda and I was rather taken aback when he said, 'Fine friends you've got!' I asked him what he meant. He said he had known Korda a long time, from his days in Berlin and Vienna. So when it came to casting *Pygmalion*, knowing that Korda had all the best actors and actresses in England under contract, he had gone to him and asked him, as a favour, to release the most suitable of his stars to

Gabriel Pascal (left) with Vincent Korda

play Professor Higgins. 'I needed a great actor,' said Pascal, 'and whom do you think he offered me? Whom do you think he dared to suggest?' I had no idea. 'That cheap ham, Laurence Olivier, that's who. He's a nothing.' I said I thought that if Alex had suggested him, he probably had something in his favour. 'He's a nobody. He would have ruined my picture,' said Pascal. Finally he cast Leslie Howard in the part, who of course was no mean actor, but I couldn't see that there would have been anything wrong with Olivier as Higgins. I thought back to the time when I had been told that Greer Garson wasn't photogenic and had no screen presence, and six months later she was a star. Now Laurence Olivier was a third-rate actor not good enough for *Pygmalion*. I began to wonder how talent was measured or appreciated in the world of films.

Pascal suddenly became very friendly. He had heard some of my scores (by this time I had done four or five for London Films) and liked them, and asked if I was free at that moment. As a matter of fact I was, because this was between my coming back from Paris and starting work on *The Four Feathers*. He said he was in great trouble. William Walton had agreed to write the music for *Pygmalion*, but because the picture had been delayed for one reason or another and because Walton now had to work on a commission from Heifetz for a violin concerto, he was no longer available to do the score. Pascal needed a composer, and asked if I would be interested. I said I thought I would and we arranged for me to go to Pinewood Studios the following day to discuss it.

I drove out the next day and found Pascal's office full of people. He was storming about cursing the English in Hungarian, saying that they had no business to be making films, they were ruining his picture for him and they had no right to live if they wouldn't do what he wanted. He said he would play some of my recordings to Shaw who, after all, used to be a music critic and was to be allowed a say in selecting a composer for the film. He told me he needed a big waltz for the ballroom scene.

I was supposed to ring Pascal a week later. When I did, he told me some complicated cock-and-bull story about William Walton meeting Honegger in Paris and promising him the score, and that Pascal no longer had any say in the matter himself. If I had known the business better I would have realised that Walton had no right to make that kind of promise, but I said I understood the position and congratulated Pascal on his new composer. Honegger did in the end write the score for *Pygmalion*, but when the picture was released in America, the music was not 'sweet' enough for Hollywood's taste so it was 'fixed up' by some local genius. It was just as well that I didn't do the music for *Pygmalion*, however, because soon after this Zoltan Korda returned from the Sudan and *The Four Feathers* was ready for its score.

One night at the beginning of the war I was invited to dine with the three Kordas at their house in Denham village, where Pascal was also to be a guest. After the ladies had left the room at the end of the meal Pascal flopped down in an easy chair with one of Alex's enormous Havanas and started to tell us that his next production was to be a non-Shavian one; in fact, not fiction at all but the 'true story' of Amelia Earhart, the aviator who disappeared so mysteriously with her plane. Gaby warmed to his theme and began to stride about the room waving his cigar like a baton. He alleged that he had forced Amelia's husband, the publisher Putnam, to tell him the truth about her disappearance. It was a love story. She and her co-pilot were hopelessly in love, and had decided to crash their plane in the ocean, ending their lives in a *Liebestod*. The music had already been written, too, by Stokowski. He had composed the most beautiful melody, which was to be synchronised to the bubbles rising from the sinking plane. The last tragic note, the last bubble: end of picture and the music swells up.

It was a masterful selling speech — only Korda wasn't buying. Stokowski's name was well-known at the time, partly because of his appearance as himself in *A Hundred Men and a Girl*, and partly because he was travelling about Europe with Greta Garbo. Gaby ignored the fact that Stokowski wasn't a composer and never claimed to be one. But he was a good name to end the sales-talk with, and I could see how Pascal had persuaded Shaw to allow him to film his plays, and why Aldous Huxley once called him 'the Hungarian Baron Münchausen'.

Incidentally, a friend of mine once asked Stokowski about his much-publicised 'romance' with Greta Garbo. 'Well,' said the Maestro with resignation, 'it was all rehearsals and no performance.'

When not actively engaged in films of my own I sometimes did odd musical jobs like helping other composers with orchestration. Once I even ghost-wrote an entire score for another composer, who shall be nameless. Muir Mathieson conducted; I was standing behind him when we recorded the title-music, and it was with mingled astonishment and fury that we saw the legend come up: 'Music composed and conducted by (Mr X).' This kind of fraud isn't unusual in the entertainment business, but I shouldn't have been a party to one.

Korda was responsible for the teaming of the English director Michael Powell with the Hungarian writer-producer Emeric Pressburger, a partnership which was to bear fruit in some of the finest British films of the forties and fifties (e.g. *The Red Shoes* and *Black Narcissus*). *The Spy in Black* was their first collaborative effort, and I did the music for it. Some years later in Hollywood I got a telegram from Powell asking me to join him in Canada to research Canadian folkmusic and then to return to London to do the music for *49th Parallel*. I had to refuse since at that time I was committed to Korda and he wouldn't let me go; in the event I was glad I did, since that film marked the cinematographic debut of the composer who at that time was the undisputed leader of music in England, Ralph Vaughan Williams.

London Films and Denham Studios had been financed by the Prudential Life Assurance Company, and apparently, though Korda had made a great many films between 1935 and 1938, the income wasn't quite as much as the Prudential had hoped. So it was decided that the company should take over the running of the studios and rent out the space, while Korda formed his own private company, Alexander Korda Films. All Korda's employees were moved to what was known as 'the old house', a lovely building at one end of the studios beside a gently flowing river, and the big studio, the old London Films Studio, was now no longer under the control of Alexander Korda.

In a way this was all to the good, because Korda always did his best work when he was concentrating on a single project, and not when ten separate films were being made at the same time, all demanding his constant attention. He was a member of the American company, United Artists, which had been set up to finance and distribute the films of Charlie Chaplin, Douglas Fairbanks Senior, Mary Pickford, Samuel Goldwyn, David O. Selznick and Korda. This meant that his films were assured of immediate release in America and were shown all over the world.

After the great box-office success of *The Four Feathers*, Korda's biggest since *Henry VIII* and *The Ghost Goes West*, Alex asked me to come and see him. He told me how pleased he was with the music and announced that the next picture I was to work on was very important from a musical point of view. This was *The Thief of Baghdad*. He told me the story, which was an Arabian Nights fantasy, and said that my contract would run from that day and that he was increasing my salary by a large amount. I must admit that my salary had been rather low up until then. The last thing I would have done would have been to ask for a rise, but now Korda was giving me one without my having to ask.

The film was already in preparation. I read the script and thought it not very good; and apparently that was the general opinion. Directors came and went. Korda tried several for a couple of weeks each but couldn't decide on the right one. Eventually he announced that he had settled for a German by the name of Dr Ludwig Berger. Berger had recently made *Les Trois Valses* in Paris with music by Oscar Straus, the famous Austrian composer of operettas such as *The Chocolate Soldier*. Berger arrived at Denham to start work on *The Thief of Baghdad*, and

Muir Mathieson   Ludwig Berger

shortly afterwards Korda summoned me to his office for a private meeting. He had a serious problem: Dr Berger wanted Straus to write the score for *The Thief of Baghdad*. Not only had Korda promised the job to me and had me under contract to do it, but he did actually want me, and not Straus, to compose the score. But everything was ready for the production to start: sets were constructed, actors were hired. A number of musical sequences were necessary before shooting began and Berger was insisting on Straus. Korda had to start production in order to keep the support of his financial backers, for he needed their money to pay his employees' wages. He was obliged, for the moment, to go along with Berger and engage Straus, but he wanted me to trust him to see me right in the end. Naturally this came as a shock, but I told Korda that I trusted him completely and would do whatever he wanted. He had already talked the matter over with Berger and it was understood that while all the pre-production music would be provided by Straus, all the dramatic and colouristic music would be written by me. In any event, I was still on the production team. I agreed — I had no choice.

Slowly the music began to arrive from Vichy, where Straus was taking a cure. It was impossible — typical turn-of-the-century Viennese candy-floss. I stuck to my promise to Korda and didn't say a word, but Muir Mathieson was outspoken in his denunciation and went round telling everyone, including Vincent Korda, that these songs would ruin not only the picture, but the company as well.

The next day Mathieson and I had a cryptic summons from Alexander Korda's office to report to him at ten the following morning. When we arrived his secretary looked very cowed and said, 'He's in a vile temper this morning. I don't envy you having to see him.' Dr Berger arrived and was shown straight into Korda's office. A few minutes later Korda called us in with an imperious 'Boys!' It was always a bad sign when he addressed you as 'boy', and he sat there behind his desk glowering ferociously at us like a Thundering Jove, a Jupiter Tonans. 'Boys', he said again, 'I understand you have been making disparaging remarks about Mr Straus's songs. Is this true?' Mathieson immediately lost his temper and let fly at Korda. 'It certainly is,' he shouted. 'His music stinks to high heaven and it is my duty as your musical director. . . .' Korda heard him out and then said, 'Right. I want it clearly understood by the pair of you that in all artistic matters the sole and final arbiter is Dr Berger. It that quite clear? That's all.' Mathieson stormed out in a rage and Dr Berger went away grinning like a Cheshire cat. Just as I was about to leave, Korda called me back, and asked me my opinion of Straus's music. I told him that frankly the music would be quite charming for a Viennese revue of 1900, but that it was completely unsuitable for an oriental fantasy. He then told me to go ahead and write the music as I thought it should be written, and to report back to him when it was done. Meanwhile I wasn't to tell a soul what I was up to, not even Mathieson.

A week later I rang him up to tell him I had finished and did he want to hear what I'd done? 'No,' he said. 'What I'm going to do is give you an office next to Dr Berger's. Keep playing your music until he comes in and listens to it. Don't say I told you to do it, just say you wrote it off your own bat and let him hear it.' So I moved into the office next to Dr Berger's and from ten in the morning until five every evening I thumped out my music as loudly as I possibly could. The secretaries in the offices above and below me complained that it was impossible for them to get any work done with all the noise, but I just kept on playing. The first day nothing happened. The second day I could hear Berger's voice through the wall, so I played more loudly than ever, but still he didn't come in. On the third day, he stormed into my room and said, 'I've been listening to this now for two whole days. Do you mind telling me what's going on?' I was all wide-eyed innocence. 'Well, you see, Dr Berger,' I began, 'I had a few ideas for the picture and I wrote them down I thought you might be interested to hear them.' He said, 'We've already got all the music we want and we won't even know what we need from you until after we've finished filming. So what are you up to now? Mind you, there was one melody I rather liked. You can play me that if you want.' So I told him I had written the music for the 'Silvermaid's Dance'. He advised me that Straus had already done that. I said I knew he had, but I had one or two ideas of my own, and I played them to him. He didn't say a word. I played Sabu's song, then another piece I had written. He paced up and down the room and left the room telling me not to go and that he would be back shortly.

About ten minutes later he was back. 'I've been to see Mr Korda,' he said. 'I told him that I much prefer what you've done to what Straus has sent us, but how am I going to tell the old man?' Now Korda had a genius for this kind of manipulative diplomacy. He was like a brilliant chess player, moving his pieces round the board, always half-a-dozen moves ahead of his opponents. It was incredible how he had manoeuvred Berger into this position, and it made me very pleased that I had put my trust in him.

A telegram was sent to Oscar Straus who alleged that his reputation was being ruined and threatened to sue, but Korda paid him his full fee and I was formally reinstated as the sole composer on *The Thief of Baghdad*.

The day after Berger had changed his mind about Straus, Korda called me into his office, looked at me, smiled and said, 'It worked.' I thanked him for the confidence he had shown in me and he said, 'My boy, I know your music. I had every reason to be confident.' He told me the lyrics were to be written by his friend Sir Robert Vansittart, chief diplomatic adviser to the British Foreign Office. I didn't know that Sir Robert was a lyricist, but Korda said, 'He is a fine poet, a good writer, and I think you will like him.' I did. He was, without doubt, the finest human being I have ever met in my life.

I knew very little about his role in British politics. First of all, I understood nothing about politics; secondly, all I did know was what I read in the newspapers, and Vansittart wasn't somebody who appeared in the limelight very often. He was the Grey Eminence, the power behind the throne at the Foreign Office. As far as I was concerned, he was my collaborator and lyric writer. He was over six foot, lean, active, with a strong profile, a born diplomat. He would have been about fifty years old at this time. He never treated me as a 'bloody foreigner'. We were equal partners: he wrote the words and I wrote the music.

There were several jobs to be done. Sir Robert was working on the script with Miles Malleson, who as well as being a fine actor — he was playing the part of the Sultan — was also a writer. The three of us discussed the songs which would have to be written. For the opening in Basra harbour we needed a song about the sea; we also needed one for the Genie, who was to be played by the popular Negro actor, Rex Ingram, already well-known in Hollywood and on the New York stage. And, of course, Sabu had to have his song.

During the whole summer of 1939 I spent every weekend at the beautiful, sixteenth-century Denham Place, Sir Robert's home. Throughout 1938 there had been grave fears that war was imminent, and I stood in Piccadilly Circus with thousands of others watching the illuminated headlines on the night that Chamberlain came back from Berchtesgaden with the promise of 'peace in our time'. There was great rejoicing. Few people would have admitted that it was only a temporary reprieve and that war, sooner or later, was inevitable. Sir Robert had played a key role throughout this difficult time.

On my last visit to Paris I had completed my *Three Hungarian Sketches* and played the work to Charles Münch, who was enchanted with it and thought it better than my *Variations*. He was going to conduct it with the Lamoureux Orchestra. I asked his permission to dedicate the piece to him and he granted it. On my return to London I wrote and told him of the problems I was having with *The Thief of Baghdad* — this was before I had become the one and only composer working on the film. He sent me a postcard in reply: 'You have your problems with The Thief of Baghdad. We have ours with The Thief of Berchtesgaden.'

Sir Robert (later Lord) Vansittart

He also told me that he had invited Karl Straube and his Thomanerchor to Paris to perform Bach's B minor Mass and that Straube had expressed a wish to see me again. I went over to Paris for the performance and afterwards at the reception I renewed my friendship with Straube. He had suddenly grown older and his hair was snow-white. He was sixty-five and he seemed terribly tired after the performance. He congratulated me on my success; he thought it a pity that Breitkopf & Härtel hadn't published my *Variations*, but he knew why they hadn't. It was typical of his generous nature, particularly as he had himself been responsible for my early contact with Breitkopf to say that it didn't matter who published the piece; the important thing was that it was a huge success.

It was a strange, rather disturbing gathering. Frau Straube expressed strong Nazi sympathies. She kept referring to 'these little Austrians,' and said, 'They all thought they were going to get the best positions in their country when we took over. That's ridiculous. We put our own people in the best positions.' Straube himself said nothing. The boys in the choir were all new to me, of course. They all looked strikingly blond and Teutonic and in their stiff behaviour there was something reminiscent of the Hitler Youth. Münch made a speech in his Alsatian German, saying that music was the only truly international medium, that it brought people together and created strong emotional bonds across radical differences of language and culture. 'We are French,' he said, 'and you are German. We are happy to have you here among us and I hope our friendship, rooted in music, will grow and flourish for many years to come.' Poor Charles Münch. How could he know that less than a year later these same boys would be back in Paris in uniforms with machine guns in their hands?

Eulenburg wrote to tell me that my *Three Hungarian Sketches* had been accepted for the International Music Festival in Baden-Baden. This was a major piece of luck for me, because all the top conductors and critics in Europe would be attending. A little later the conductor of the Baden-Baden Festival wrote to say that seven rehearsals were scheduled and he was inviting me to attend them as well as the festival itself, all my expenses to be met by the German government. He also sent me the full programme for the festival, which looked very interesting. Every nation was represented, and my piece was the official Hungarian entry. The BBC Chorus was giving a complete evening concert of new English choral music.

The papers were full of the worsening political situation. Austria had already been annexed; Czechoslovakia was gone, and Poland, with its vulnerable Danzig Corridor, was under constant threat. The newspapers were beginning to advise British subjects not to travel in Germany. Although I wasn't a British subject I felt I owed allegiance to Britain. I rang the BBC and asked if the BBC Chorus were still intending to go to Baden-Baden and was told that the trip had definitely been cancelled. I told the gentleman at the BBC what my own position was, and he advised me not to go. I decided not to. I wrote to the conductor and told him I was very busy — which was true — and couldn't afford to take a whole week to come to the festival. After the performance he sent me a telegram to say that the work was a great success and the reviews were outstanding.

I was warned by Eulenburg that I would be committing artistic suicide and ruining him as well if I persisted in dedicating the *Sketches* to Charles Münch. In his experience, no conductor would be interested in a piece dedicated to another, especially an up-and-coming conductor like Münch. But I had already asked Münch's permission for the dedication and he had given it, so Eulenburg proposed printing only six copies with the dedication in place, two for Münch and four for me. I hope dear Münch never found out.

Shortly afterwards I received another letter from the publishing firm, but this time it wasn't signed by Eulenburg but by Schulze, his business manager. He told me that Eulenburg had been sent to a concentration camp and asked me for help on his behalf. Unfortunately, of course, there was nothing anyone in London could do. Then, just before war was declared, I received a letter from Eulenburg himself, from Switzerland, informing me that he and his family were now safely together in Basle.

So the storm clouds were gathering in 1939, but I was so busy and excited about *The Thief of Baghdad*, now with a script that had been improved beyond all recognition, that I was almost unaware of what was going on in the world around

At work on *The Thief of Baghdad* (with Toscanini's tacit disapproval)

me. Naturally enough, not everything was plain sailing — it never is when a film is being made.

Berger wanted me to do the market scene in the manner of a musical; that is, he wanted the music first, to which he would then shoot the action. The scene introduced Sabu as a thief in the market place: everybody was bustling around selling while Sabu was busy stealing. We worked out the scene in terms of action and choreography and ended with a sequence over five minutes long. After I had written the music Berger went over it with me and I made many adjustments, slipping in an extra two bars here, re-introducing Sabu's theme there. Finally we were all satisfied and we recorded it. Then came the playbacks, and Berger wanted the actors to move in strict synchronisation with the music. Naturally enough the result was chaos. Little Sabu was expected to move like a puppet in a puppet theatre, the actors like dancers in a pantomime, but to appear at the same time to be acting quite spontaneously and naturally. They just couldn't get it right, and after a week's work we had practically nothing to show. When Korda saw the result he all but burst into tears, it was so awful. He called me in and asked me if I could adjust

Sir Robert Vansittart
l'éminence grise
du Foreign Office
écrit des textes du film
« Le voleur de Bagdad »

Il y a dans la triste Europe des millions et des millions de braves gens qui attendent une éclaircie dans le ciel politique, chargé d'orages. Pourquoi ne pas leur signaler un tout petit fait, gros de sens, si l'on y réfléchit?

Le Chief Diplomatic Adviser de M. Chamberlain, sir Robert Vansittart, le *power behind the throne*, le (pouvoir derrière le trône), l'Eminence grise du Foreign Office, pour tout dire, écrit les textes du film *Le Voleur de Bagdad*, qu'Alexandre Korda va tourner à Londres.

Félicitons-nous de cette bonne petite nouvelle. Si sir Robert a le temps de faire du cinéma, c'est qu'il n'y a pas de danger imminent en Europe.

Sir Robert fait des couplets sur les airs du compositeur Miklos Rozsa. Et comme celui-ci est Hongrois, sir Robert peut même se donner l'illusion d'avoir ramené Budapest vers l'axe Londres-Paris.

On the set of *The Thief of Baghdad* with June Duprez   The *Figaro* article about Vansittart

the same music to the scene *after* the sequence had been shot; I told him of course that was perfectly possible, whereupon he put a stop to any further antics of this kind.

In the end the only sequences shot to pre-composed music were those involving special effects — the gallop of the Flying Horse and the Silvermaid's Dance. The scene with the Flying Horse, in which the Sultan is so enchanted by the magic toys and the ride across the sky above Baghdad that he gives his beloved daughter's hand to Jafar the Magician, was a collaboration between Vansittart, Miles Malleson and myself. The script and the music were conceived as a single entity; the three of us spent all day at the piano at Denham Place working out the details.

Vansittart and I never established a fixed pattern of working together. Sometimes the music came first, sometimes the lyric. In the case of the 'Lullaby of the Princess' he wrote the poem first, which I then set to music and which in fact became the main love theme of the picture. With 'Sabu's Song', again an important song because it had to reappear throughout the film, the tune came first and the words followed later.

I soon became almost a permanent fixture in Vansittart's home. He spent the week at his flat in London, but every weekend we were together at Denham Place, and I soon got to know his enchanting wife. We never discussed politics, but these were critical days for Britain. Stafford Cripps was in Moscow trying to forge an alliance with the Russians, but was pipped at the post by Ribbentrop. The Russian–German agreement came as a great shock to England, but whether Vansittart was expecting it or not I am unable to say. Sometimes we would be working at the piano and the butler would come in to call him to the telephone. When he came back he never revealed whether it had been good or bad news (though sometimes he looked ashen-faced) and I never asked him. We would simply carry on from where we had left off.

Somehow the foreign press got wind of the fact that he was writing the lyrics for *The Thief of Baghdad*. It was at about this time that *Figaro* in Paris printed an article to the effect that if the chief diplomatic adviser to the British Foreign Office had time to write lyrics for a motion picture with me, there could be no immediate danger of war. A fortnight later, on 3rd September 1939, war was declared. Thereafter my relationship with Vansittart changed. He opened up and talked about subjects I wouldn't have dared mention to him. He told me fascinating things about the people he met in diplomatic circles, and about the past few years when he had constantly and unavailingly been trying to warn the British government of what was happening on the continent. He talked about the 1936 Olympics at which he and his wife had met Hitler. He spoke fluent, idiomatic French, and also German and Arabic, just as a senior British diplomat should. Even in 1936 he had been thought of as a Germanophobe and a warmonger. Hitler had been told that he was a swarthy little Jew and was shocked to be introduced to the tall, imposing British gentleman who spoke perfect German.

Vansittart presented me with two volumes of his poetry, suggesting I might find something in them to set to music. One collection, *The Singing Caravan*, he had written at the time he was British Ambassador in Teheran. I set two of them for contralto and piano, 'Beasts of Burden' and 'Un Jardin dans la Nuit'. I found the latter title too close to Debussy's 'Jardins sous la Pluie', and asked him if I could change it. It became 'Invocation', published later in America and re-published now in England.

There was panic in London at the outbreak of war because people were caught unprepared. On that Sunday, soon after Chamberlain had come on the radio to announce that 'a state of war exists between Germany and England', I was driving towards London when there was an air raid warning. It was a false alarm, but of course all the traffic was stopped and we had to get out and lie down in a ditch. Petrol rationing was introduced and I moved to a little cottage in Chalfont St. Peter only ten minutes away from the studios to make things easier. The Korda brothers set up home together in Denham village.

Slowly *The Thief of Baghdad* progressed towards completion. Two additional directors, Michael Powell and Tim Whelan, were put to work on it, but still sequences were missing and the picture took shape in a very haphazard manner, not as originally envisaged. Not until February 1940 did we get to the final recording sessions.

Sabu menaced by the Djinn (Rex Ingram)

I had met Maurice Martenot in Paris and I had once written a *Berceuse* for the electronic instrument he had invented, the Ondes Martenot. I decided it would be the right instrument to use for the Djinn. It would be an unworldly tone-colour for an unworldly happening, the Djinn escaping from his bottle and later flying through the Grand Canyon with Sabu on his shoulders. We wrote to Maurice Martenot asking him to bring his instrument to England and he agreed, but by the time of the recording he had been called up and was somewhere defending his country. So I had to forget about the Ondes Martenot for the next five years.

Eventually Berger returned to Holland leaving Bill Hornbeck to cut the picture together as best he could. Alexander Korda left for the States. My work on the film seemed to be complete, but one day I heard from David Cunnyngham that arrangements were being made to shoot the missing scenes in America and that United Artists were putting up the money. Everyone who was directly involved in the production would be needed in Hollywood to finish the film.

I had never even dreamed of going to America. My *Variations* had been well received when performed in Chicago, but America was a long way off and it took five or six days to get there, so you had to have a good reason for going. Well, I had to go now. I had fought so hard to write the music for *The Thief of Baghdad*, and if I didn't go to America now it would be finished by someone else, which was the last thing I wanted. David Cunnyngham explained the various ways I could make the journey. American and English passenger ships were no longer crossing the Atlantic directly, but I could get an American ship from Genoa, though that route too was likely to be closed shortly. I could take the train from Paris to Genoa, but getting from London to Paris was going to be the difficult part. There were two possibilities. I could either make the dangerous sea crossing, or I could fly. I had never been up in a plane, and I was a poor sailor. Cunnyngham said drily, 'You stand a good chance of being shot down over the Channel, which at least has the virtue of being a quick death. Or you could be sunk, which would be considerably less pleasant. It's up to you.' Sometimes I find the British sense of humour a little hard to take. I told Cunnyngham I had never flown in my life before and asked if he had. He looked at me from behind his glasses and said casually, 'Oh yes'. When I told this story to a friend later he burst out laughing. It turned out that Cunnyngham had been an ace RAF pilot in the First World War and that his answer to me had been a typical piece of British understatement.

I was sad to be leaving London. I had been happy there, I liked the English and I had felt at home. I had been able to write both my own music and music for films in the way I wanted to, always bearing in mind the kind of contribution Honegger had made to the cinema. I was sorry too to be saying goodbye to my beloved Trinity College and to the Civil Service Orchestra, who were still meeting every week to play good music badly but with great enthusiasm.

My plane left from Croydon, and I expected the journey to Paris to last about an hour and a half. After five hours or so, while we were still in the air, I began to wonder whether it would have been better to take the risk of being sunk by a submarine. Then suddenly I saw the Eiffel Tower. I learned that we had had to take a roundabout route via the Channel Islands to avoid German planes. The sight of Paris was incredible. We had had ten months of blackout in London; the foggy, unlit streets were a constant danger for the pedestrian, for even car headlights were masked. But Paris was lit up like a Christmas tree, another world altogether. Nobody seemed worried — they trusted their Maginot Line. I saw all my friends, said goodbye to them and caught the train for Genoa where I found my ship in the harbour.

The trip took ten long days. We were to call at Gibraltar on the way. I spotted a familiar face: it was Noël Coward. He usually sat reading in a deckchair. I was sure everybody must have recognised him, but he talked to no one, and no one bothered him. When we dropped anchor at Gibraltar a cutter came alongside and took him off. We waited about ten hours, then the boat brought him back and we set sail again. Later I read that he had been sent to America by the authorities for propaganda purposes, and I assumed that his short visit to Gibraltar was to meet the Governor or to receive a final briefing.

Charles Boyer's mother was also on board, a lovely, elegant, elderly lady. When at last we arrived in New York, there were Charles Boyer and his wife to meet his mother, and Gertrude Lawrence waiting for Noël Coward. They embraced and seemed overjoyed to see each other again.

After a few days at the St. Regis Hotel in New York (Korda's favourite), I set off for Hollywood. I went there, as I thought, for a month or so, forty days at the most. Now, forty years later, I am still there.

6: A Hungarian in Hollywood

That journey was a revelation. I was accustomed to European trains where eight people would be crammed into each compartment. American trains were quite different, more like hotels on wheels. The journey from New York to Hollywood took three days. You started on the 20th Century Limited to Chicago; this was the business man's train and left at 6pm from Grand Central and arrived in the morning. The food was superb, and you were all by yourself in your own compartment, with its own wash-basin and lavatory.

The train from Chicago to Los Angeles was called the Chief, and was just as beautiful and luxurious. That journey took three nights. It was on the radio in the Club Car that I heard Jack Benny for the first time, with Rochester, his stooge. To my great embarrassment American humour was so incomprehensible to me that I was unable to join in the screams of laughter of the other passengers. I was veritably in a new world.

America was *immense*. Three days in the train took us through vast areas that were completely uninhabited. I was astounded; in Europe the shortest trip takes you into another country. On the third day I awoke to see palm trees; we had reached California.

The steward (they were all black, and all angelic) asked if I were getting out at Pasadena, which, he told me, was where all the 'film folks' disembarked in order to avoid reporters. I was certain that there would be no reporters waiting for me, and pressed on to Los Angeles.

In common with most Europeans I had expected some sort of Sin City, a Californian Babylon. In fact Los Angeles looked normal enough to me, and I was both relieved and disappointed. Bill Hornbeck, Korda's editor who had come to meet me, told me that none of the Hollywood people ever went to Los Angeles proper, except to get on or off a train. The city sprawled for miles before we got anywhere near Hollywood. At last, on La Brea Avenue, Bill pointed out the first magic name — the Chaplin Studios. I had admired Chaplin for years, and was surprised to see how small the studio was. Round the corner, on Santa Monica Boulevard, we drove into the much larger United Artists Studio, where the Korda offices were to be found. Nobody was about because they were all on location in the Grand Canyon with Zoltan Korda shooting the backgrounds for the Djinn scenes. But I was pleased to see a few familiar faces from London.

They found me an apartment in the Chateau Marmont on Sunset Boulevard, and I was allowed to bring in a piano for my work. It was a lovely old place, but I knew that I wouldn't be able to work there. I can't bear being overheard trying things out and changing them. How my music is composed is a secret I cannot share with anyone else. I found a little house in the Hollywood Hills, a part of town I quickly came to like both for its relative remoteness from the movie world and for the magnificence of its views over the San Fernando Valley. Here I have lived all my Hollywood life, and my family and I have occupied our present house on Montcalm Avenue for well over thirty years.

The Kordas rented General Service Studios where bungalows were available for their staff, so I moved into one of these. I also acquired a secretary, to my amazement. I had never had a secretary and couldn't imagine what she would be doing. Still, she went with the job and I was told that I was now Musical Director of Alexander Korda Films Inc.

I did what remained to be done on *The Thief of Baghdad* and conducted the new music myself at the recording sessions. In London Muir Mathieson had had to conduct, but by dint of watching him at work I had managed to equip myself with most of the techniques relating to the fitting of music to film. From then on I always conducted my own scores.

After *The Thief of Baghdad* Vincent Korda also came over to join his brothers and to work on *Lady Hamilton,* which was to star Laurence Olivier and Vivien Leigh. Julien Duvivier was already preparing the picture to follow, so, as they say in America, we were in business.

Let me attempt at this point some sort of evaluation of the three Kordas as I saw them. Alex was the eldest. He was the head of the family, and without any question the most brilliant. He was urbane, while the other two had a certain rusticity about them. Alex was tall and lean, rather grand, and resembled a distinguished professor of philosophy. Only in his cigar did he at all suggest the conventional image of a Hollywood producer. He was intelligent, well read, and spoke English, French and German fluently, all with a Hungarian accent. He never thought like Hollywoodians; his whole way of life and the working of his mind were based on European culture. He was a very astute business man, and totally honest; I don't think he ever broke his word. A recent biographer writes that his irresistible personal charm enabled him to wheedle money out of big businessmen. This is completely untrue. It was his reputation for honest, straight dealing, his sound business sense and the tremendous success of his films that brought him the money. Another statement in this biography tells us that Korda knew nothing of music, which is also untrue. He might have confused one Beethoven symphony with another, but he *knew* his Beethoven symphonies, which is rather unusual with film producers. The story that he could recognise 'God Save the King' only because people stood up is a malicious invention.

He was incredibly generous and lavished money on people everywhere. When it came to production, money was no object in realising his dreams. He lived like a prince and had the manners of a prince. He knew how to put people at ease. He liked to laugh, and his laugh was infectious. It was impossible to lie to him — he always knew, and saw through you with X-ray eyes. He virtually created the British film industry, and for this alone deserved his knighthood. After the war Churchill remarked that the logical president for the new Hungary would be Alexander Korda, as long as he had Rockefeller for his Finance Minister.

During the cutting of *The Thief of Baghdad* I witnessed clashes between Zoltan and Alex. Zoltan was incapable of accepting any criticism of his work, especially from his brother. In one scene Zoli wanted a great gush of blood from the face of a black man during a sword fight, which Alex objected to. He pointed out that this was a fantasy, and that such extremes of realism were inappropriate; which made Zoli denounce his brother as a faker. This sort of thing went on all the time. Zoltan was two years younger than Alex, stocky and good-looking. His manners, his comportment, his attitude to life were entirely different from his brother's. There was no doubt that Zoltan loved Alex, but beneath it I sensed some kind of resentment, envy or rivalry, which went back to their childhood. Zoltan was hostile to any form of authority. He often got into trouble when he worked with other producers for big companies like Columbia or Universal. He would cause terrible scenes when the 'authorities' decided on a change of some sort, a cut, a modification to the story line — anything. The worst rows of all were with his own brother; they were famous. But one thing shouldn't be forgotten and that is that he was a sick man. He never entirely recovered from the tuberculosis he contracted during the First World War, which was followed by malaria and other illnesses. He was very neurotic and thought paranoically that people were out to thwart him; whereas in reality he was a lovable man, very popular with his co-workers. But a single word, the slightest breath of criticism, was enough to make him break off relations with the critic forever. He could love deeply and hate deeply, with no half-measures.

The youngest Korda brother, Vincent, was a brilliant draughtsman and painter. He studied at the Academy of Fine Arts in Budapest and, like most painters of his generation, ended up in Paris. When Jacques Feyder introduced us at Denham Studios he described him as 'très Montparnasse'. He was; he had spent his youth with the painters of the twenties in famous cafés like the 'Coupole', the 'Dôme' and the 'Rotonde' on the Montparnasse and had absorbed their peculiarities and philosophies. His style of painting derived from the Post-impressionists, from Van Gogh and Cézanne, but developed a recognisable personality of his own. When Alex came back from Hollywood and started production in England he brought Vincent over from Paris and made him his art director. Vincent's sets for *Things to Come*, *The Thief of Baghdad* and *The Jungle Book* were miracles of beauty and imagination, and fortunately, unlike many of his colleagues in the film world, he wasn't only an artisan but also a creative artist. That was what Alex needed. Vincent lived for fifty years in England, had two English wives and four English-born children, but his English remained as incomprehensible as it was on the day he first arrived. Often when I visited him at his home in Chelsea he tried to call me a taxi. No luck, nobody understood him. He tried again and again until finally he angrily called over to one of his sons saying, 'These idiots don't understand me, talk to them.' In Hollywood we became friends and remained so until his death. After Alex's death he lived on in their glorious past and told the same stories over and over again. I urged him to take up painting again; sometimes he did surprisingly good work, but he was unable to recapture the strength and brilliance of his youth.

Vincent Korda at work on set-designs for *Jungle Book*

His last letter to me arrived on the day of his funeral, and with him my last link with the Korda era was severed.

My responsibilities as Korda's one-man music department left me little time for my own non-film music, but my name gradually became known through concert performances. Within a year I was accepted in Los Angeles as something more than a 'film composer'. In 1941 the Los Angeles chapter of the Pro Musica Society organised a concert of my chamber music with the participation of the best local performers.

In the autumn of 1940 my old friend Antal Doráti arrived from Australia with the Russian Ballet, whose conductor he was. It was under his direction that I had

The Crescendo Club honouring guest Paul Whiteman (centre). Among its members pictured here are Aaron Copland (back row, 3rd from right), myself (middle row, 2nd from right), John Crown (middle row, 4th from right), Castelnuovo-Tedesco (front row, extreme right)

first seen *Firebird* and *Petrushka* in London. He rang to say that the ballet master, Adolf Bolm, wanted to meet me, and that, by the way, Stravinsky and his wife would be there as well. It was a lovely evening at Doráti's, and I sat listening in fascination to Stravinsky. He knew everything about everything — politics no less than the arts were analysed by his razor-sharp mind. He spoke with anger about several conductors who were playing *their* conceptions of his music as distinct from *his*. All he asked was that the conductor should play what was written on the page. Doráti was relieved to escape censure in this respect. As for Adolf Bolm, the first Moor in the original 1911 production of *Petrushka*, he wanted to work now at the studios as a choreographer. I was not used to this approach at the time, but later learned that in Hollywood when you are invited to dinner because somebody is very interested to meet you, it is because they want your influence to get them a job.

The news from Europe was very bad. I was driving down Sunset Boulevard when I heard the announcement of the fall of France. The newscaster told us that at that very moment the Germans were marching down the Champs Elysées. Then his tragic tone changed to glee as he shouted excitedly, 'But, ladies, we have good news too. For only a dollar fifty you can get your dishes cleaner than ever before!!'

There was a strongly pro-German feeling in America. Whether this was because of the large number of citizens of German descent, the activities of the German Bund, the three pro-German senators in Washington or the misguided opinions of the American hero Lindbergh, I don't know. The media were full of propaganda against involvement in another foreign war, England being represented as trying to drag in the United States. Europe should solve its own problems.

California was at that time a haven for European refugees. An extraordinary number of great men lived there: Paul Dessau, Castelnuovo-Tedesco, Szigeti, José Iturbi, Stravinsky, Schoenberg, Alexandre Tansman, Ernst Toch, Erich Wolfgang Korngold, Bruno Walter, Alma Mahler and her husband Franz Werfel, Aldous Huxley, Thomas Mann, Bruno Frank, Christopher Isherwood, Emil Ludwig, Heifetz, Rachmaninov, Rubinstein, Piatigorsky, Stokowski and countless others. Musicians used to meet once a month in the Crescendo Club, whose president was a Russian singing teacher who spoke English with a Russian-Brooklyn accent. I was sitting next to Schoenberg when this man made a speech to the effect that the club had only one rule: we had to use 'foist' names. I turned to Schoenberg and asked: 'Herr Professor, should I call you Arnold from now on?' He answered without a smile: 'Herr Professor will do.' On that occasion my Sonata for Two Violins was performed. I watched his face. Every time there was a tonal melody, or a movement ended with a consonant chord, his face became contorted, in the way people react when listening to the most excruciating dissonances. When the piece was over he turned to me and asked if I had any news of Hungarian musicians. I told him that Bartók was coming to America, and that Kodály and Dohnányi were still teaching at the Academy. 'No, no,' he said impatiently, 'never mind them. What about Jemnitz?' Sándor Jemnitz was a Budapest critic and a very mediocre composer, but he was the Master's only twelve-tone disciple in Hungary at that time. I saw immediately that no friendship would develop between Schoenberg and myself.

When I conducted my first concert in the Hollywood Bowl in 1943, the Crescendo Club gave a reception afterwards. The programme of the concert had included my *Jungle Book Suite* in which the contralto soloist was Anne Brown, the first Bess in Gershwin's *Porgy and Bess*, a fine artist and a perfect lady. Naturally I brought her along with me to the reception. During the course of the evening I was aware of some commotion in the club, but knew nothing of its cause; later I was told that one of the members, a music critic, had left in a state of indignation — why, I didn't know. The following morning I was astonished to get a call from this critic accusing me of having insulted him and his bride by bringing 'that nigger woman' into the club. He was quite happy for the 'niggers' to serve him in restaurants and on trains, but the idea that he should be expected to meet them socially on equal terms was outrageous. He demanded an apology from me and from the club. Needless to say, he didn't get one from either. Instead the club gave him an ultimatum: either *he* apologised to *me* and to *them*, or he would be expelled from their midst. Of course he failed to apologise in his turn and was duly shown the door.

The Crescendo Club came to a rather tragi-comic end. It was situated in a quiet residential part of Los Angeles, and the old Russian singing teacher and his

Rehearsing in the Hollywood Bowl

daughter were scandalised when they suddenly started receiving calls at all hours of the night from men demanding women. It turned out that in a house quite nearby there lived a woman who ran a so-called 'Escort Bureau' which, at a time when the town was full of soldiers, plied a most profitable trade. The founder of the Crescendo Club complained to the police, but the Escort Bureau lady evidently had better connections in the police department than he had, since she retaliated successfully by denouncing the singing teacher for giving lessons in his home — i.e., for carrying on a business in a private residence. The upshot was that the singing teacher was ordered by the police to leave his house. From that moment the club should have changed its name to the 'Diminuendo', for it quickly disintegrated. Its defeat was no doubt watched in triumph by the madam of the 'Escort Bureau', which continued to flourish.

The fine English conductor Albert Coates and I became great friends. Coates had come to America before the war and had conducted concerts with all the great orchestras. His marital status was unfortunately not in order. He was living with a lady who couldn't get a divorce in England, and he was unable to divorce his wife. For this reason he was soon ostracised by Society. In musical America 'Society' means women's organisations, and if they are against you, you are through. His lady, who was a great lady, wasn't received, he was offered fewer and fewer concerts, and eventually they had to go back to England. Finally they married and went to Johannesburg where he died. He was one of the finest conductors, especially of Russian music, that I have ever known. He gave the first English performance of my orchestral *Jungle Book Suite*, playing it on the piano at the Wigmore Hall and speaking the narration himself — surely one of the most bizarre performances my music can ever have received.

I made serious efforts to get to know the music of my new colleagues in the film world, but frankly I was not impressed. Each score was credited to a different composer, but the music all sounded much the same. The only man whose music I found in any way worthwhile was Erich Wolfgang Korngold, and he, of course, was a composer with an established reputation in Europe. The interesting point was that many of these composers were taking lessons from important teachers like Schoenberg, Toch and later Castelnuovo-Tedesco. What had happened was that with the advent of sound, 'background' music became necessary in large quantities, and the studios brought in men who were conductors of Broadway shows or cinema orchestras. The cinema no longer needed live orchestras, so their musical directors turned to composing. Hitherto the 'background' music they had provided had consisted of fragments of symphonies, light classical music or collections of pieces designed for the purpose — chases, love scenes, melodramatic moments and so on.

The great difference between the Europeans and the Americans in Hollywood was this: we in Europe had studied first, and on the basis of a sound classical training had found employment. The commercial boys, however, were clever enough to get a job in Hollywood first and then start studying. At a party given by Albert Coates I met one of his conducting students who was already under contract

My Hollywood Bowl debut concert, 1943

With Albert Coates in the Hollywood Bowl

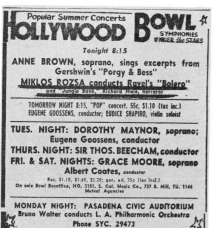

95

to a major studio as a composer. He told me that his room-mate some years back had been making more money as an arranger than *he* had been as a glove salesman. So he had had a few piano lessons, and now here he was employed as a professional composer. I asked him if he had studied harmony and counterpoint, but he told me that they were unnecessary; it was quite possible to compose and conduct without them. There were dozens of these people, and they were nothing better than hacks. The studios loved them — they were willing, versatile, indefatigable, and the music they provided was in execrable enough taste to please even the studio heads.

It was in Hollywood that I had my one and only meeting with Béla Bartók. There had been large advertisements in the local Hungarian newspapers announcing that the 'famous Hungarian pianist' (*sic*) would be giving a concert at the Wilshire-Ebell Theatre and that all Hungarians should attend to pay due tribute to him. I had already heard that Bartók was in town but that he was 'unapproachable', so I decided just to go to the recital. It was, I think, the saddest concert I have ever been to in my life. There was hardly any audience, and what there was (no more than a hundred people at the most) was scattered over the front few rows. Then out on the stage came this very thin, ethereal-looking figure with snow-white hair who sat down at the piano. When he was about to start playing, two young Hungarian girls wearing the phoney national costume he hated so much came out and presented him with flowers and tried to make a speech in English: they kept stopping and restarting and Bartók just stood there, embarrassed, in silence. When they had finally finished telling him how honoured the Los Angeles Hungarian community was to welcome him, they retired, and Bartók shoved the bouquets under the piano stool and started to play. The programme started with some early Italian music he had transcribed himself (Veracini and Frescobaldi) and went on to include works by himself and Kodály. The critic of the Hearst afternoon paper left in indignation during the interval: the others later wrote that Bartók had played badly (which wasn't true) and that his works were experimental, dissonant and unpalatable. Of the many European composers living at this time in Los Angeles hardly any came to the concert. The only musicians I saw there were Eugene Zador, a Hungarian composer who knew him personally, Jakob Gimpel, a Polish pianist who had met him at a festival in Europe, Ingolf Dahl, a Swedish pianist/composer, and Joseph Achron, a Russian violinist/composer. Bartók had toured America a few years earlier under the aegis of the Pro Musica Society, but this series of concerts (he later went to San Francisco) was on a strictly commercial basis; as it was, his manager lost everything and refused afterwards to handle him any more. After the concert I was introduced to Bartók, who looked tired and ill. When he heard my name he said, 'Oh, are you Hungarian?', and when a friend whispered to him *sotto voce* that I was a composer he said, 'Oh yes, you have several works published by Breitkopf & Härtel, don't you?' and proceeded to name most of them. I tried to say something to him, but the small room was so full of people that it was impossible to have a conversation. So when I got home I wrote a letter to him, simply explaining what he meant to Hungarian composers and to Hungarian music in general. Later, when I was in New York to record *The Jungle Book*, I met a close friend and pupil of his and asked whether it would be possible to visit Bartók, who was also at that time

Bartók rehearsing his *Contrasts* with Josef Szigeti (violin) and Benny Goodman (clarinet)

living in New York. The friend, however, said that Bartók wasn't interested in seeing anyone or hearing anyone else's music. Few people played his music because it wasn't to the taste of the American public; Rachmaninov was more in their line. Only Fritz Reiner performed a few works during this period and Spivakovsky played his violin concerto in New York. Menuhin came into his life towards the end, but for the others he didn't exist.

In 1944 I was invited by the Dean of the Music Department of the University of Southern California to teach a summer course in composition. I would have loved to accept but was so overwhelmed by film commissions that I had to turn the offer down. I suggested Bartók instead (the Dean wasn't even aware that he was living in America), but clearly nothing came of it, because a minor young American composer got the job. Even though Bartók needed the money, he always refused to teach composition, only piano, a policy he had stuck to throughout his life. He was a proud and difficult man who couldn't accept charity. Szigeti established an anonymous research fund for him at Columbia University; and then Koussevitzky (rather in the manner of the mysterious stranger of Mozart's *Requiem*) commissioned the *Concerto for Orchestra* from him when he was very ill in hospital. Fortunately he was able to hear its first performance and enjoy its immediate success.

I used to meet Stravinsky and his wife Vera quite often at the house of the

Tansmans. Alexandre Tansman was a Polish-born composer who had come as a refugee with his family from France to Hollywood at the invitation of Charlie Chaplin; that is to say, Chaplin sent them their tickets but failed thereafter to take the slightest notice of Tansman. One night Tansman and Stravinsky told me that they had been offered a film; since Stravinsky had never written a film-score Tansman had been engaged as his assistant and adviser. It was a war picture called *The Commandos Strike at Dawn*, set in Norway. They asked my advice on all sorts of technical matters, while I was more interested in establishing whether or not they had received contracts. No, they said, but their agent said it was all settled. A month later I met them again. There was still no contract, but they showed me the Prelude Stravinsky had written based on Norwegian folksongs. It was in full score, in his immaculate hand, on paper where, as always, he had drawn his own staves with a little gadget of his own devising. I read it through — it was a lovely little piece — and asked again about the contract. Nothing. At last it became apparent that the producer had cold feet. His alleged reason for not engaging the man he called 'the great Maestro' was that he knew that the Maestro would need a huge orchestra to do justice to his magnificent music (in fact, after *The Rite of Spring* Stravinsky's orchestra tended to be *smaller* than average, rather than larger) and the budget could only run to a small one. So with the greatest regret. . . . Well, Stravinsky learned his lesson, but the music wasn't wasted. Later he published what he had written under the title *Four Norwegian Moods*. Anthony Collins, the composer and conductor, told me that a producer once asked him for something like *The Firebird*. Collins suggested Stravinsky — after all, here he was in Hollywood! The producer replied scornfully, 'He couldn't do it!' Sometimes the bigwigs would decide they wanted a 'modernistic' score, having heard something on the radio of Copland or Stravinsky, but they would never approach these people themselves; they always preferred to get one of the tame studio hacks to imitate the style. They were ignorant, but they were in charge and their word was law. One of the most celebrated studio heads issued a direction to the music department that no minor chords were to be used (minor chords, of course, meant dissonances for him). Another told the composer that the heroine's music was to be in the major key, the hero's in the minor, and that when the two were together, the music should be both major and minor! Bi-tonality *à la* Hollywood.

Stravinsky told me he always had to laugh when he heard my name, since in Russian 'Rózsa' sounds like a slang word meaning 'mug' in the sense of 'face' ('gueule' in French). From then on he always addressed me as 'Monsieur Gueule'. I couldn't retaliate, because 'Stravinsky' doesn't mean anything in Hungarian.

Stravinsky had only one pupil in Hollywood (or anywhere else for that matter): a well-to-do, middle-aged inventor who was also an amateur composer. He paid Stravinsky liberally for his lessons and also helped with his correspondence. He had a son-in-law who was a local conductor, a pupil of Monteux. One night my wife and I were invited to a party given by the son-in-law in the father-in-law's house and we were promised that the Stravinskys would also be there. By the time we arrived our host was already the worse for wear, standing on top of a table and splashing spaghetti into the plates (and faces) of his guests. Stravinsky and I and one or two others retired upstairs. Little peace was to be had there either, for a local musician proceeded to regale us with improvisations at the piano based on Sabu's song 'I want to be a sailor' from *The Thief of Baghdad*. Stravinsky asked petulantly what the music was, and I said I didn't know. Some time later Mrs Stravinsky came upstairs in a state of agitation, said a few words in Russian to her husband and peremptorily took him away. When another husband was likewise claimed by his wife I decided to go downstairs and find out what was going on. It seemed that one of the guests, an elderly man, had tripped on the stairs and broken his foot. I didn't realise at the time that in California, if a man sustains an injury on the premises of a householder, the latter is legally responsible. If a burglar breaks his leg in the process of 'burglarising' your premises, he can sue you. In this case our gracious host, by this time drunk to the point of no return, had got it firmly fixed in his mind that the 'accident' was merely a put-up job, its purpose being to hold him liable and take him to court for a vast sum of damages; so he had grasped hold of the man in question (who really had broken his foot and was in great pain) and literally kicked him out. The conductor-son-in-law had called an ambulance and had had him taken off to hospital, the whole scene being enacted to progressively more elaborate variations on Sabu's song from upstairs, which continued in blithe unconcern and with ludicrous dramaturgical inappropriateness. I tried to imagine a similar scene in a European context. It made the same incredulous impression as the man who called one day trying to persuade my wife and me to commit ourselves to somewhat premature burial arrangements in Forest Lawn Cemetery. When, in order to get rid of him, we pretended not to be residents of California but visitors from New York, he replied that that was no problem — the bodies could be shipped across on ice!

Stravinsky liked his house and the California climate, but not the non-existent cultural life of Hollywood. In the long run he realised he was being treated with complete indifference, and left forever. The only real recognition he got was from a small circle of musicians who gave the Monday Evening Concerts. Their director was proud to announce that they had given more Stravinsky premieres than Diaghilev (albeit of works of somewhat lesser importance).

At a time when Bartók was still unrecognised in the United States, Stravinsky and Schoenberg were the leading names in contemporary music. They lived quite near each other but never met, and I think they despised each other's music. I once asked Stravinsky his opinion of Schoenberg, and he described him as the 'Alchemist of Music'; I still wonder whether he found any gold. This non-relationship between Stravinsky and Schoenberg reminds me rather of Wagner and Verdi towards the end of the last century. They were the two giants of opera in that period, and Verdi, even if he didn't like it, respected Wagner's music (a sentiment not reciprocated by Wagner). Towards the end of his life Wagner spent a lot of time in Italy (he died in Venice) and a meeting could have been arranged, but apparently neither of them desired it. Franz Werfel's story of Verdi deciding finally to pay his respects to his great colleague and arriving in Venice only to learn that Wagner had just died is of course the purest fiction.

Generally in Hollywood great names received little recognition, but one day a music critic called C. Sharpless Hickman went to the mayor of Los Angeles to tell him that the great Schoenberg was about to reach his seventieth or seventy-fifth birthday, and that it would be nice if the mayor were to write him a letter of appreciation. The mayor agreed, but as he knew nothing of music asked Hickman to compose the letter, which the mayor signed. The next day Schoenberg rang Hickman, whom he knew, to tell him, with great emotion, that he had received the most beautiful letter from the mayor, and that, because his English was not perfect, he would like Hickman to compose a letter of thanks. Hickman wrote back (to himself) a letter addressed to the mayor and signed by Arnold Schoenberg.

Another European composer who found his way to Hollywood was Ernst Toch. In my Leipzig days, Toch was a very prominent composer, second only to Hindemith in the number of performances his works received. His music was astringent, linear, contrapuntal and somewhat like Hindemith's. I heard his piano concerto played by Ellie Ney under Furtwängler. My old teacher Grabner once said to me that at heart Toch was a romantic, but that he forced himself to be dissonant and 'contemporary'. He was popular with the young, rather less so with the older generation and the critics. He had to leave Germany when the Nazis took over and worked for a while in London for Korda. In Hollywood he did some original scores, but was more successful as a teacher at USC.

Emmerich Kálmán, the composer of *The Gypsy Princess*, *Countess Maritza* and other operettas once popular the world over, also lived in Hollywood during the war years. I met him once when he was invited to a private screening of *The Thief of Baghdad*. During the performance he displayed no emotion of any kind, nor did he make any comment afterwards; to the great annoyance of Korda his only concern was to get his cigar lit and summon a taxi to take him home. (He didn't drive, and once when walking near his Beverly Hills home he was arrested, so suspicious is it in Los Angeles for people to be seen walking for pleasure.) Once during the early years of the war he gave a large party in honour of Otto von Hapsburg, who was in America trying to enlist support for the idea of a Danube Confederation. The whole Austro-Hungarian colony was invited, and I agreed to go as soon as I had finished recording at the studio that day. When I arrived at about six o'clock there was a strange hush among all those gathered there, and at the far side of the room a large throne was to be seen. Apparently Kálmán, who had spent his whole life writing operettas about crown princes, had felt so honoured by the presence of a real Hapsburg (a crown pretender) that he had borrowed a throne from the prop department of MGM and had had it installed in the living room. When Otto arrived and saw it he was terrified, refusing not only to sit on the throne but also to sit down at all unless everyone else did. He certainly gave a royal lesson in democracy to his over-solicitous host.

The American composer George Antheil arrived in Hollywood. I had first heard his name as a student, when he gave a piano recital in Budapest. I hadn't been there, but heard that when the audience had laughed at some of his 'modern' music he had risen from the piano, pointed a revolver at them and said, 'If you don't stop laughing, I'll shoot!' I got very angry with the fellow-student who had told me this and accused him of making it up. No one pulls a revolver on the podium. Years later Antheil and I became friends and when his book *Bad Boy of Music* came out I

Castelnuovo-Tedesco, myself, Lawrence Morton (founder-director of the famous
Los Angeles 'Monday Evening Concerts'), George Antheil

was discomfited to learn that the story was true, though the pistol had been a toy
one. He had some success in Hollywood and wrote some good film scores, though
in a style much mellower than his percussive and spiky music of the twenties; in
those early days he was a follower of the *Rite of Spring* school and used all sorts of
outlandish instruments like airplane engines to shock the audience. He had much
succès de scandale, and in the twenties, at least in America, was definitely a Name.
Later, as Virgil Thomson said, he became the *good* boy of music. I have never met a
composer with a more brilliant mind and with such a deep and far-reaching
knowledge of so many subjects. During the war he wrote editorials for a Hollywood
evening paper which were masterly in their analysis of the war; the articles appeared
under the editor's name, however. He wrote a series of articles about endocrinology
for *Esquire,* and once explained existentialism to me so brilliantly and clearly that I
understood what had previously been a mysterious word. He died far too early, and
it is sad that his name is now largely forgotten. He once urged me to write my
memoirs, but I protested that I was too young, and that I couldn't write anyway.
'When you do,' he said, 'tell me, because there is a trick to it. The trick made my
book a success, and I'll pass it on to you.' Well, now he is dead, and unfortunately I
never learned his trick.

The Korda office advised me to set about applying for American citizenship,
since it was obvious that the United States was not going to remain aloof from the

war in Europe, and I had decided by this time to settle in America; my career was developing well and there seemed little point in returning to a war-ravaged, Korda-less England. The process involved applying in person at the U.S. Embassy in a foreign country. I went to Mexico as the closest. The day I applied who should I meet doing the same thing but Josef Szigeti, the eminent violinist, whom I knew well. When it was my turn to go in for the interview, I was surprised to be questioned probingly about Szigeti, to which I could only reply that he was a fine violinist. When I next met Szigeti, he told me that all *his* questions had been about me! Fortunately neither of us had felt inclined to say anything to the detriment of the other, so we were able to return to the U.S. as fully-fledged 'first paper' citizens. After that there would be some years to wait before we received full citizenship.

There was no one in Hollywood whose acquaintance I more earnestly desired to make than Aldous Huxley. I admired his colossal erudition in so many fields — in art, in science, in music, in history — over the whole spectrum of human existence. I often saw him in the street or in the studios, but there was nobody to introduce us. I didn't flatter myself for a minute that my intelligence was anything approaching his, but thought that there were areas where we might find a common interest.

In 1950 I sailed to Europe on the Queen Mary and discovered that Huxley was on board. We would pass each other on the deck from time to time, but there was no one to introduce us and we never spoke. Then in Rome I would often find myself at the same café on the Via Veneto as Huxley and his wife, but again there was no one to introduce us.

Back in Hollywood I was invited to be a guest speaker at a dinner and was excited to discover that the other speaker was to be Huxley. Now, surely, we would meet. He spoke first; his theme was the difficulties of young writers. When my turn came I addressed my whole talk to him. I spoke of the struggles of young composers to find a publisher. I had just read Honegger's autobiography *Je suis Compositeur* and I quoted some of the facts therein. Debussy's *First Arabesque* took twelve years to sell its first printing of four hundred copies. Ravel's *Bolero* (the piano version), published at the height of his career, sold its 2,000 copies in the first year, which was regarded as a triumph. I congratulated Huxley on becoming a writer rather than a composer, and he laughed. Afterwards we were surrounded by questioners, and when finally I escaped to look for him, he was gone.

Zoltan Korda worked with him on the screenplay of *Mortal Coils*, a short story of his from *The Gioconda Smile*, and although I was invited to write the music, I never met Huxley. *Mortal Coils* was released under the frightful title *A Woman's Vengeance* — the studio heads were afraid that the New Yorkers might mis-hear the title as 'Mortal *Goils*', i.e. girls.

At a Festival concert for Stravinsky's 75th birthday I, as local president of the American Federation of Composers and Conductors, had to present him with a scroll and make a short speech. Aldous Huxley was to be the principal speaker. Now, surely, at last, I would meet the great man. At the rehearsal Franz Waxman took the orchestra through Stravinsky's own paraphrase on 'Happy Birthday to You', written for Monteux's 80th birthday. Stravinsky was standing there with a stopwatch and when Waxman came backstage he congratulated him: exactly one

Stravinsky (right) with Franz Waxman at his 75th birthday concert during which Waxman conducted the 'Greeting Prelude'

minute long, as it should have been. In other words, one minute and two seconds would have been completely wrong! But again I had no luck with Huxley, for by the time I got to the artists' room at the end of the concert he had gone. It was obvious that for some reason the gods did not wish us to make each other's acquaintance, and I gave up.

In 1940 Gabriel Pascal came to Hollywood, and I was instructed by Korda to help him with modifications to Walton's score for *Major Barbara*. I was hesitant about tampering with the work of so eminent a colleague* but Uncle Gaby (as I used to call him) told me that he was not satisfied with Walton's arrangement of *Onward Christian Soldiers* which served as the main title. He wanted me to arrange it in a sarcastic, Shavian way. I told him this wasn't really possible, that the piece was itself, no more, no less. The best I could do, I suggested, was to give the tune to brass and woodwinds, with a light, bustling counterpoint on the strings. He agreed.

---

* The only other occasion when I let myself in for rewriting part of someone else's score was in the 1950s when I was on the music staff at MGM. Producer Sam Zimbalist came back from London with a picture called *Beau Brummel*, dissatisfied with the music provided by an English composer. He felt that the whole beginning and end were wrong, and asked me to provide new music. My contract with MGM specified that I should not interfere with any other composer's music, nor should anyone interfere with mine. However, since Zimbalist was a personal friend, I agreed to make an exception in this case, on condition that I received no screen credit. Now that the composer whose music I replaced is dead, there seems no harm in saying that the whole of the final scene, where Beau Brummel takes his leave of the dying King, is mine.

When we came to try it through with the orchestra, Pascal was not satisfied. It wasn't funny. 'Let's try it *spiccato* (bouncy)', I said to the strings. No, Uncle Gaby didn't find that funny either. Finally I suggested *pizzicato* (plucked). 'That's it!' cried Pascal. '*Pizzi* can do! Now everyone will know that this is a comedy!' If we laughed at that moment, it wasn't at his picture.

I had to re-do another scene, where Walton had underlined every funny remark with a 'wah-wah' on the trumpet. He wasn't to blame — it was the style of the time, and I had done exactly the same in *The Divorce of Lady X* on the advice of Muir Mathieson, who told me that we had to learn from Hollywood. Pascal wanted me to produce a different sort of 'wah-wah', and I spent half an hour with the trumpeter trying every possible sort of 'kva-kva' (as Pascal called it). Nothing satisfied him. We tried every sort of mute, every conceivable way of playing, but nothing was any good. At last Pascal shouted 'It's hopeless! The man has no sense of humour!' When we saw the finished edit, the 'kva-kva' we had finally chosen (after endless wasting of time and Korda's money) was inaudible under the dialogue.

Once the *Thief of Baghdad* was finished I set to work on *Lady Hamilton,* one of Korda's most prestigious productions. Out of the great love story of Emma Hamilton and Horatio Nelson a beautiful screen drama was evolved by Walter Reisch and R. C. Sheriff. Then I got a letter from Lord Vansittart, with whom I had remained friends after our collaboration on *The Thief of Baghdad.* He begged me to persuade Alex not to do a picture about 'that shallow lady' at this time. I asked Vincent Korda's advice and he told me to say nothing to Alex. It was too late, the sets were built, Alex would never agree. So the picture went ahead, eventually to become the favourite of Winston Churchill. He saw it dozens of times and every time he saw the great death scene, and heard Nelson's famous line 'Kiss me,

With Vivien Leigh and Sarah Allgood

Letter from Vansittart

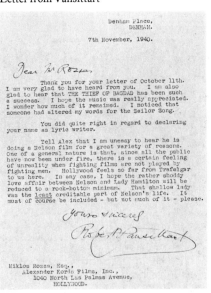

Laurence Olivier and Vivien Leigh in *Lady Hamilton*

Hardy', he would shed tears. *Lady Hamilton* was no war-mongering picture, but it was obvious that a film about Napoleon would strike a responsive chord with the English when Hitler and Mussolini were terrorising the world. One scene when Sir William Hamilton, the husband of Emma, made an impassioned speech against dictators, had a great effect upon the English audiences at this time, which was precisely Korda's intention. In the scene where Nelson returns to Emma after losing an eye, and the two rush together in a passionate embrace, Alex Korda told me that the music should express the culmination of their great love. The audience must be transported. I told him he had given me only ten seconds in which to treat this great emotional moment. 'My boy, that's your problem,' he said, and left the studio. But behind my back he instructed the cutter to give me as much footage as I wanted.

We also discussed what to do with the opening titles. (I detest the Hollywood term 'Main Titles'. This derives from the old silent days when there would be other titles throughout the picture to explain what was going on, and it is meaningless today.) At first Alex wanted me to begin with Beethoven's 'fate' motif from the Fifth Symphony, which was being used by the BBC throughout the war as a V for Victory sign, but I was against it, thinking it too jingoistic. I suggested *Rule*

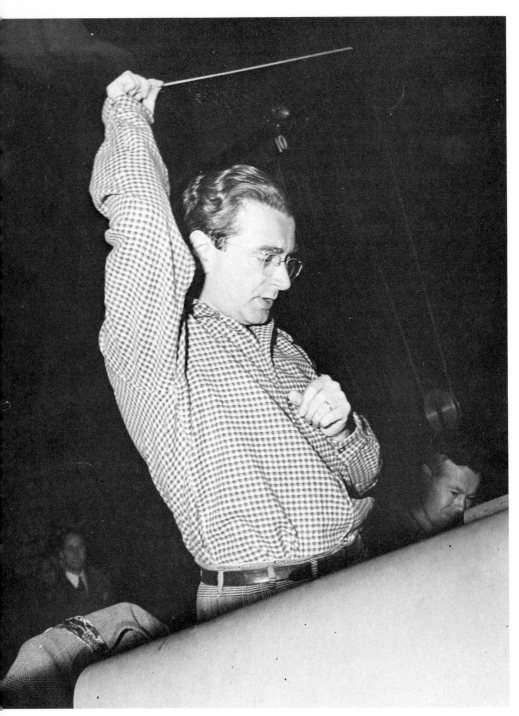

Conducting *Lady Hamilton*

Britannia, which Alex accepted, and we recorded it with a chorus. Two days later two of the American executives in Alex's company told me that the song was completely unacceptable as it was British propaganda. I went to Alex with the news. He told me to use *Rule Britannia* without the chorus as the executives would not recognise the melody without the words. At this same meeting I learnt that he had been summoned to Washington for a Congressional examination on a charge of being a British spy. A couple of days before the hearing the Japanese attacked Pearl Harbour and that was that. America had entered the war, and there was no more investigation.

Korda's agreement with United Artists was for a certain number of pictures, but during his two years he had made only four. This meant that he had to use other people to help him fill the quota, and one of these pictures was based on the life of Schubert. In Budapest I had seen Walter Reisch's picture *The Unfinished Symphony* which I had found charming. Our picture was called *New Wine* and when I read the script I was horrified; Schubert was represented as a complete idiot. I went to see Korda, told him I would do my duty as his Musical Director and provide music, but that I wouldn't allow my name to appear on the screen. Korda was surprised and couldn't understand why, but he hadn't read the script.

After I had prepared a score from fragments of Schubert's music I told the producer what I had told Korda. I wouldn't do the final recording and I refused to have my name attached to such a travesty. It seemed that I was not the first to ask for his name to be removed. The producer agreed to our request, but warned us that when the picture was a 'smash hit' and we all came begging to have our names restored, it would be too late. I told him I would take a chance. As it happened, the picture deservedly sank without trace very soon after its release.

My only other unpleasant experience on a Korda picture was *To Be or Not to Be*. It was directed by a master, Ernst Lubitsch, and starred Carole Lombard and Jack Benny. The idea had come from Melchior Lengyel, a Hungarian writer I knew well; we used to meet in the Hungarian restaurant on Sunset Boulevard, but before that I had seen many of his plays in Budapest. His most famous film is *Ninotchka*, and his best known short story, *The Miraculous Mandarin*, was made into a pantomime by Bartók.

I read the script and again I was appalled. It made huge fun of Hitler's occupation of Poland. The story concerned a group of Jewish actors who impersonate S.S. officers and outwit the German forces. I found this in terrible taste at a time when the newspapers were telling us what in reality was happening to the Poles and the Polish Jews. I told Korda, who shrugged and agreed to give the picture to another composer, although I would have to do some work on it until someone suitable could be found.

I had to write an anti-German song for the Polish officers, to lyrics by Ira Gershwin. Ira Gershwin was a dear man, quite different from the Tin-Pan-Alley type I had expected. He was very simple and modest. He and his wife Lee lived in the house that had been his brother George's until his death a few years earlier. The music paper he handed to me to jot down a few lines had 'George Gershwin' printed on it.

The Mowgli dynasty

Lubitsch didn't like our first attempt; it was too venomous, he wanted something more lightly humorous. Eventually we used an old army song. Werner Heymann was engaged to do the rest of the music for the picture and I gladly washed my hands of it, though of course offering him any assistance he might require. Then I went home happily to get on with my own music for *The Jungle Book* which was already underway.

My happiness didn't last long. A frantic call from the studios where Heymann's music was being recorded summoned me there. It seemed that Lubitsch wasn't pleased, and in fact when I got there he was very angry. For one dramatic scene Heymann's music was grotesque, and used the 'Mickey Mouse' technique whereby everything on the screen is directly mimicked in the music. It was all my fault, Lubitsch told me. I was the Musical Director, I should have supervised and approved. Now it was up to me to put it right. He wanted to know what I was going to do about it. It was ten o'clock in the morning, and come what may the music had to be recorded and completed by six — there wasn't enough money to call another session.

I went back to my office and ordered two orchestrators and two copyists. I saw the scene, got a cue sheet with the timings and started to compose. As I finished a page I passed it to the orchestrators; as they finished they passed their pages to the copyists. At four o'clock we got back to the studio, gave out the parts and recorded the music, three minutes of it. Lubitsch embraced me.

Two days later Heymann thanked me most kindly and gave me a Boxer puppy which I had been thinking of adopting for some time (he had consulted my secretary for clues). I called the dog Mowgli and we spent a very happy twelve years together.

Mowgli stories are legion. Once when I was staying at a hotel in Palm Springs I

With Mowgli

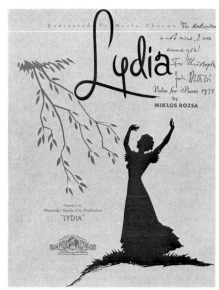

Lydia Waltz with its unauthorized dedication

was sitting in the courtyard and saw him appear on the balcony of my room, several floors above me. I motioned to him to come down. The next thing I knew he was sailing through the air! He had been ordered to come down, so down he would come by the most direct route. I closed my eyes. When I opened them there was Mowgli standing beside me, completely unscathed, wagging his tail frantically. Another time I was at Vincent Korda's studio and Mowgli appeared in the doorway with blood pouring from his mouth. Closer investigation revealed that he had been drinking his fill at one of Vincent's pots of red paint. I once left him in the care of Korda's secretary while I popped in to see the great man. When I came out I found Melchior Lengyel raging and laughing at the same time. 'Your dog ate my hat!'

When we first had him we feared he might be jealous of our children as they arrived. But he accepted them totally — they could pull his ears, punch him, bite him — he loved it. In fact he became their guardian, and would growl menacingly if any of our friends attempted too close an inspection of the babies. He founded a dynasty and at one point there were four enormous Boxers in the house. As he controlled us, so he controlled his family; he was a highly respected and feared paterfamilias. He appeared to enjoy the sensation as his head, resting on my feet, rose and fell as I played the piano. One of his sons was Fitzi, a diminutive of FitzMowgli, so named because he was born out of wedlock. Fitzi longed to join his father under the piano but this Mowgli never permitted; a head on my pedal-foot was his privilege alone. Eventually Mowgli died — he was old and tired — and my wife dared not tell me until the next day because that evening I had to conduct *The Jungle Book* which she sat through with tears streaming down her face. I sat down sadly at my piano and began to play. Suddenly I felt a soft doggy head on my foot. It was Fitzi's turn now.

After *To Be or Not to Be* came a very Americanised remake of Julien Duvivier's *Carnet de Bal* known as *Lydia*. Here we experimented a little: in one scene it was decided never to have music and dialogue at the same time. Merle Oberon (who played the title role) would speak, then there would be music, then she would speak again, and so on. The idea worked well, and showed how inventive a great director could be in treating music as something other than mere wallpaper. Apart from this the picture had many opportunities for music inasmuch as one of the characters was a blind pianist for whom I had to write a set of piano improvisations and a concerto-finale. The 'Lydia Waltz' which was one of the main themes won considerable popularity, and I was more amused than annoyed to see that when a printed arrangement for piano solo came out the title page bore the inscription 'Dedicated to Merle Oberon'. Korda's publicity man must have been responsible for this 'dedication', for certainly I was not.*

At last came *Jungle Book*, which I had been looking forward to for so long, for I had loved Kipling since my childhood. It was Zoltan Korda's picture, beautifully designed by Vincent. The script was no more than adequate, with little of the poetry of *The Thief of Baghdad*. The young Indian actor Sabu I already knew, of course. He had been 'discovered' in the stables of the Maharajah of Mysore by the great director of documentaries, Flaherty. He was an actual elephant boy and his family name was Dastaghir. Flaherty brought Sabu back to London, together with his older brother, his only relative, to take care of him. The brother, Shaikh, spoke English; Sabu didn't. He was no actor; all he could do really was smile, but this smile smiled him into the hearts of millions.

According to English law a child actor had to have a tutor if he couldn't go to school, and Korda engaged a young man to teach him English. Sabu was about eight when he made *Elephant Boy* and this was followed by *The Drum*, *The Thief of Baghdad* and lastly, *Jungle Book*. For the first Christmas in England Korda sent the two Indian brothers and their tutor to St. Moritz in Switzerland for a holiday and for some publicity pictures to be taken. He told the tutor that although the best hotel was the Palace, he always went to another which was almost as good and much cheaper, and he had booked rooms for them there. The next day there came a frantic telephone call from St. Moritz. The tutor reported that Sabu had found out that the Palace was the best hotel and wanted to go there. Considering that a year earlier he had slept in an elephant stable, he had certainly familiarised himself as quickly with the Western scale of values as he had become aware of his own importance.

We met once after the war and he seemed happy to see me, and was surprised to learn I was still writing music. He assumed that one graduated from composer to producer, from producer to high-ranking executive. He made me a wonderful proposition. He told me that he had bought a young elephant and that if I would write suitable songs for him, we would engage an orchestra and travel from town to

---

* In the late 1940s my *Lydia* music, adapted and developed (with my blessing) by Mario Castelnuovo-Tedesco, underwent a second incarnation for Robert Siodmak's film *Time out of Mind*. In addition to the dramatic sequences themselves the two set-pieces (a concerto-fragment and a symphony-finale entitled New England Symphony) were all based on my themes from *Lydia*.

Newspaper picture of Sabu and me   Sabu and friend

town, he singing my songs from his elephant, I conducting. He assured me that in this way both of us would quickly become millionaires. As it would have been useless to tell him I was neither a songwriter nor an itinerant vaudeville conductor, I pointed out how expensive the orchestra would be. 'How much for a week?' he asked. I told him the Union rate. He couldn't understand how I could be so naïve. 'All we have to do is offer them half!'

After the success of *Jungle Book* RCA Victor offered to make an album of the music. They thought that as Prokofiev's *Peter and the Wolf* was so good with its narration here too the music should be linked by a recital of the story, and Sabu would be a natural choice as narrator. I agreed, and Anthony Gibbs put together a text derived partly from Kipling, partly from the picture. The words of the lullaby sung by Mowgli's mother had already been written for the picture by Arthur Wimperis. 'Wimpy', well-known in England as a writer of lyrics for musical comedy, was one of Korda's old guard; in collaboration with Lajos Biro he had written the scenario of what is probably Korda's most celebrated picture, *The Private Life of Henry VIII*. He was a darling man, one of those perfect English gentlemen to whom I have always been drawn. During the war (by which time he was in his seventies) he was called to Hollywood to work on the screenplay of the pointedly pro-British *Mrs Miniver*. The boat on which he was travelling was sunk by German torpedoes, and Wimperis spent four days and nights in a lifeboat with adults and children dying all around him. (One of those who died was a distant cousin of mine, a Hungarian newspaperman working in London who for some reason was on his way to Canada.) Wimperis, being a tough old bird, survived to be picked up by a British destroyer and taken back to England. Undeterred, he bought himself a new set of clothes, took the first available boat and arrived more or less on schedule in Hollywood. Korda asked him to set lyrics to the *Jungle Book* lullaby. He sat down with me at the piano and after half an hour produced the lovely words sung by the contralto solo:—

111

See the silver moon,
Hear the breezes croon
Jungle's cradle tune: lulla-lullaby.

We recorded the *Jungle Book Suite* in New York, and I was thrilled to be conducting Toscanini's great orchestra, the NBC. I coached Sabu in the text, which he found no difficulty with except the line, 'The woman . . . teaches him the first word of the man speech: "Mother".' Sabu was an orphan who had never known his mother and the line meant nothing to him. The word was snapped out in a matter-of-fact way in spite of all my efforts.

Sabu was instantly recognised on the streets of New York in his red turban, and crowds were always thronging round us. He was very proud of being famous but always remained a delightful child, quite natural and unaffected. Unfortunately he made the same mistake in his life that all child stars, from Shirley Temple to Mickey Rooney, have made — he grew up. When he first appeared on the screen as a young boy he enchanted millions all over the world; when he returned after the war a grown man, the charm was gone. Jobs became few and far between; he occasionally played an Indian prince or appeared on television, but that was all. When his brother was shot dead in his furniture store one day, it came as a tremendous shock. He had never known his own father, so his brother had been like a protector and parent to him. After that life became more and more difficult for him, and he finally succumbed to a heart attack in 1963.

The period after finishing the recording with Sabu was a lovely time. I thoroughly enjoyed myself in New York, taking in the concerts and museums and revelling in the general atmosphere of culture. It was like coming back to civilisation again, and Hollywood receded to the back of my consciousness.

The Jungle Book was the first American film score to be commercially recorded by a major film company, so RCA started to arrange some promotional interviews. I had previously had the waltz from *Lydia* recorded by RCA, but this was something quite different, and I was thrilled. Here was an opportunity to start something new in America. The Suite became quite a popular concert item in America; I conducted it several times in Hollywood, once in Portland, Oregon, with Lionel Barrymore as narrator, and in the 1950s I made a new recording in Nuremberg with Leo Genn. The original Sabu version is now available on LP and still sounds well. The newest recording is with German narration on Colosseum Records.

The journalists who came to interview me were all intelligent men, and we talked about music in Hollywood and the 'factory methods' (as I called them) employed there, whereby a number of composers collaborate on a score in order to shorten the composing period. I forgot I had to return to Hollywood. All my remarks appeared in print and, when I did get back to California, friends came up to me and asked why on earth I had said what I had. Apparently there had been an article in one of the trade papers attacking me, saying if Europeans who came here to work didn't like Hollywood methods they had better go back where they came from; another paper had the headline 'Hollywood Composer Abhors Factory Methods'; and so on. I told them I had just stated my opinion, but clearly that wasn't tolerated in

About the time of *Jungle Book* (1942)

The original *Jungle Book* record album, the
first commercial recording of a film-score
ever released in America

Eugene Ormandy's dinner last night at the Beverly Hills Hotel in honor of Mme. Alma Mahler-Werfel, widow of the Austrian composer, Gustave Mahler, included 11 noted Hollywood composers among the 100 guests. Left to right are George Anthiel, Eugene Zador, Arthur Bergh, Italo Montemez- zi, Miklos Rozsa, Richard Hageman, William Grant Still, Igor Stravinsky, Ernst Toch, Louis Gruenberg, and Erich Wolfgang Korngold. Ormandy will conduct Mahler's Eighth Symphony, dedicated to Mme. Mahler-Werfel, in Hollywood Bowl on July 29.

Newspaper report of a concert in which Eugene Ormandy conducted Mahler's Eighth Symphony before a particularly illustrious audience

Hollywood. And the fact of the matter was that, for ten months after Korda went back to England, I couldn't find any work; when my agent mentioned my name the musical directors at the studios said, 'Oh *that* one who doesn't like us. . . .' This at least gave me the opportunity to resume the other part of my Double Life, for in New York I had heard great orchestras and again felt the urge to write something substantial. It was there, too, that I met the conductor Eugene Ormandy for the first time — a meeting which later blossomed into a long friendship. He invited me to one of his concerts at Carnegie Hall, and later to Philadelphia. The whole trip had been invigorating and inspirational, so by this time I was more than ready for something new and non-cinematographic. The piece I wrote was for string orchestra and I called it Concerto for Strings.

As Bruno Walter was in town I asked my concert agent to find out whether he was interested in seeing the new Concerto for Strings. He was, and invited me over to his lovely little house on Chevy Chase Drive in Beverly Hills, very close to where Alma Mahler-Werfel lived. I took Mowgli along, but left him sitting in my car. The Walters saw him there and insisted that I bring him in as they were great dog-lovers. This certainly helped to break the ice: Mowgli was a perfect charmer.

Margaret   Bruno Walter

I played the Concerto for Walter, who said that though he liked it he would prefer a work for full orchestra which he could perform in New York. When I showed him my *Capriccio, Pastorale e Danza* (alias *Three Hungarian Sketches*) he was again complimentary but warned me against the danger of becoming categorised as a *genre* composer, saying his favourite was still my *Variations*. The latter piece had already been performed in Chicago, but this didn't worry him; he wasn't a premiere-hunter like many conductors. A few days later we went over the score together and he made several useful suggestions regarding the orchestration and recommended certain cuts. I agreed wholeheartedly to almost everything he proposed, and the present form of the work, listed as Op. 13a, is largely due to Bruno Walter.

At the Walters' home I met Mahler's widow, Alma Mahler. Walter had been a protegé and friend of the Mahlers all his life; he was a devoted exponent of Mahler's music and always treated Alma with great deference. I once met her at a dinner party at the Ernst Tochs'. She asked me how it was that Bruno Walter had performed my music, when she knew that he liked hardly any music written after about 1910. I couldn't answer, except to say that I supposed he liked my music. I think she was annoyed on account of her former son-in-law Ernst Krenek, whose music, in spite of her urgings, Walter seldom performed. 'Bruno was born an old man,' she said. To keep conversation going I told her how much I had enjoyed her book about Mahler. She thanked me, and told me she had just written another, about Men. 'Men?' I asked. 'Yes,' she said, 'I've known so many men, and not only erotically.' Well, perhaps.

A friend of hers, Walter Slezak (son of the great tenor Leo Slezak) told me she had once remarked that two of her husbands had been Jews, and did he know what they did in bed? Slezak was highly embarrassed, but Alma had pressed on. 'I'll tell you what they did in bed. They talked about Jesus Christ!'

Walter invited me to the New York performances of Op. 13 but I didn't go, for three reasons: (i) I had heard the piece often and New York was 3,000 miles away; (ii) I had just got married; and (iii) I had a job lined up.

I had met Margaret Finlason at a party given by the actress June Duprez who had played the part of the princess in *The Thief of Baghdad*. Margaret was born in Liverpool, started as an actress in the local repertory theatre and was working at Denham when I was. She used to sit in the tea-room next to the recording stage at the studio, listening to my music as it was being recorded. We saw each other often

Five Graves to Cairo: von Stroheim and Anne Baxter

Notturno
The newly-weds, Margaret and I

in the train or at the studio, but no one had introduced us. This oversight was corrected later in Hollywood when she came there as secretary/companion to Gracie Fields. In August 1943 we were married, and the Concerto for Strings is dedicated to her.

Just after I had finished the Concerto my agent told me that Paramount wanted me for a picture by Billy Wilder called *Five Graves to Cairo*. I went over to Paramount and met Wilder and his associate Charles Brackett. They were entirely different personalities: Brackett was a reserved New England gentleman, literate, cool, composed and well-behaved; the volatile Wilder was all jokes and wit and couldn't sit still for a moment. They were like solid iron and quicksilver respectively. Brackett had contributed to *The New Yorker* for a long time, and Wilder had also previously been a writer; this was only his second Hollywood film as a director. He told me bluntly that he had actually wanted Franz Waxman (a friend from his Berlin days) to do the music, but Waxman unfortunately was under contract to Warners; however, he promised that, if I did a good job on this film, I would be his first choice on the next. I was a bit taken aback by his blunt-spokenness, but that was a Wilder trait; and he certainly kept his promise later on.

So Billy and I became friends. I was very fond of him: he was an entertaining and creative man and I enjoyed sharing his ideas and playing over my music to him on the piano. Film-making is a composite art, a Wagnerian *Gesamtkunstwerk*, and film music should be written this way. Billy wanted as much music in *Five Graves to Cairo* as possible, and this I was happy to supply since the picture was good. It was a re-make of a play by Lajos Biro (head of Korda's script department) called *Hotel Imperial*, about a Polish girl and a Hungarian officer in the Austro-Hungarian army. Paramount had originally filmed it with Pola Negri, but Brackett and Wilder had invented a completely new background, transplanting the whole idea to North

The concert Bruno Walter never conducted—the young, hardly-known Leonard Bernstein stepped in at the eleventh hour. Andrew Schulhof was also for a time Bartok's concert agent in America.

Bernstein being congratulated by members of the New York Philharmonic after his last-minute début conducting, among other works, my *Theme, Variations and Finale*

Africa during the Second World War. Erich von Stroheim played Rommel. My contract with the picture was for four weeks, which left me about three weeks to write some 45 minutes of music. I could not do it today, but I was full of enthusiasm for the picture and my work went well. I also knew I *had* to succeed for, with all due respect to Korda's pictures, they had been considered 'outside work'; *Five Graves to Cairo* was my first real Hollywood engagement in a major studio.

As it turned out both Billy and Charles Brackett liked the score, but the studio's Musical Director was not so sure. Their chief composer was Victor Young, a kind and charming man whom I liked very much, but who wrote in the Broadway-cum-Rachmaninov idiom which was then the accepted Hollywood style. My own music was not like this at all, and despite Wilder's and Brackett's praises the Musical Director became very perturbed. He once asked me why I had so many dissonances in my music. 'What dissonances?' I asked. 'Well, in one spot the violins are playing a G natural and the violas a G sharp. Why don't you make it a G natural in the violas as well — just for *my* sake?' When I refused he became furious — one thing you don't do in Hollywood is disagree with an executive. However, Billy Wilder came to my aid and told him that he wasn't in the *Kaffeehaus* where he once played his violin and that he'd better stay in his office in future and leave the composing to me. This was all very embarrassing, but the man finally left in a rage and let us finish the picture in peace. Afterwards, however, the usual thing happened: the film needed cutting and was handed over to the so-called music editors, whose sole basis for deciding where to cut was to find two identical notes the required number of feet apart. What this practice did to the music's continuity and logic was another matter, and they never thought to consult me in any way. Shortly after the premiere Bruno Walter remarked to me, 'You had a few modulations I didn't quite understand. . . .' I had to explain that these were the work of a pair of scissors and not of the composer.

The New York performances of the *Theme, Variations and Finale* took place soon afterwards, in November 1943, at Carnegie Hall. There were four performances, the last of which was broadcast. Walter conducted the first three but due to sudden illness had to delegate the broadcast to one of his assistants, the young Leonard Bernstein. My piece came just before the interval and was splendidly performed; there was a youthful drive that not even Walter could have equalled, and a bravura that I have hardly heard since. I myself was twenty-six when I wrote it, and Bernstein the same age when he conducted it, so perhaps we shared the same kind of musical passion. I heard later that Bernstein was given no rehearsal time and, as far as my own piece was concerned, simply had one session with Walter during which they went through the score together. The reviews the next day were fantastic, the press acclaiming him as the first American-born top-flight conductor. The rest is history, as the cliché has it.

Later that same year, oddly enough, my career again made fleeting contact with Bernstein's in a way that proved significant for him. A then practically unknown dancer in New York's Ballet Theatre, Jerome Robbins, had been given the opportunity to choreograph an original ballet, his first; its subject was a group of sailors on leave in wartime New York. On the recommendation of Antal Doráti he asked me to write music for it, but after I had done a piece called 'First Sailor's Dance' he realised it was much too un-American to suit his purposes. So the dance became the finale of my children's piano suite *Kaleidoscope* and Robbins went to Leonard Bernstein. The result was Bernstein's first big theatrical success, *Fancy Free*.

In my naïveté I imagined that all this prestige would enhance my reputation in Hollywood — that there would be cries of 'Hail Rózsa!' when I walked into the studio the next day. Nothing of the sort: film people didn't listen to the radio and the musical directors wouldn't have gone to a concert if you had paid them. Once again I had the feeling that civilisation was three thousand miles away.

120

7: *Hollywood in the 1940s*

My Double Life began to take more pronounced shape after *Five Graves to Cairo* and the New York performance of *Theme, Variations and Finale*. Eugene Ormandy performed the latter in Philadelphia: Hans Lange conducted the *Three Hungarian Sketches* and the Concerto for Strings in Chicago, and in Hollywood, as nobody had objected to my music for *Five Graves*, the studio's chief saw no reason not to offer me more pictures. They were all unremarkable and done 'safely' one after another; I had no wish to jeopardise my career unnecessarily at this stage, since I knew that Billy Wilder was already working on his next film, *Double Indemnity*. True to his promise he asked if I would write the music. I read the Chandler novel on which it was based and was fascinated by its brutal, fearless portrayal of American life; and when I finally saw a rough-cut of Billy's film I thought it brilliant — three fine performances by Fred MacMurray, Edward G. Robinson and Barbara Stanwyck, a faultless script, and inspired direction by Wilder.

When Billy and I discussed the music, he had the idea of using a restless string figure (as in the opening of Schubert's Unfinished Symphony) to reflect the conspiratorial activities of the two lovers against the husband; it was a good idea and I happily accepted it as a basis to work on. As usual, I played sections of the score on the piano to Billy as I went along; he was very enthusiastic and we understood each other completely. Enter now the figure of the Musical Director who, when the time of the recording came, made no secret of the fact that he disliked the music intensely. Wilder finally turned to him and snapped, 'You may be surprised to hear that I *love* it. O.K.?' At this point the musical director disappeared and we didn't see him at the sessions again. Later I was summoned to his office where, in the presence of his assistant, he reprimanded me for writing 'Carnegie Hall' music which had no place in a film. This I took as a compliment, but he assured me that it wasn't intended as such. He suggested I should listen to Herbert Stothart's recent score to *Madame Curie* to learn how to write properly for the movies and, when I pointed out that that film was basically a love story, he described my title music to *Double Indemnity* as being more appropriate to *The Battle of Russia*. He was convinced that when the artistic director of the studio, Buddy de Sylva, heard the score it would be thrown out and all of us would suffer. Soon after this lecture the film was previewed in Long Beach, and Buddy de Sylva called the man over as he tried to make a hasty exit afterwards. He walked over like Louis XVI going to the guillotine, expecting heads to roll. De Sylva, however, began praising the music to the skies, saying that it was exactly the sort of dissonant, hard-hitting score the film

Fred MacMurray and Barbara Stanwyck in *Double Indemnity*

needed. The only criticism he had to make was that there wasn't enough of it. By this time the musical director was grinning from ear to ear and put his arm around de Sylva, saying, 'I always find you the right guy for the job, Buddy — don't I?' Well that, it seemed, was the Hollywood way.

From then on I had to dance less and less to the tunes of musical directors and studio executives. After *Double Indemnity* proved a big success, I had many offers and did as many pictures as I could. My Double Life also flourished. Alfred Wallenstein, the new conductor of the Los Angeles Philharmonic, had heard the New York performance of the *Theme, Variations and Finale* and invited me to conduct the premiere of my new Concerto for Strings. My favourite Musical Director was present at the concert (which was my first with the orchestra outside the Hollywood Bowl) and I heard that he was duly scandalised by the piece: the Hollywood grapevine is both fast and thorough when it comes to bad opinions. Later the same gentleman told me that one trouble with my music was that I wrote too many fugues. When I pointed out that there wasn't a single fugue in the score in question he said, 'Of course there are. There's that place where one part starts pom-pom-pom-pom-pom and then another part answers pom-pom-pom-pom-pom.

122

That's a fugue!' This was news to me; the fifty or sixty fugues I had written for Grabner at Leipzig obviously hadn't taught me anything at all . . . but I was eager to learn.

I had another music lesson many years later when I did *The Power* at MGM in the late sixties. An MGM Records executive met me and started to proffer his advice on what was wrong with my music. 'You know, you write too many themes. I counted the ones in *King of Kings* — fourteen. It's too many — one is enough. Look at *Doctor Zhivago*! That had only one theme and the album sold a million and a half copies!' Again it was my turn to learn.

One day in 1943 I received a call-up card for the United States army. At the time I was working on a picture called *So Proudly we Hail* for Paramount, a war film with Claudette Colbert and Veronica Lake. A general from the U.S. army was acting as technical adviser and I jokingly remarked to him on the set one day that we were soon to become colleagues. But when later I turned up at the induction centre I was rejected as medically unfit, so the U.S. Army had to win this one without me. Instead, I made my contribution to the war effort through my Hollywood war pictures and often conducting for the soldiers in the Hollywood Canteen.

Soon afterwards I was asked by Columbia to act as musical adviser, arranger and orchestrator on a biography of Chopin called *A Song to Remember*. I have already recounted my unfortunate experience with the life of Schubert as represented, or rather travestied, in *New Wine*, and I was naturally afraid that Chopin would be subjected to similar maltreatment. In fact he was not, but escaped only by the skin of his teeth. *A Song to Remember* was a remake of a German picture, a romanticised fantasy built round the pivotal facts of Chopin's life and dressed up in the grand Hollywood manner. It was often totally wrong from the historical point of view, but there was little I could do about that; I merely pointed out the more idiotic inconsistencies, and my advice of course was totally disregarded. The pianist who played Chopin's music on the soundtrack was José Iturbi, who had achieved a certain notoriety then for acting in MGM musicals like *Anchors Aweigh* and had become an idol of the 'bobby-soxers'. He was a fine pianist, with a particularly delicate touch in Mozart and Spanish music, but he ruined his concert career by becoming a Hollywood actor. Strangely enough, although he was so popular at the time, he received no screen credit for his work in *A Song to Remember* since the studio did not want to destroy the illusion that Cornel Wilde, as Chopin, was playing the music himself.

This was my first experience of having to adapt a great composer's music for a film. Often it would have been much simpler to write my own music for a scene, instead of having to wade through all the sonatas, nocturnes and waltzes just to find an eight-bar phrase to fit a specific situation. On those occasions where I could find nothing suitable I wrote in Chopin's style: I hope no one can tell where Chopin ends and Rózsa begins! Later I did the same with Rimsky-Korsakov's music for Walter Reisch's highly fictionalised and romanticised 'biopic' entitled *Song of Scheherazade*.

Publicity was part of the Hollywood way. Some composers even had their own publicity agents in addition to the studio publicity departments: these people didn't care what lies they fabricated about their clients as long as they made 'good copy'. In addition there were the two gossip queens of Hollywood, Hedda Hopper and Louella Parsons, each of whom wielded tremendous power over actors, producers and directors. Intellectually there was little to choose between them. Hedda Hopper once wrote something to the effect that 'there is no one in this country who knows more about sharps and flats than Maestro Arturo Toscanini. I hope that one of our smart producer boys will get him to do a musical in Hollywood as soon as possible'. This struck me as so ludicrous that I cut it out and sent it to *Musical America* (a very good serious monthly) with a note suggesting that Toscanini should be engaged to do the music for the next Abbott and Costello or Carmen Miranda picture. When Miss Hopper read this she couldn't wait to get even with me, and when *The Lost Weekend* opened shortly after *Spellbound* she wrote: 'Miklós Rózsa has repeated note-for-note his *Spellbound* score in *The Lost Weekend*'. Well, I admit that both of them featured the novelty of the theremin, but the important thing was that she had her revenge, which I duly survived. It was really disgusting to see everyone in Hollywood cowtowing to these two gossip-mongering illiterates.

I had already heard Toscanini in Bayreuth, Paris and London and had thought his performances masterly. His presence in America was especially important as he towered like a colossus above the excesses and liberties of Stokowski. His orchestra, hand-picked, was the NBC Symphony, and their broadcasts were national events. He was a tyrant. His rages during rehearsals were famous, and his players both loved and feared him. He used to conduct the opening of Mozart's G minor Symphony angularly and unemotionally. Now one day Bruno Walter, whom Toscanini categorised as a sentimental fool, was the guest conductor. He rehearsed the same symphony with gentleness and love; the opening had to be played *dolce* and *amabile*. The rehearsal went well but at the concert the players, to their consternation, saw Toscanini sitting in the front row. His stern expression froze them with fear, and no matter how Walter encouraged them with his lovely smile they played the opening theme as they aggressively as they played it under Toscanini. On one occasion when he brought his orchestra to Los Angeles they played Weber's *Invitation to the Dance*. Suddenly a scantily-clad woman ran up to the platform and started to waltz about. The old man was petrified when he became aware of her, looked at her incredulously and put down his baton. Ushers came running up and ejected the impromptu ballerina. It turned out that she had done it for publicity and hoped for a job in films. Nothing came of her ambitions (the press ignored her completely), but poor Toscanini was in a state of shock for weeks.

At the end of the war I read a book by Marquand, a fine American novelist, in which I came across a quotation from Ecclesiastes: 'To everything there is a season.' The beauty of these words and the philosophy behind them made an immediate impression on me. Later I came across the same quotation in a copy of *Reader's Digest*; and then, when I happened to see it a third time in a Gideon Bible which lay open at this page in a hotel bedroom in Palm Springs (where I always went to recuperate after finishing a film score), I told myself that all the signs pointed to my setting this text to music. The only choral works I had written since my Leipzig days were two madrigals for female voices, and now I felt ready to compose a motet

The original *Spellbound* soundtrack album

Salvador Dali with some of his designs for the
dream-sequences in *Spellbound*

to this text. The passage ends with the words, 'A time for war, and a time for peace',
and since it looked as if peace was at last coming I added a final 'Alleluia'. I sent the
finished composition to Associated Music Publishers in New York (Breitkopf &
Härtel's agents) and had a reply from the Managing Director saying that he
regretted he couldn't publish anything which admitted that there could be 'a time
for war and a time for hate'. I wrote back sarcastically saying that it wasn't in my
power to change the Bible. Happily Breitkopf & Härtel published the piece after the
end of the war when normal communications with Germany were resumed, since
when it has become my most popular choral piece (excluding the short choruses

125

from *Ben-Hur* and *King of Kings*). I later dedicated the motet to the memory of my dear mentor Straube, from whom I learnt my choral technique and who died in 1950.

Cinematically the year 1945 was a very busy one. Alfred Hitchcock had liked my score for *Double Indemnity* and told David O. Selznick that I would be a good choice for *Spellbound*, a 'psychological thriller' which he was then making with Ingrid Bergman and Gregory Peck. After terms had been agreed between my agent and Selznick's business manager, I went to meet Hitchcock and Selznick in person. I was only to see them twice during the whole job, and this was the first meeting of the two. Both gentlemen were most amiable, and Hitchcock told me his precise requirements: a big sweeping love theme for Ingrid Bergman and Gregory Peck, and a 'new sound' for the paranoia which formed the subject of the picture. I immediately suggested the theremin, an electronic instrument bearing the name of the man who invented it.

I have already described how I tried to use a close relative of the theremin, the Ondes Martenot, in *The Thief of Baghdad* back in 1940. The following year, since the Ondes Martenot didn't exist in America, I tried to persuade Henry Hathaway and Walter Wanger to let me use the theremin in a war picture called *Sundown*. The film was set in Africa and contained a scene showing a *habari* (the negro word for a premonition of death); the director and producer wanted an eerie sound for this, but neither was interested in my high-flown idea, so I finally used a musical saw. Anyway, here at last, in 1945, came my third chance. Hitchcock and Selznick hadn't heard of the theremin and weren't quite sure whether you ate it or took it for headaches, but they agreed to try it out, telling me first of all to go and write the two main themes.

In the meantime *Spellbound* was previewed in Pasadena with a temporary music track (more-or-less appropriate music derived from other film scores). This was a regular practice and in this case (unlike the later *Lost Weekend*) was well done. Coming out of the theatre afterwards I immediately jotted down the love theme — it came to me, as it were, straight from the picture. I record this merely for interest's sake, because, although it isn't my own favourite, it has since become my most recorded film theme. When I played this and the 'paranoia' theme to Selznick and Hitchcock, they liked the melodies but were still not sure about the theremin. Selznick finally suggested I should write and record the razor scene (in which Gregory Peck stands over Ingrid Bergman with a cut-throat razor in his hand) in order to see whether my concept would work or not. This was my second and final meeting with these two gentlemen. Instead, after a try-out recording (which they approved of), I was bombarded by the famous Selznick memos, which virtually told me how to compose and orchestrate the music scene by scene. One dealt with the scene where Bergman passes Peck's room after their first meeting and sees the light coming from under his door. 'Be sure to sell Ingrid's love when she sees the light under the door (cymbals).' I never asked what he meant by 'cymbals' (a cymbal-clash is too intrusive a dynamic to be used in any but big noisy dramatic scenes) and thereafter completely disregarded all his 'musical' ideas. I 'sold' Ingrid's love in my own way and with my own theme.

Neither Selznick nor Hitchcock turned up for the final recording sessions, so afterwards I just had to sit and wait for their reaction. (Selznick was quite capable of throwing out a complete score if he didn't like the finished result, and had, in fact, done so on his previous picture.) Next day I had a call from one of his secretaries asking how many violins I had used in the title music. After I had told her, she called back to say that Selznick had checked Franz Waxman's score for *Rebecca*, found that he had used more and wanted me to re-record the Main Title with the same number. This I happily did, but whether half a dozen extra violins made any difference only Selznick could tell.

It seemed I was 'up' for his next picture, *Duel in the Sun*. In order to find the 'best' man for the job Selznick had decided to put six composers on trial. They were each to be given two weeks' salary and set to score a specific scene. Then Selznick would sit in judgement and decide which composer was the 'best'. That composer would be engaged to do the entire score but, inasmuch as he had already done two weeks' work, the two weeks' salary would be deducted from his overall fee. I was one of the lucky composers selected to undergo this humiliation. I instructed my agent to reply that even if Mr Selznick had never heard a note of my music I would find his proposition an insult. Insofar as he had heard and apparently approved my *Spellbound* music, I regarded it as an outrage, and never wanted to hear his name again.

It seemed I was not to be rid Mr Selznick so easily, however. After *The Lost Weekend* (which followed *Spellbound*) I received a frantic telephone call from his secretary asking me if it were true that I had used the theremin in my new picture as

Ray Milland and Howard da Silva in *The Lost Weekend*

well; apparently Selznick considered he had a monopoly on the instrument. I flew into a rage and told the lady yes, I had used not only the theremin but also the piccolo, the trumpet, the triangle and the violin, goodbye!

The Lost Weekend was directed by Billy Wilder. Wilder had recently enlisted in the army and had to go off to England and Germany, but before leaving he approved my idea of using the eerie theremin to depict alcoholic delirium. To begin with, the film was previewed with a disastrously inappropriate temporary score. The opening shots of the New York skyline had some jazzy xylophonic Gershwinesque music (in the Hollywood musical vernacular New York means Gershwin), and when Ray Milland was fishing in the whisky bottle the audience roared with laughter. As soon as they began to realise the film was actually a stark drama about alcoholism many started to leave. No applause was forthcoming at the end. Next day the studio was full of gloom, and there was talk of shelving the whole picture. I

Lev Theremin playing the instrument he invented and which I made the official Hollywood mouthpiece of mental disorders

tried to explain to Charles Brackett that the music was to blame since it led the audience to expect a comedy. He was very depressed and not totally convinced, but he told me to go ahead and do what I felt was right. Much to the discomfort of the Musical Director, I wrote an intense, impassioned and dramatic score in which the weird sound of the theremin became the official 'voice' of dipsomania.

Once again the Musical Director kept calling my music too dissonant, too aggressive, too noticeable beneath the dialogue, but Charles Brackett supported me unreservedly. In fact it was he who asked me to write a stronger version of the famous Third Avenue sequence, when Ray Milland walks the streets and tries to pawn his typewriter; this is the version that now appears in the film, but at the time, as was to be expected, the Musical Director complained bitterly about the wasting of money. I remember his castigating me on one of my early pictures for giving only one note to a triangle-player in a sequence, saying that I should either give him

Receiving my *Spellbound* Oscar from Ginger Rogers

more to play or not use him at all. Here was the studio making thirty or forty million dollars' profit a year and he was worried about losing the company money by not giving a solitary triangle-player enough to do!

When *The Lost Weekend* was re-previewed with the final score it got an ovation at the end and the rest is now cinema history. The film received all the important Academy Awards of that year except that for 'Best Music', which went to *Spellbound*. I was sorry about this because, though *Spellbound* had the more popular theme, *The Lost Weekend* was an infinitely stronger score: but I was consoled by the fact that, when we all walked into dinner afterwards holding those stupid little statuettes, the one man who was hoping for reflected glory — the Musical Director — was a sorry sight. Later, on the fly-leaf of my score for *The Strange Love of Martha Ivers*, he wrote, 'Dear Miklós — let's hope this is "it" for 1947' — 'it' of course, being, the coveted Oscar, which to these people meant more than life itself.

I had met Jerome Kern at the Academy of Motion Picture Arts and Sciences and found him a most lovable, kind, unassuming man. You would never have known that this was the world-famous composer whose songs so far transcended the tawdry conventions of Tin Pan Alley. He became a good friend of ours, and we were often invited to his lovely house in Beverly Hills. I still have, unopened, a bottle of Irish whisky he once gave us with a dedication. It wasn't until he told me one day that 'we' were going to publish the *Spellbound Concerto** that I discovered that he was a co-owner of Chappell's Publishing in New York, along with Cole Porter and the Gershwin Estate. It was Kern who had urged the company to publish my work, and I am grateful to him. The theme is constantly being re-recorded, and in the language of Broadway, it has become a 'standard'.

After the success of *Spellbound* and *The Lost Weekend*, offers began to pour in and I found myself in the position of being able to choose exactly what I wanted. My personal joys came in a very different sphere, however: in 1945 I finally became an American citizen and my daughter Juliet Valerie Alexandra was born; the following year my son, Nicholas John Reginald, arrived. Juliet has graduated in Library Science, and Nicholas has made his profession out of what has been a life-long hobby of mine, photography. My 1946 *Kaleidoscope* for piano (later orchestrated) consists of six easy pieces, three for each of my children.

About this time I did the music for two Deanna Durbin comedies at Universal, *Lady on a Train* and *Because of Him*. They weren't really my kind of film, but I needed some relief after doing two heavy psychological dramas in a row: it was, too, a pleasure to work at this studio. The musical director there, Milton Schwarzwald, never tried to interfere with my music: he never asked to me play the love theme in fox-trot tempo to see if it could be exploited on records, as had happened before.

I worked with two important men at Universal whose memories I cherish: Fritz Lang and Mark Hellinger. Lang had long been a hero of mine. In my youth I had been very impressed by *Die Niebelungen* in Budapest and later, while waiting for

---

* This title was originally applied — very misleadingly — to a purely *orchestral* suite I made of the *Spellbound* music for concert performance. Later I re-worked it in the form of a proper one-movement concerto for piano and orchestra, of which Leonard Pennario made the premiere recording. In recent years Semprini and Daniel Adni have both made recordings.

Family group in the 1970s: with Nicholas, Juliet and grand-daughter Maria

Furtwängler in Berlin, by his thriller, *M*. Lang did not have a very good reputation in Hollywood: everyone talked of him as some sort of Teutonic monster, a schoolmaster-like slave-driver who always demanded the impossible of people he worked with. I was surprised, therefore, to find him one of the most charming, witty, cultured and entertaining men I had ever met in a film studio. He had the same elegance and fine manners as Jacques Feyder. He told me he had seen *Spellbound* and *The Lost Weekend* and that finally I was going to get a psychological picture in which the psychology was correct. It was to be called *The Secret Beyond the Door*. In actual fact its script was not as good as those two earlier pictures, but it was none the less a great pleasure to work with Lang and we became friends and, indeed, partners. With Alfred Hitchcock there had been no partnership at all: we had never really clicked — I disliked his overbearing attitude and he, I presume, was uninterested in my music, since he never came to the recording sessions and never bothered to congratulate me on winning the Oscar (even Selznick had had the

131

Fritz Lang

courtesy to send me a telegram). With Fritz Lang, however, it was entirely different: I said I would like him to hear the music as I wrote it, and he readily agreed provided he could do so along with the picture. So we met in a small projection room and I played from my manuscript while he watched the film. He liked my work and made certain constructive suggestions, and wasn't afraid to give new ideas a try. For one sequence I said I wanted to write a passacaglia, and though he didn't understand the technical term he was happy to have it explained to him. For another, when Michael Redgrave opens the doors behind which lie his secrets, Lang wanted an unusual sound and, since I refused to use the theremin again, we experimented with having the orchestra play their music backwards, recording it back to front on the tape, and then playing it back as usual; the end result sounded the right way round but had an unearthly quality. Lang and I also mixed socially. Going to his house for dinner was a great pleasure because the atmosphere was totally un-Hollywoodian — it was like being in Paris again. He was a charming host; in fact on one occasion I was rather overwhelmed by the variety of wines and drinks he served at dinner and passed out on the bed upstairs. As a non-drinker I should have marked better the lessons to be learnt from *The Lost Weekend*.

Lang and I worked together once more many years later, on an MGM picture called *Moonfleet*. The film was already completed when I learnt about it, and naturally I accepted the job with alacrity, hoping for the same kind of working relationship with the director. When I met him, however, he told me he was

Michael Redgrave and Joan Bennett in *Secret Beyond the Door*

finished with the picture and was leaving the next day to start another; John Houseman, the producer, would supervise the recording and dubbing. It was a melancholy lunch we had together, but that was the system of the time; the producers and the front office had the power, and the rest of us — writers, actors, directors, composers — were considered mere employees. On some pictures I didn't see the director at all; people often ask me what it was like working with Douglas Sirk, for example, on *A Time to Love and a Time to Die*, and they are surprised when I say I never ever met him.

The other personality I worked with at Universal at this time was the producer Mark Hellinger, who had been a well-known New York columnist before coming to Hollywood, where he produced a few pictures for Warner Bros. before setting up his own company and producing for Universal. I was assigned to his first picture for them, *The Killers*, adapted from a short story by Ernest Hemingway. It was also the first film of a former circus acrobat named Burt Lancaster, and the first important American film of the German director Robert Siodmak. Hellinger was the kindest and most appreciative of men. We had little contact up to the time of recording the music — though I remember our meeting in his studio bungalow one morning and discussing my idea of using a short, distinctive musical motif to characterise the killers whenever they appeared* — but after I had completed the score he invited

---

* This later became world-famous as the 'Dum-da-dum-dum' motto of the TV series *Dragnet*.

133

me over one day and told me he was already preparing a new picture, *Brute Force*, and asked if I would do the music for that too. I told him I would be delighted to work on anything of his.

The Killers was a violent film, and my score, which was also brutal and dissonant, predictably ran into a certain amount of heavy critical weather at the studio. Milton Schwarzwald reported the front office's unfavourable reaction to me, but since the film was Hellinger's and not really theirs, there was little they could do about it. *The Killers* inaugurated my 'third period' in film scoring. The first had been the 'oriental', in which the films had had exotic locations — *The Four Feathers*, *The Thief of Baghdad*, *The Jungle Book*, *Sahara*, *Sundown*. The second had been 'psychological' — *Spellbound*, *The Lost Weekend*, *Secret Beyond the Door*, *The Strange Love of Martha Ivers*, *The Red House*. Now came these hard-hitting *films noirs*, dealing with American urban low-life and the underworld, which demanded a new approach. Berlioz once said that for each new dramatic subject he attacked he had to change his style; in fact, he only *thought* he changed it, because, whatever the subject, his music always sounded as if only he could have written it. The same, I would like to think, applies to me — though in those days to have a distinctive style was no positive asset in Hollywood.

Hellinger's *Brute Force* was about a prison break and again starred Burt Lancaster. It was a fine picture with a strong script by Richard Brooks and excellent characterisation, and again I wrote a tough, stark score which Hellinger loved. The front office, as I heard again from Schwarzwald, did not. Finally came *The Naked City*, directed by the talented Jules Dassin, a former B-picture director at MGM who had been asked to leave because he was suspected of left-wing sympathies. Hellinger was happy to use him, however, and we had agreed that I would do the music. One day, though, he called me in and explained frankly that he was in a quandary: Dassin wanted him to use instead a composer-friend who had also lost his job at MGM, though for a different reason. I remembered Berger, Straus and *The Thief of Baghdad*, so I told him that, if that was what Dassin wanted, it was all right with me; there would be other opportunities for us to work together in the future, and I would have no hard feelings. Hellinger was such a sweet man; he embraced me (it was early in the morning and he had had a few brandies already) and said, 'You're really not mad at me?' 'How could I be?' I replied, 'when I love you?' So that was that, or so I thought.

I then did a picture at Paramount instead (*Desert Fury*, yet again with Burt Lancaster), and when I was almost finished with it I heard that Hellinger had had a heart attack while on location in New York. Normally in such cases the patient is kept immobile in bed for at least six weeks; Hellinger stayed in hospital for only three days before returning to the set. The film was his responsibility and he felt he had to be there. He always used to wear a dark shirt and a white tie, but when I saw him on his return to California his face too was white. He looked drawn and old, a good ten years in excess of his real age of 43. In the meantime, Dassin's composer scored the film. There's a saying in Rumania that one never knows where the bandit ends and the gendarme begins: in Hollywood one could say the same about arrangers and composers. Dassin's friend (whom I didn't know personally) was

Burt Lancaster (photo inscribed to my daughter Juliet)

The Killers: Burt Lancaster and Ava Gardner (right)

Mark Hellinger (right) and actor Don Taylor during the shooting of *The Naked City*

really only an arranger, and when Hellinger heard this man's score at the recording session he almost had another heart attack. He ranted and raved and swore that, come what may, that music would never go into his picture. The next day I received a call with the familiar voice at the other end. He began by asking if I had finished the picture I was working on and whether I had heard about what had happened the previous day. I said I had, and there was a long, dramatic pause during which he searched for the right words. In the end he just said, 'Would you . . .?' and my heart overflowed. 'You know I would, Mark,' I replied. 'Bless you,' he said. That was our last conversation together: next morning I heard on the radio that he had died during the night from another heart attack.

A few days later I went to his funeral and afterwards had to go straight from there to the studio to view the picture. The film opens with shots of New York and his voice saying, 'This is Mark Hellinger speaking.' This barely an hour after we had buried him. Milton Schwarzwald knew that Hellinger had wanted me to do the music but explained that there was a problem: the premiere date was already fixed and left just two weeks to write and record the music. It was an impossible deadline for me to meet, and I refused to accept any 'help' from other composers (a regular Hollywood practice, which I was to fight against in my MGM contract, whereby other composers work uncredited on individual sequences using the credited composer's thematic material). So Schwarzwald suggested that Frank Skinner, a staff composer at Universal, score the less important dialogue sequences while I cover all the 'foreground' areas — a proposal I agreed to as long as Skinner received screen credit along with me. For the final scene, which again features Mark Hellinger talking about New York, I wrote an epilogue as an *in memoriam*, subtitling it 'The Song of a Great City'. As a final tribute I assembled a *Mark Hellinger Suite*, using two pieces from each of the three scores I had written for him. It was later recorded under the unfortunate title *Background to Violence*, which hardly did justice to the more lyrical sections of the suite — but one can do little in the face of the decisions of record companies or publishers who know all there is to know about commercial titles.

I made few real friends among studio musicians and composers, but one exception readily comes to mind in connection with Universal — Hans J. Salter, an excellent Viennese-born musician who spent well over thirty years at the studios but remained totally untouched by all the blare and ballyhoo. To this day we meet regularly; he is one of that rare breed, a professional composer for films who is also interested in music. Most handle it as a commodity.

During the war, through the International Red Cross, I received a note from my French aunt in Paris: 'Votre père est mort'. My father was dead. It was a hard blow, this tiny note, and harder still that it was impossible to write to my mother because, in the craziness of war, Hungary had declared war on America and there was no communication between the two countries. At the end of the war I was relieved to receive a letter from her in which I learnt that she and my sister were both all right. My mother wanted to join me in America. By this time I was an American citizen and the law allowed me to ask for my parents to join me; so I wrote to her telling her that I had applied for a visa for her. I was working with Fritz Lang on *Secret Beyond the Door* at the time she arrived in Hollywood, heartbroken because the U.S. Customs had confiscated the salami she had brought with her; I must have mentioned it to him because she was greeted with a huge bouquet of beautiful roses with a card which read: 'Welcome to America — Fritz Lang'. This was the ogre the whole of Hollywood dreaded.

We moved into a new house in the Hollywood Hills. With our two children and my wife's parents, and now with my mother's imminent arrival, there simply wasn't enough room in the old one. The new house had previously belonged to the actor Richard Green and his actress wife Patricia Medina, and had been built by the silent picture stars John Bowers and his wife Marguerite de la Motte, who threw lavish parties. Like so many silent actors, they both lost their jobs with the coming of the talkies. Bowers forfeited what money remained by investing unwisely, and the bank took possession of the house. He went to Santa Monica, hired a little boat, and sailed out to sea, never to return. This sad story was actually dramatised in the picture *A Star is Born*.

My mother liked the house and its beautiful garden, but began to miss my sister. The law didn't allow me to apply for an immigration visa for her, and although she was supporting herself perfectly well in Budapest as a piano teacher my mother would frequently burst into tears at the thought of her. We managed to solve the problem when we discovered that she had been corresponding with a Hungarian-

American, an officer in the Marines, who wanted to marry her. If he did so he could, of course, bring her to America. To comply with the law the marriage had to take place off American soil; so it was arranged that the couple would meet and marry in Guatemala.

All went well until my sister reached London, whence she was to fly direct to Guatemala. But revolution broke out in that country and all flights were suspended. To make matters worse, because she had intended merely to change planes in London she hadn't applied for a visa for Britain. Now she was trapped at the airport, forbidden to enter the country, with the authorities insisting that she return to Hungary. My wife rang me at Universal to tell me. 'Do something!' she said.

William Goetz, the head of the studio, rang his brother Ben who was the head of MGM in London. I sent a telegram to my friend Emeric Pressburger, and through the intervention of these two my sister was let into England, provided Pressburger would vouch for her.

Finally the law was changed in the States: it was enough for the bridegroom to send a declaration to the embassy in London. This was done, and in 1948 they were married and are living happily together to this day.

Back at Universal I began work on my last patho-psychological picture *A Double Life*. The script was by Garson Kanin and his wife, and the producer his brother Michael; the director was George Cukor. The story concerned an actor, played by Ronald Colman, whose involvement with the role of Othello gradually takes over his own life, with the inevitable tragic result. I discussed with Cukor the idea that whenever *Othello*, the play itself, was presented in the film we should have 'Shakespearian' theatre music. Cukor agreed in principle, but suggested that the music be not 'Elizabethan' but rather 'Venetian', and I proposed the Venetian composer Giovanni Gabrieli as a model for the style. Cukor borrowed records of

Gabrieli from Aldous Huxley so that he could hear what I had in mind.

My 'Venetian' music worked well and for the rest of the picture I continued in my best patho-psychological vein: as always I tried to illuminate rather than illustrate, to underline the characters' emotions and help transmit them to the audience. I wrote a strong driving theme for the opening titles and the picture was previewed with my music, as it was ready in time.

The next day the front office complained that the title music was 'too modernistic' and ordered it be changed. I rushed over to Cukor's bungalow, where he was reading the enthusiastic comments the public had made on their cards, and told him what had happened. Cukor grabbed me and shouted 'If you change one note, I'll kill you!' I was glad to send a message back to the front office politely suggesting that they jump in the lake, Toluca being the closest. The picture went out with the score as written, and for it I received my second Oscar. Sometimes it pays to be stubborn. Needless to say, I was asked to take publicity pictures with the studio heads, which of course I refused to do.

During this period picture followed picture and I was very much in demand. I had little time for my own music, but did manage to write a piano sonata, which I

Ronald Colman and Signe Hasso in *A Double Life*

Nursing my *Double Life* Oscar, smilingly encouraged by the reigning *prima donna assoluta* of Universal at that time, Deanna Durbin

count among my best works. It was first performed by my dear friend John Crown, professor of piano at USC, where I also was a member of the faculty by this time; for in 1945 I had been invited to start a course on film music composition, the first of its kind in America. I had taught ordinary composition before, first as Grabner's assistant, and later to private pupils, but I was a novice in the teaching of film composition. I gave my students a short history of film music to begin with, and then a series of dramatic ideas to which they had to write music. That took up the first semester. The second was devoted to writing music for a specific film to be made by the cinema department, and for which the music would be recorded by members of the student orchestra. The students experienced exactly the same difficulties as I had when I began. They found the tyranny of the stopwatch irksome and had to train themselves to compose not in pursuance of classical ideals or their own individual inclinations, but in accordance with the specific needs of the drama. I found the course tiring because I was working so hard all the while at the studios, but I did it not only because I liked it but because I felt it was my duty to pass on my acquired knowledge.

My pupils often asked me about the writing of music for cartoons, a subject about which I knew nothing. But MGM had a whole cartoon department, and the music was under the direction of Scott Bradley. I invited Bradley to come along and talk to the class, which he agreed to do. He explained that music was the most important element in a cartoon, especially for laughter — the music underlines the gags in a unique way. He illustrated this by showing a *Tom and Jerry* cartoon, without and with the music, telling the class beforehand that there would be very little humour in the silent version. He showed the latter and the class rocked with laughter. Music or no music, Tom and Jerry were very funny. I think he was rather annoyed at this, but anyway he pressed on and said, 'Now we'll have the version *with* the music, and you'll see immediately how much funnier it is.' But a joke is funny only once. The music went wild — xylophones clattered, bass drums thumped as the characters fell about — and nobody laughed. They may have smiled, but they didn't laugh. I was acutely embarrassed, and poor old Scott immediately changed the subject and started talking about something else.

One year I arranged a symposium in which I invited a number of colleagues to participate. Quixotically, perhaps, I rang my friend Bernard Herrmann to invite him; whereupon a species of volcanic eruption took place at the other end of the phone, the gist of which was that the course, the University and everyone connected with them (which presumably included myself) should go to the Devil, and with all convenient speed. I knew my Benny and left it at that. Sure enough, in no time at all he called back and, sheepishly and with the greatest show of reluctance, asked for details of what he would be required to do. He came — and absolutely stole the show. He was in top form, and the students adored him. Why then the preliminary tantrum? But that was Benny all over. First the lion had to roar; then he would become docile as a lamb.

John Crown gave a brilliant performance of the Piano Sonata, and the second printing of the piece is dedicated to his memory. He was my closest friend in Hollywood, a perfect gentleman; our friendship started when I first arrived and lasted until his untimely death, which left an unfillable void in my life.

Simultaneously with my contract with Universal for a certain number of pictures, I had a contract with Hal Wallis at Paramount. Our first film was the already-mentioned *Strange Love of Martha Ivers*, for which I was told a 'theme song' was wanted. This was the fashion now, a tune to which lyrics could be added and broadcast as a 'plug' for the film. I had to try. I looked back to my Parisian days as Nic Tomay and wrote a 'love theme', which, combined with its specially-written lyrics, became the song 'Strange Love'. It never became a hit but had several recordings and the studio was happy.

Then came *Desert Fury*, when again I was intimidated by the head of the music department, who gave me long lectures about lovely main titles with swooning violins and the rest, and this time I composed a title so conventional that even he smiled when we recorded it. A few days later he rang with a voice of doom to tell me that Wallis didn't like it, no doubt because the music wasn't melodious enough — the studio wanted hit tunes in the manner of Victor Young. I went over to see Wallis, but in fact his complaint was very different. He had listened to many of my 'black' pictures. They were strong, gripping, powerful. What had happened? This music was wishy-washy and non-committal, like that of any other second-rate composer. I didn't think it fair to reveal where my inspiration had come from, so I apologised and asked permission to write another piece. I did and we were both happy. As can be seen in situations like this, the producers and directors themselves were hardly ever to blame. The trouble stemmed from the heads of the music departments, men from jazz bands and theatre pits who hadn't the faintest notion of music as an adjunct to drama, and always wanted to 'play it safe' (literally). They were the arbiters of musical taste in Hollywood, and since they employed hacks when real composers were available they caused the ruin of many potentially good films.

By now the forties were coming to an end, and with them my status as a free agent. Twice before MGM had invited me to join them, and both times I had refused. I couldn't see myself as a staff composer; hitherto I had picked and chosen as I liked. The idea of checking in and out every day sounded frightful, but in 1948 my agent gave me some advice. The war was over, television was coming in, films were already in difficulties. Independent producers were on the way out, and he felt that this was the time to take a safe job. MGM had made a third offer for me, and he advised me to accept. I had to think of my Double Life and hoped that in future, being more secure as an employee of a major studio, I should have more time for my own music.

We went to see the Managing Director, L. K. Sidney. I had expected an ogre and instead found one of the kindest and sweetest men I had ever met in the studios. He knew all my films and all my music, and in very pleasing words told me that MGM needed me. He said that MGM was the most important studio in the world, and that, in his opinion, I was the most important composer of film music.

After some consideration I decided to accept, but felt I had to lay down certain conditions. Nobody was to add a note to any of my pictures, nor was I to be asked to add anything to anybody else's. I was not to be required to attend the studio if I had no work to do at the time. I was to do my composing in the privacy of my own home. My teaching job at the University of Southern California was not to be called in question. Sidney was a sensitive man, and told my agent that he could see from these conditions that I had been hurt in the past. He accepted all the points except the one about my teaching at USC. He said the studios had nothing to do with the universities and the interests of the former must come first. Through my agent I remained adamant. No USC, no deal. The next day the studio accepted and engaged me, and I began a period of fourteen years as a member of the music staff of MGM.

8: The MGM Years

I had heard much bad and little good about MGM before I arrived there: that its immense and relentless conveyor-belt-style productivity depended on a constant ingestion of new creative talent, but that artists counted for little or nothing apart from their ability to deliver the goods. Well, I can only report that, in my early days at least, I saw little or nothing of this. I was treated in all quarters with the greatest kindness and consideration. Louis B. Mayer was at that time still the head of the studio, but all my dealings were with Sidney, and I never had cause for complaint.

My first two pictures were of no great consequence, but they seemed to please because I was then assigned to *Madame Bovary*, with Jennifer Jones and the young Louis Jourdan. The title was magic to me. As a child I had read the novel in French, and loved it. Now I re-read it, and Flaubert's other novels. I had a collaboration with Vincente Minnelli of a kind I had enjoyed previously only with Lang, Wilder and the Kordas. Usually one is called in when the picture is finished and told, 'There's the picture — compose!' I love to be in from the planning stage, to give and receive suggestions. This is the only way a work of art — assuming one thinks of a film as a potential work of art — can come into being.

Minnelli was a sensitive artist and director, and he made a masterpiece of *Madame Bovary*. The set-piece of the film was the great waltz in the ballroom. During our discussions I would refer to Flaubert, he to his script. If he mentioned something that wasn't in the book, I would open Flaubert as a priest would his breviary. Flaubert describes the waltz in detail and Vincente wanted to recreate it accordingly. He told me exactly how long each part, each incident should be, and I was able to write the music to match and in a spirit of dedication, knowing that in this instance the camera would be following my music, not my music the camera. For the pre-recording I arranged it for two pianos, one of which was played by a very young member of the MGM music department called André Previn.

Minnelli was so excited by the waltz when the two pianos played it that he asked his wife, Judy Garland, to come over to hear it. There is a sudden modulation in the piece where the big tune lurches into an unexpected key, and at that moment Miss Garland gasped in thrilled amazement and goose pimples appeared on her arms. (Always the actress!) Minnelli shot the scene to the two-piano track, which was later replaced by the orchestrated version.

We went to the out-of-town preview with some trepidation, because nobody knew how an American audience would react to a hundred-year-old French story. The waltz scene is quite long — about five minutes — and I remember with a

With Clark Gable (*Command Decision*, 1948)   Vincente Minnelli in later years

certain pride that at the end the whole audience burst into applause. Of course this wasn't necessarily only for the music, but for the brilliance and excitement of the scene as a whole.

No pictures of great importance followed immediately, apart from *The Asphalt Jungle* of John Huston. I wrote the prelude and asked Huston to come and hear it. He didn't like it. He said it was doing what innumerable preludes had done already, telling the audience that what they were going to see was super-colossal, tremendous, fantastic, the greatest picture of all time; and then came — just a picture. What he wanted was a tense but quiet opening, and that is what the picture has now. Interestingly enough, this was Marilyn Monroe's first major film. She was splendid in the small dumb-blonde part she played. We had the same agent, Johnny Hyde, and one day he rang me to ask if I would have lunch with his protegée. I did, and found her charming and uncomplicated — a normal Hollywood girl who wanted to get into pictures. When the film was shown, the audience gave her a good rating on their comment-cards, but these were disregarded by the new studio head who was gradually taking over from Louis B. Mayer, and he let her go. She was immediately snapped up by 20th Century Fox, and within a year was a number one box-office attraction.

Another part of my agreement with Sidney allowed me first refusal on MGM's most prestigious films; furthermore, I could request any film that took my fancy. *Quo Vadis* was in preparation, and of course I was interested in it. It was to cost seven million dollars, an unheard-of sum then. In an attempt to keep the budget as low as possible it was being made in Italy, where labour was very cheap in those days, and various European composers were being considered, also to save money.

Sidney called me to his office one day to show me a list of suggested composers. There were some impossible names on the list, but also William Walton. He asked my opinion. I told him Walton was a great composer, the best. He seemed surprised and said, 'But I want you.' I told him that I was grateful, but that if it was a choice between Walton and me, he should take Walton. Again he gave me a quizzical look and thanked me, and I left his office. A couple of days later I learned that I was assigned to the picture.

This was the begining of a long period of really interesting pictures which I feel brought out the best in me because I enjoyed my work so much. For that reason alone I am grateful to MGM. My Historico-Biblical period — my fourth — had begun.

I was very lucky that MGM brought to *Quo Vadis* a genuine quest for historical accuracy. An Oxford classical scholar, Hugh Gray, was assigned to write a résumé of the first-century Roman world. It was a fine piece of work, dealing with architecture, the arts, customs, family life and, particularly interesting for me, the musical instruments of the period. This study laid the foundations for the script, the sets and costumes, and the music. Gray was also commissioned to write the words for the songs and hymns in the picture.

Some of the music was *musique de scène*; that is, music which is actually a *part* of the action, as opposed to dramatic incidental music which subliminally *supports* the action. In the case of *Quo Vadis* this *musique de scène* had to be written before the

Madame Bovary: the 3 a.m. waltz, the highlight of the film and of my score

145

Quo Vadis: with Hugh Gray (and musical props) in Rome

shooting, so that the lips of singers and the movements of the dancers would coincide with the music. Mervyn LeRoy, the director, was amazed to learn that I hadn't been sent to Rome to supervise these scenes, particularly an important 'Bacchanale'. He stormed into L. B. Mayer's office and, I heard, made a scene, with the result that I was despatched to Rome along with everybody else.

Hugh Gray's constant supervision ensured that no anachronism found its way into the picture. In my own field, I had copies of the ancient instruments made in Rome, though, of course, they made no sound. For this we made do with modern instruments approximating as closely as possible to the sounds that ancient ones of a particular size and shape would presumably have made.

Now it is not easy to know exactly what music the Romans played on their instruments, since none of their written music survives. But several examples from Greek monuments and tombstones have been deciphered by scholars, and as Greek civilisation dominated Rome so completely in the fields of religion, architecture, literature and drama, it seemed reasonable to employ these Greek sources as a basis for my music. Nero's song is an authentic Greek melody, and every piece of 'source music' is based on something from the period. Sometimes a short fragment was enough to serve as a point of departure.

Another problem was the music of the early Christians. The earliest 'Christian' music is Ambrosian chant, which is some four hundred years too late. Before this their music would no doubt have drawn largely on Jewish and Greek sources, and I discovered the work of a Jewish scholar called Idelsohn who had collected the songs of Yemenite and Babylonian Jews. The way of life of these peoples had remained unchanged from ancient times, so it seemed reasonable to assume that their music also had changed little. Certainly their liturgical music was completely different from other Jewish music, and some was identical with hymns in the Gregorian liturgy. So my early 'Christian' music was derived from these sources.

On my first evening in Rome, Hugh Gray and I walked about exploring. I don't have to unveil the city to my readers, but the great monuments of the ancient world and St. Peter's by night were impressions I will remember all my life. Since that evening, Rome and I have been 'going steady'. They say you must throw a coin into the Trevi fountain to ensure your return. I have thrown in many coins, and have returned many times.

The studio told me I would have to find an assistant because I wouldn't be able to stay in Rome for the whole period of the shooting — they needed me back in Hollywood. I interviewed at least ten Italian composers and discovered that none had any idea of how to synchronise music to picture. I called Muir Mathieson in London, and he suggested a young man called Marcus Dods. When Dods arrived I found him agreeable and competent and was able to put my confidence in him.

Some of us were invited to a private audience with the Pope. We waited in the sumptuous throne room — Sam Zimbalist, Robert Taylor, Deborah Kerr, myself and others. One of the Swiss guards whispered to his neighbour, 'Look, it's Robert Taylor!' They all became very excited — after all, the Pope they knew every day — and clustered round nice, unaffected Bob Taylor asking for his autograph, which he willingly gave. Then we were conducted to a smaller room whose ceiling was covered with gold. The Monsignor told us this was the first gold brought back by Columbus, sent to the Pope as a gift from Ferdinand and Isabella.

At last we met the Pope, Pius XII. When he learnt that we were from Los Angeles and commented on the beauty of that city, I began to have my doubts about Papal Infallibility. I was presented, and he asked me whether I was going to use Gregorian or Ambrosian chants in my music. I had to tell him that both were some centuries too late for that period. After he had blessed us we were all given a special tour of the Sistine Chapel, which on that day was closed to the public. I have been

The MGM Music Department gave me a farewell lunch on the eve of my departure for
Rome. Among those visible are John Green (on my immediate right); cartoon-composer
Scott Bradley (second from *his* right); David Raksin, composer of *Laura* (foot of right-hand
table); producer Saul Chaplin (on Raksin's right); André Previn (on Raksin's left);
Conrad Salinger, orchestrator/arranger extraordinary (on Previn's left); (moving now from
Salinger upwards) orchestrator Robert Franklyn; composer Eugene Zador; composer
Bronislau Kaper; musical director/composer Adolph Deutsch; (top of table) orchestrator
Paul Marquardt

there many times since, but it is always crammed with visitors. On this occasion
there were only a few of us, and the Monsignor was able to speak with knowledge and
true appreciation of Michelangelo's masterpiece, the greatest achievement of a
painter. It was an experience I shall never forget, and one which, perhaps, later left
its mark on the Prelude to *Ben-Hur*, during which the film's titles are superimposed
on the *Creation of Adam*.

For the 'Bacchanale' at Nero's banquet I interviewed several choreographers, but
they all turned out to be variety dance-arrangers and were no use to me. I discovered
that Serge Lifar, one of the few survivors of the Diaghilev era, was at the Maggio
Musicale, so I went to Florence to talk to him. He was very interested and asked if
he could bring his own dancers from Paris, to which I agreed. Lifar told me the
story of his so-called 'collaboration' with the Nazis during the war, which had led to
his banishment from the Opéra afterwards. The day the Germans arrived in Paris
he had been woken at two in the morning by the concierge who told him that 'Itlair'
was in the Opéra building demanding that Lifar, as its Director at that time, show
him Renoir's painting of Wagner. Lifar hurried to the Opéra, met Hitler, but

claimed not to know where the picture was. He told me proudly that he had saved the painting for the French nation. I gave him the dates when the Bacchanale was set to be photographed, but unfortunately he had to go to South America at that time and asked us to postpone the shooting, which of course was impossible. The next day I interviewed Aurelio Miloss, the Hungarian choreographer of the Rome and La Scala opera houses, and engaged him.

The 'Assyrian Dance' was easy — we needed only one dancer. The 'Bacchanale' was a tougher nut to crack. I had already recorded the music with a small ensemble in Hollywood, and Miloss listened to it and began to formulate his ideas. All our discussions had to be with Zimbalist because LeRoy was impossibly busy all the time. The best dancers of Italy were engaged.

At this point I had to go to London, a trip that eventually made a great difference to my life. MGM had finally succumbed and let me go to Rome only on the condition that I do an additional picture in London, to which I gladly agreed. The picture was the second 'Mrs Miniver' — *The Miniver Story* — and I was going to have to use some of Herbert Stothart's themes from the original. I didn't care; I would have done a picture on the moon for the chance to return to Europe. Just before I was about to leave for London a message came from LeRoy to the effect that he could spare me a little time. I hurried to the stage with all my music, ordered a piano, and found him directing a scene with Bob Taylor. At the end of the scene he came over to me at my piano. He said that he understood that I was going to London the next day — would I pick up some cigars for him? We would talk about the music on my return. This was our first and last discussion about music.

I took the train to London. About seven in the morning I awoke, and we were still in Italy. The most beautiful vista of bay, mountains and blue sky stretched before me. It was Rapallo. I decided then and there that this was a place where I would like to write some music.

In London I finished my work in about ten days and took the train back to Rome.

MGM in the Vatican, including Deborah Kerr, Robert Taylor and myself

London 1950—with Muir Mathieson   With Peter Ustinov

Again I saw that unbelievably beautiful landscape, and again I knew that I would return to it.

One day LeRoy telephoned me to tell me that a musician had come to the Cinecittà with an ancient Roman instrument, on which he said he could play ancient Roman music. I was to go to one of Alfredo's famous restaurants and ask for Mario. I took Hugh Gray along. After dinner a swarthy little man appeared and asked me whether I was the *direttore musicale*. This was Mario, and he showed me his 'ancient Roman instrument'. It was an ordinary mandolin, maybe twenty years old. I wanted to hear the 'ancient music,' and he started to play Enesco's *First Rumanian Rhapsody*. I wouldn't have been *un vero direttore musicale* had I let this pass, so I told him the composer's name. He became very angry, and swore that it was his own composition, based on ancient Roman tunes. We thanked him and promised to report our findings to Mr LeRoy. 'And who is going to pay me for the day I lost in Cinecittà, waiting for Signor LeRoy?' he shouted angrily. I had to tell him that I certainly wouldn't be the one. He became furious, and we left the restaurant under a torrent of abuse. The next day I waited for LeRoy to ask me about the man, but he never did.

Peter Ustinov, who played Nero, was a man with an encyclopaedic knowledge. He could talk about composers who were only names to me. He could sing Mozart operas in Italian. He loved to laugh and tell funny stories, which he did incomparably. To sit with him at one of the cafés on the Via Veneto was the best entertainment one could wish for. I arranged for him to be coached in Nero's songs, and also to have lessons with a harpist, so that he would be able to strum his lyre

150

Sightseeing in Rome with conductor Antal Doráti (left) and my uncle Lajos, friend of Doráti *père*. In the background is the Villa Medici where many French composers (including Debussy) had stayed as a result of winning the Prix de Rome

convincingly. We became close friends, and when I returned to Hollywood we wrote to each other frequently. I was touched when he wrote to tell me that he wanted to dedicate his new play *The Love of Four Colonels* to me. I was just finishing the String Quartet, so I was able to reciprocate by dedicating it to *him*. The ending of this story is rather disappointing. The Quartet came out with its dedication to Ustinov, but unfortunately when his play appeared it was *not* dedicated to me. Well, I am philosophical about such things.

The business manager who was sent from Hollywood to oversee *Quo Vadis* was the typical Ugly American. He treated the Italians like dirt, and there was a terrible fracas when he announced that nobody working on the picture would have a holiday on Ferragosto — the great Italian summer holiday which combines the feast of the Assumption of the Virgin which an ancient festival dedicated to Augustus. He didn't give a damn about Italian traditions — they were wasting valuable American money. The poor people were distressed but had to comply. The night before the holiday a terrible storm blew up and completely destroyed the magnificently furnished tent which had been erected to house the set for Nero's banquet. The next morning the Italians arrived, beamed at the devastation, and said, 'Augustus did it for us.'

When I got back, the dances were under way and everything seemed to be going well. Of course in pictures nothing ever goes well for long, as I should have known. A telegram arrived from MGM, summoning me back to Hollywood immediately; apparently they needed me for something unspecified. There was nothing I could do because the agreement stated that I would set up the production in Rome and

151

then hand over to an assistant. I did not know then that my departure would mean disaster for the wonderful scene that the 'Bacchanale' could have been. I took an Italian ship and during the ten-day trip composed the slow movement of my String Quartet. When I got to the studio I was told that there was nothing for me, and that I should take my two weeks' holiday. I could have murdered them, knowing that my presence in Rome was so necessary. My salary kept coming in. I was able to finish the quartet, but it was outrageous that I could not be in Rome to help *Quo Vadis* along.

My music was undergoing a change during this period. *Madame Bovary* had been romantic, luxurious and expressive, but at much the same time, in 1948, a new style began to appear in my Piano Sonata — more percussive, contrapuntal, aggressive. The String Quartet continued this vein. Maybe it was an inner protest against the excessive amount of conventional music I had had to write for conventional pictures. The Quartet was premiered in Los Angeles by the Compinsky Quartet, whose leader Manuel Compinsky, an excellent London-trained musician, had helped me over the years with all my problems relating to the technicalities of stringed instruments. Later he performed my *Sinfonia Concertante* with the cellist Nathaniel Rosen, and Gregor Piatigorsky came to a rehearsal. 'Stoppp!' he shouted at one point when we were apparently getting carried away. 'Jascha (Heifetz) and I couldn't play it this fast!' We slowed down.

In Hollywood I began to get alarming letters from Miloss and Dods. The 'Bacchanale' was fine, they reported, but they couldn't get LeRoy to come and see it. It was important that he *did* see it, because it wasn't just a set-piece but an integral part of a larger scene. At last word came. The day before the shooting of the scene LeRoy had seen the dance. It was much too elaborate; all he wanted was a few girls prancing about behind the emperor and his wife. Everything else could go. That was that. Marcus Dods was a very able musician, but of course he was a young man and didn't have my authority and had to obey his orders, which were simply to forget about *my* orders. The 'Bacchanale', which could have been a tremendous Roman spectacle, was reduced to shots of a few limp showgirls.

Trapped in Hollywood while the picture was still going on in Rome, I tried to make the best of things. I had already insisted on composing as much as possible while the cutting was in progress, because the film was a long one and I didn't want the usual four-week scramble at the end. But the rushes were being sent back to Hollywood for cutting at the same time as they were being cut back in Rome. In other words, there were going to be two versions of every scene and the timings were not going to correspond. Even so, I set to work so that at least something was ready, even if it had to be modified later. I worked with the Chief Supervising Editor, Margaret Booth, whose technical knowledge is incomparable; she has saved more pictures from ruin than anyone I can name.

Finally the Rome contingent arrived home with their version. It wasn't so very different from the one that Margaret had put together, and there were no insuperable problems. Sam Zimbalist was amazed and delighted when I had all the music ready in three weeks, thanks to the work Margaret and I had already done.

I chose the Royal Philharmonic in London to record the music, and this turned

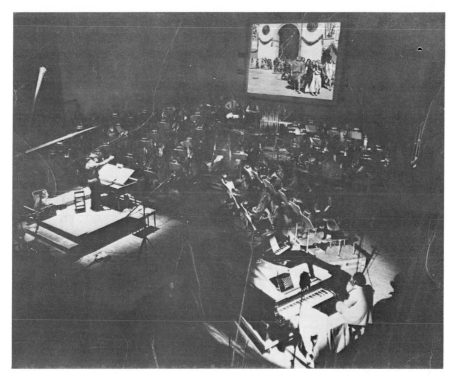

Quo Vadis '50—the Christians entering the arena

out to be the beginning of a happy association that has lasted to this day. They were a revelation to me. The Hollywood studio orchestras consist of excellent musicians, but there is no style whatsoever — or, at least, a Hollywood style inappropriate to the lean and hungry music I had contrived for early Rome. But, to be fair, when Hollywood studio musicians were engaged it was on the basis of their ability to play popular music and jazz. Hollywood demanded a particular expertise for her musicals which was totally unsuited to symphonic music. It took my orchestras a long time to realise that for me they had to play differently. When we first recorded *The Thief of Baghdad* the leader ('concertmaster' in America) played his solos with the most nauseating vibrato and glissandos. I complained and he said, 'Oh, it's the gypsy in me!' To which I replied, 'No, my friend, it's the MGM in you.'

As well as the Royal Philharmonic we had the BBC Chorus — over a hundred singers. The early Christian hymns had to be recorded out of doors in order to obtain the right acoustic, which meant working at night when there were no planes or cars about. The same thing applied to the great wind band which played Nero's triumphal march.

I was sure that the music of *Quo Vadis* was going to be interesting not only to the audience but also to musicologists, on account of its authenticity. Unfortunately this did not turn out to be the case. Sam Zimbalist was a dear personal friend but had no ear for music. He didn't understand its function. He knew I was a good

Quo Vadis '50—recording Nero's *Marcia Trionfale* outside at night with a band of massed woodwinds, brass and percussion

musician and trusted me, but didn't use the music in any way as effectively as he might have done. After all the trouble I went to, much of my work was swamped by sound effects, or played at such a low level as to be indistinguishable.

At the dubbing sessions Zimbalist listened with closed eyes instead of watching as well, and at the end of every dialogue scene he complained that the music was too loud. Even when there was no dialogue, for example in Robert Taylor's wild chariot ride to Rome, we heard horses' hooves, the chariot, the wind, but not the music which actually brings the scene to life. Every department had made an all-out effort in the interests of authenticity. I had done likewise, but in the event I need hardly have bothered. It was a great disappointment to me.

Quo Vadis, because it was produced abroad, was completely boycotted by Hollywood and received no Academy nominations. When Korngold was asked if he was going to nominate the music, he replied that he couldn't nominate what he hadn't heard. Months later, when MGM issued a record of about thirty-five minutes of the score, Sam Zimbalist rang to tell me that he had just listened to it and that it was the greatest music ever written for a motion picture. I was flabbergasted, but the reason was, of course, that he was hearing the music for the first time.

I made a concert suite of four movements based on *Quo Vadis*: 'Ave Caesar', based on Nero's Triumph; 'Romanza' (the love theme); 'Assyrian Dance', and finally a paraphrase on 'Quo Vadis Domine', the music for the miracle and the end of the picture. Twenty-seven years later, in 1977, I re-recorded selections from the score for Decca in London, again with the Royal Philharmonic, and was delighted to recognise three players who had been in the orchestra at the time of the original recording.

154

Quo Vadis '77—recording 'Quo Vadis Domine' for Decca Phase-IV Stereo with the Royal Philharmonic Orchestra and the Saltarello Choir

The music of *Quo Vadis* established me as a composer of 'epic' scores. I became apparently a specialist in historical pictures, much to my delight. Whether as films they were good or bad, the subject matter was invariably interesting and worth spending time on.

Such a picture was *Ivanhoe*. The book was a favourite of my youth, in Hungarian translation, of course. I re-read my Scott and was again delighted. When I read the script I was less delighted. It was a typical Hollywood historical travesty and the picture for the most part was cliché-ridden and conventional. So I turned back to Scott, and Scott it was, rather than Robert or even Elizabeth Taylor, who inspired my music.

In *Ivanhoe* I went back to mediaeval musical sources; the next picture found me in Jacobean England. I didn't use any actual music of the period, but projected my own music into the framework of the style. The picture was *Plymouth Adventure*, the story of the Pilgrim Fathers. I found out that these people had had with them on their boat the Ainsworth Psalter, consisting of musical settings of the Psalms. I chose a striking melody called 'Confess Jehovah thankfully' (another form of which may be found in J. S. Bach's *St. Matthew Passion**), and used this to express the faith of the Fathers' great endeavour, their momentous voyage into the unknown. The picture was lacking in any real spirit of heroism or passionate aspiration; this I tried to supply with my music.

MGM was changing. A new chief of production replaced Louis B. Mayer. With the new regime a new music director came to the studio, the Harvard-educated John Green who set a sorely-needed standard of culture and good manners. But his first

---

*In the final chorus of Part I.

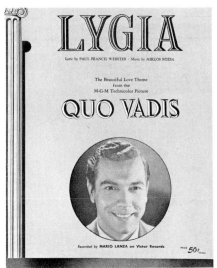

Quo Vadis '77—the 'Bacchanale' with its Wagnerian array of harps

Even MGM's Mario Lanza played his part in promoting the music of *Quo Vadis*

departmental meeting, when he had to pass on to us a directive from the new head was (at least for me) disturbing. The new chief wanted to hear the tunes in the musicals and not the orchestrations. (This was a thrust at the enormously-gifted Conrad Salinger, the arranger responsible for most of the MGM musicals' musical distinction.) If in the dramatic pictures he had to choose between the 'Steineresque' and the 'Coplandesque', he preferred the former. (Surprise, surprise!) I asked meekly whether I would be permitted to continue to be 'Rózsaësque', but my sarcasm wasn't much appreciated. Green became a buffer or middle-man between the front office and the music staff; he saved us from being molested by those in authority, and he had the good sense not to interfere with our work himself. Now, thirty years later, his glamour and sense of humour have still not deserted him.

The year 1953 was one of the most productive in my life. Not only did I do five major pictures — *The Story of Three Loves*, *Julius Caesar*, *Young Bess*, *All the Brothers were Valiant*, and *The Knights of the Round Table* — but I also wrote my Violin Concerto in the three months I took off in the summer.

My first three years at MGM had been on a fifty-two week basis with two weeks' holiday a year. This began to tell on me. I felt that I was growing older and hadn't yet said all I wanted to in terms of my own music. I needed time to live the other part of my Double Life. So when the time came for the renewal of my contract I said I would be glad to continue, but it was important that I have three months off, unpaid, each summer. They were amazed — it must have been almost unheard of for anyone to ask for *less* money in Hollywood. I told my old friend L. K. Sidney why I needed these months, what I wanted to do with my life, that I wanted to enjoy the company of my family during the vacation. At first the studio said they couldn't guarantee that the three months would always be in the summer — if there was an important picture at that time they would be in a difficult position. But finally they agreed. Somehow I always got everything I wanted at MGM. L. K. Sidney kept his word and watched over my career like a father.

The Story of Three Loves was a delightful picture. It was produced by the admirable Sidney Franklin, a charming man of impeccable taste and good manners, qualities very thinly spread among Hollywoodians: in a word, a gentleman. He used to be a fine director but was now a producer. Vincente Minnelli and Gottfried Reinhardt were the directors of the three love-stories that made up this picture.

The first thing I had to do was to produce a ballet, since in the first story Moira Shearer played a dancer. I discovered that she had already arrived from London and that the choreographer, Frederick Ashton, would be here in a week. Could I write a ballet in a week? The schedule demanded that one be completely rehearsed and ready in two weeks' time. I had to tell Franklin honestly that although Rossini wrote an opera in ten days, I couldn't do an original ballet in so short a time. He told me in that case to find something suitable in the repertoire, something romantic. I went through all the music that came to mind, avoiding the obvious, and thought of the ravishing love-music in César Franck's symphonic poem *Psyché*. When I played it to Franklin and Reinhardt they didn't like it at all. Shortly before, I had conducted the *Rhapsody on a theme of Paganini* of Rachmaninov at the Hollywood Bowl (with André Previn as soloist)*, and so I approached them again with the eighteenth variation. This time they were delighted. We had to get permission from the publishers, which was granted with the proviso that not a note of Rachmaninov's music should be changed. It wasn't, but of course for the dramatic incidental music required I was free to write my own variations on Paganini's original theme.

Frederick Ashton and Moira Shearer rehearsed every day, and at last Sidney Franklin came to see the ballet in the big rehearsal room. He was enchanted. He described the dancing as lyrically beautiful and aesthetically pleasing — words rarely heard in a film studio. The usual reaction was 'It's OK, it has great commercial possibilities'; but Franklin was an artist.

---

* This was not my only encounter with the still-teenaged André Previn in my pre-MGM days. In 1947 I did an independently-produced film called *The Other Love* in which Barbara Stanwyck played a concert pianist. At one point the script called for her to play some jazz, which I couldn't write because I knew nothing about it. The film's editor happened to be Steve Previn, who suggested his brother André. André was already under contract to MGM and had no right to be working for any other studio, but we promised him anonymity and he wrote the music we needed. Then we discovered that André's hands looked on camera much more like Barbara Stanwyck's than those of the lady pianist hired for the film, so he did that job too, and the hands you see playing the piano music in *The Other Love* are actually André's. I later repaid André by inadvertently 'spilling the beans' about his breach of contract to the head of the MGM music department, who flew into a rage and wanted to dismiss him. Fortunately for all of us I managed to persuade him not to! When *Asphalt Jungle* came along I was able legitimately to engage André to do the jazzy 'source' music, since that was an MGM production; and I am proud to claim the credit for making him use a proper full orchestral score at recording sessions rather than the 'piano-conductor' parts in vogue at the studios (often to make things easy for 'composers' or 'conductors' who could scarcely even read music). André was kind enough to pay written tribute to my mentorship both in his book *Orchestra* and in the Martin Bookspan – Ross Yockey biography, but at the studios it was a real and rare pleasure to come into contact with someone who both was musical and loved music.

With Moira Shearer (*The Story of Three Loves*)

The picture was moderately successful. It was too poetic for popular consumption, and not all the episodes were even in quality; the third was rather tedious. I went to MGM records and told them about the beautiful variation of Rachmaninov which had appeared so prominently in the film. After I had explained who Rachmaninov was, and that I thought the theme would sell well as a single, they grudgingly consented to apply to New York for a go-ahead. The reply came back that New York wasn't interested; the piece had no 'commercial possibilities'. Well, the picture came out, and in no time the eighteenth variation became the most popular non-pop tune in America. All the big record companies pulled out that variation from their recordings of the piece. Out they came on singles, and sold by the hundreds of thousands. The only company who knew about it months ahead was MGM records, but the New York office had pronounced it not commercial and 'too high-brow'. They always knew best, and today it is no different.

In 1953 the studio still had a very large staff in every department. It is hard to realise that there were seven or eight composers, an orchestra of fifty, four or five orchestrators, about ten copyists, librarians and assistants, all under permanent contract. The studio decided that since they had such a well-staffed music

Agnes Moorehead and Moira Shearer in *The Story of Three Loves*

department they wouldn't hire free-lance composers from outside. Now when *Julius Caesar* came along, John Houseman, the producer, wanted his old friend Bernard Herrmann to do the music. This proposal was turned down by the studio because I was under contract. I didn't know Houseman, but I presume he knew my work, because he accepted me. Of course, I only heard about all this much later. And it was only later, too, that I met Benny Herrmann and we became friends.

Julius Caesar was, and is, my favourite Shakespearian play, Brutus my favourite Shakespearian character. I knew of the great talents of Houseman and Joseph Mankiewicz, the director. The text was Shakespeare; there were a few cuts but no 'improvements'. I put it to both Mankiewicz and Houseman that this time I wouldn't write 'Roman' music as I had for *Quo Vadis*; this should be music apt for a Shakespearian drama. They agreed, and I waited till the picture was finished before starting. I had no opportunity of working with Mankiewicz because the moment the picture was finished he had to hurry off to direct *La Bohème* for the New York Metropolitan Opera. I referred instead to Houseman, and it was a very happy collaboration. He was a man of talent, taste, learning and intelligence. He usually came to my bungalow where I would play him the scenes I had composed. He had

159

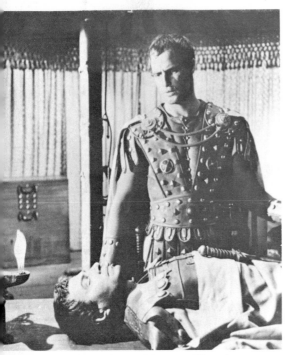

Julius Caesar: Mason and Brando   John Houseman

very little to say, but he knew what he wanted and when he did say something it had substance.

Stereophonic sound had just been invented and studios were using it in an attempt to combat television (another gimmick was the wide screen). Although Disney had already experimented with six-channel sound in *Fantasia* in 1940, stereophonic sound was now being presented as the newest thing. The new technique suggested new musical ideas. I discussed with Houseman the possibility of a stereophonic musical treatment of the final scene, where Brutus is awaiting the arrival of the victorious Octavian and Antony. I would combine the music for the noble Brutus with a march for the approach of his foe, Octavian. To do this it was necessary to use a click-track,* something I usually avoid. The clicks had to be matched to the steps of the marching soldiers; then we cut to Brutus and superimposed his music, still using the clicks of the march. Everything worked well when fitted together. The march started at one side of the screen at a low level and gradually moved across, growing implacably louder as it progressed; and over this Brutus's tragic music was superimposed with ever-increasing intensity. I must admit that this was not entirely my own idea. Bizet used it in the final scene of *Carmen* when the Toreador's music is played inside the bull-ring and the tragic Carmen motif outside.

*A mechanical (and therefore by definition anti-musical) device used to facilitate exact and immediate synchronisation of music and action.

I also suggested that there be an orchestral overture before anything appeared on the screen, as in the theatre. (Later this idea gained wide currency and I supplied overtures to many other films.) Houseman and everybody agreed. I wrote a strong, starkly Shakespearian overture, but unfortunately it wasn't used in the film. For reasons beyond my control it was decided that stereophonic sound was going to make its debut with a film of an orchestra in a concert hall playing Tchaikovsky's *Capriccio Italien* before the picture. Now I am a great admirer of Tchaikovsky, but the *Capriccio Italien* is one of his cheapest works and is certainly not an appropriate prologue to one of the greatest human dramas ever written. When I found out that this was to be the plan I asked Houseman if he knew. He didn't. He rushed to the head of the studio and protested. He was told it was too late, that the orchestra had been called to record in two days' time, that nothing could be done now to stop it. So bang went *my* overture, which remained unheard until a few years ago when I recorded it in London with the Royal Philharmonic for Polydor.

The coronation of Elizabeth II was approaching and MGM wanted to do their own homage to the new queen. A picture called *Young Bess* was being produced, with Jean Simmons as the young Elizabeth I. As the producer was again Sidney Franklin, I was delighted to accept it and immersed myself in the music of the Tudor period. The picture was not a masterpiece but had lovely scenes and fine moments; I still like the music for the mischievous little Prince of Wales, and the chaconne for strings on the 'Dies Irae' which accompanies Henry VIII's death-scene.

I could hardly wait for my three summer months to come, for a special reason. My readers may recall that at the age of twenty-one I had written an immature violin concerto (never published), and now I felt like attempting a mature one. As all great composers had written their concertos with a particular artist in mind, I wanted to do the same and decided to approach Jascha Heifetz. I had met Heifetz briefly once only, shortly after I came to America, when he gave a concert at the Hollywood Bowl, and we were introduced by Albert Coates. I did know his accompanist Emmanuel Bay, however, and asked him to approach Heifetz on my behalf. Heifetz sent back an answer that he was interested, and suggested I write one movement which we could try through together before he made up his mind. This sounded rather risky to me. Heifetz had approved the first few pages of Schoenberg's concerto, only to refuse to play the piece when it was finished — in fact a number of concertos had suffered the same fate. It was a chance, but I decided to take it.

I set off for Italy with my family. In spite of my eagerness to go to beautiful Rapallo, my friend Castelnuovo-Tedesco, who after all was Italian, had advised against it. It was no good for children, he said. There was no beach, only rocks. We should go further south, to Forte dei Marmi, beneath the great marble mountains of Carrara, quarried by sculptors and architects since Etruscan times. When we got there, we found a sandy beach as Tedesco had promised, but the place was hideous. No trees, ugly hotels; and the houses, one of which I had hoped to rent, were horrible little shacks. Admittedly the great mountains of shining white marble behind the town were an imposing sight, but everything else was loathsome. We

With Jascha Heifetz at his Beverly Hills home

spent two days there, but my wife and I finally admitted to each other that we hated it. We drove back north to Rapallo, and found the most beautiful villa; and I sat down to begin the Violin Concerto.

I talk again and again of this heavenly place, but who can blame me? Inspiration, if I can use that nowadays much-despised word, was round every corner. Ideas for the concerto flowed naturally; all I had to do was write them down. I had intended to complete the first movement only, but in six weeks the whole work was finished.

When we got back to Hollywood, Emmanuel Bay took the concerto to Heifetz and a few days later rang to say that Heifetz liked it, but wanted to talk about it. He would ring me in a month after he had returned from a tour. After six months of silence I assumed he had changed his mind, and mentioned it to Antal Doráti, who suggested sending it to Menuhin. As luck would have it, within days Heifetz rang. I made a fool of myself by thinking it was my MGM colleague Bronislau Kaper pulling my leg and said, 'If you're Heifetz, I'm Mozart.' Once past this inauspicious beginning, Heifetz invited me to his house to talk.

He said he liked the piece, but there were certain cuts and changes he wanted to propose. Would I be willing to work with him on them? I was willing, of course. It is quite usual for a soloist to advise a composer in a situation like this. We worked at intervals over a period of months.

One day Heifetz referred to a passage of repeated notes which betrayed a certain gypsy influence, saying that he had heard gypsy violinists playing this kind of thing in Budapest. How was it done? Would I demonstrate? Of course I was very embarrassed — I hadn't held a violin in my hands for so long. When he insisted, I took his priceless Guarnerius and demonstrated. He tried it; I demonstrated again. When he got the hang of it I asked him if I could henceforth describe myself as a teacher of Jascha Heifetz. He laughed, which is unusual for Heifetz.

Throughout our work together he would append the words, 'if I play the piece' to every request for a change. After perhaps four months he rang me one day at home. 'Are you sitting or standing? Standing! Well, you had better sit down. I've decided to give the premiere of your concerto.'

Some Hollywood musicians got so tired of playing movie music all the time that they used to meet together for an evening to play symphonic music for their own enjoyment. They were kind enough to spend an evening reading through my concerto so that I could check the balance of the orchestration against the solo instrument. The soloist was Werner Gebauer, a violinist friend who had worked on the piece with me before I sent it to Heifetz. It was a valuable lesson for me because I saw immediately that many passages were over-orchestrated and cancelled out the soloist.

The premiere was given on 15th January 1956 in Dallas, Texas, with Walter Hendl as conductor. Heifetz played like a god. His tone was unsurpassable and his technique the most dazzling since Paganini. At the end he motioned me to join him on the platform and there was a standing ovation. The reviews were very enthusiastic; the Dallas critic John Rosenfield wrote of a 'historic premiere'. The next performance at Fort Worth was equally well received. Later in the year when Heifetz had finished his tour, he, Hendl and the Dallas Symphony Orchestra recorded the concerto. In the interim he had been too busy to look at it since he had last played it; nevertheless he did it faultlessly and from memory. The record was made simply by recording each movement three times without stopping. When I asked him how it was possible for him to play so well without any practice, he replied, 'I practised it well to start with.' Heifetz himself selected the takes which now make up the record.

The record was well reviewed and the concerto immediately won an international success. The first European performance took place in Baden-Baden. The first American performance after Heifetz's was given at Franz Waxman's Los Angeles Festival by Spivakovsky. Spivakovsky's performance was the only one that differed from Heifetz's interpretation, and I liked his individual approach. I myself conducted the work ten or fifteen times over the years, in America and Europe, and never needed a rehearsal with the soloist alone; the performances were always duplicates of the Heifetz recording.

After my so-called 'triumph' with the concerto I fondly imagined that MGM would be happy to bask in my reflected glory. On the contrary, one of the executives called up John Green and complained that he had read in the trade papers (well, where else?) that I had written a concerto for Heifetz. How was this possible when I was under contract to MGM? He had to be told that the piece was written in my own time, in the three unpaid summer months. The executive grudgingly accepted this, but said that I ought to have been spending my holidays writing themes for future films.

From the Rapallo where Sibelius wrote his second symphony, I travelled back with my newly born Violin Concerto to the England of King Arthur. For *Knights of the Round Table* again I went for inspiration not to the film itself (which was tawdry and unimaginative) but to its literary sources, Malory and Tennyson. For the MGM authorities the film's main attraction was technical, not aesthetic: it was their first film in Cinemascope and as such it had at all costs to beat the contemporary 20th-Century Fox rival *The Robe* into the theatres (the director was one of those who found perennial favour with production heads because he could always be relied upon to bring in a picture under budget. The film itself might be — generally was — abysmal in quality and prove a box-office disaster, but that was of no consequence.) I was told therefore in early October, 1953 that *Knights of the Round Table* had to be ready for a Christmas release, which meant that a total of some ninety minutes of (for the most part heavy) symphonic music had to be written in six weeks. I demurred of course, but executives (in this case my good friend Eddie Mannix, a tough little Irishman) can be persuasive, especially when they imply that a film cannot possibly make the grade without you. In this case there was no time for musicological research, but that was of no great moment: (a) because I already had the mediaeval English experience of *Ivanhoe* behind me, and (b) because the musical legacy of sixth-century England is practically non-existent. I bore in mind the Gregorian modes for the religious sequences, and elsewhere adjusted my brush to a palette of mediaeval colours; but by and large literal authenticity played no part in the score. King Arthur, his knights and his England, are all part of legend. Theirs is the Land of Long Ago where scholars and musicologists are unheard of and unwanted. For me, legends spell romance, and in my music I must evoke them romantically.

After this marathon little of interest came up for the time being. One sequence of about twenty minutes in *Men of the Fighting Lady* needed music, a self-contained tone-poem I called 'Blind Flight' which depicted a blinded pilot trying to land his plane by radio. Then I got saddled with a film called *Green Fire*, one of Grace Kelly's last. I had to go and see it when finished, and I was sitting with the director and everybody else in the projection room bored to death, wondering what the head of the studio was going to say at the end — was he going to shout and storm and fire us all? When the lights went up he proclaimed the picture excellent, and congratulated everybody. Unfortunately as things turned out he wasn't able to congratulate the box-office.

The remainder of 1955 was not much better. There was one picture directed by my old friend Fritz Lang called *Moonfleet*, set in eighteenth-century England. The characters reminded me very much of those in my wife's large collection of Rowlandson aquarelles but the story was tedious and inconsequential. However, I managed a stirring enough seascape for the title music, which I recorded on one of my Polydor albums of the mid-1970s.

Then came *Diane*. Diane de Poitiers was a favourite historical character of mine. In this case the script was the work of Christopher Isherwood, and I expected great things. Lana Turner was, of course, as far removed from Diane de Poitiers as Sunset Boulevard is from Blois. But she was a star and did her best, though I didn't

With MGM's Ann Blyth at the time of *All the Brothers were Valiant*, for which I studied native Polynesian music

feel she cared much about looking the part historically. *Diane* was not a disgrace as a film, but it was no more than tolerable, and not a commercial success either. In America nobody had heard of Diane de Poitiers; they pronounced the title 'Die-ann' and probably expected a song of that name (like 'Laura') in the score, which I did not supply. The main theme had some popularity in an arrangement for string orchestra published under the title (not mine) 'Beauty and Grace'.

1956 started badly with *Tribute to a Badman*, a Western starring James Cagney. I had always avoided Westerns. To my ears Hollywood 'Western' music was so

Lust for Life: Kirk Douglas as Van Gogh

stereotyped that all the scores came out sounding the same, and the American folk-idiom was not one I felt sufficiently in tune with to want to assimilate. The producer, however, was my friend from *Quo Vadis*, Sam Zimbalist, and knowing that he was already preparing *Ben-Hur* (which of course I had my eye on) spurred me on to make an effort. I did not use authentic American folksongs as such, but rather my interpretation of them, much as I had interpreted the folksongs of my own country in the *Three Hungarian Sketches* and other works. Whether the species of Americana I evolved for this film would have been approved by Aaron Copland I hardly know, but I presume the music must have had some merit since I was requested to represent it on one of my later Polydor anthologies, and Morton Gould included it recently in a 'digital' spectacular.

After that I worked again with George Cukor on a much better picture, *Bhowani Junction*, set in India; but from my point of view it was very uninteresting, since for the most part all that was required was ethnic music (which I made up) to be used as a background. The plum of the year came later. John Houseman produced and Vincente Minnelli directed *Lust for Life*, the biography of Vincent Van Gogh, based on Irving Stone's famous book.

I knew nothing of painting as a child, and it was only as a student in Leipzig that my interest began to develop (I have to admit with shame that the first time I entered the Budapest museum with its magnificent Esterházy collection was when I was there in 1974). Later in Los Angeles I got to know the works of Van Gogh and he quickly became one of my favourite modern painters. For *Lust for Life* art galleries and private collections all over the world were ransacked, among them Edward G. Robinson's. This was not the first time I had drawn inspiration from fine art in the composing of a film score. In *The Thief of Baghdad* the sets and

166

scenery of Vincent Korda ravished the senses; in *Spellbound* Salvador Dali's designs for the central dream-interpretation sequence immediately suggested a musical complement, and literally coloured my concept of the score as a whole. Now I was back again on familiar and much-loved territory.

The picture was made mostly in Europe. When I first saw it it was a good hour longer than the final version. For me it wasn't long enough, it was so rich in fascinating details and character studies. But studio policy intervened. The picture couldn't be more than two hours long; who wants to see a mad suicidal painter anyway? So it was boiled down and mutilated in such a way that it lost most of its former strength and depth, just as *The Private Life of Sherlock Holmes* was made to suffer later. Nevertheless it was far better than the average Hollywood picture, and I was happy to be associated with it. A great deal of care had gone into the art direction. For example, the asylum at St. Rémy where Van Gogh stayed when his mind was going was painted by him many times. In his pictures there is a large tree outside, which by the time our film-makers got there had disappeared. They implanted one, so much did they care about authenticity.

I asked myself what sort of music Van Gogh would have known. He was a Post-Impressionist, but Post-Impressionism in music comes much later than Van Gogh's death at the end of the nineteenth century; pictorial trends are always between 25 and 40 years ahead. The music he himself knew would have been that of the eighties — Wagner, Liszt, César Franck — but I felt that mid-nineteenth-century romanticism had little in common with his work. Somehow I had to evolve a suitable style in terms of my own music. It had to be somewhat impressionistic, somewhat pointillistic, somewhat post-romantic and brightly, even startlingly colourful, much like the tenor of his paintings. I worked with Houseman again in my bungalow, playing my music on the piano. Once I was describing the scene when Gauguin arrived at Arles and makes his way to Van Gogh's house. I wanted to evoke an extrovert, south-of-France atmosphere, rather in the manner of Bizet's *L'Arlésienne*. Houseman's criticism was that I was illustrating the scenery when I ought to have been reinforcing emotion. He was right, and I substituted a brooding, self-assertive theme for Gauguin which gave the drama more positive support. I have nothing against constructive criticism when it illuminates a dramatic point. I'm annoyed by *musical* criticism from producers and directors who don't know what they are talking about. There was a great outburst of anger from Georges Auric, the French composer, when William Wyler tried to suggest changes in the music for *Roman Holiday*. 'I didn't tell you how to direct your picture — don't tell me how to write my music!' My reaction was 'Bravo Auric!' Later, on *Ben-Hur*, I ran into similar trouble of my own with Wyler.

Lust for Life afforded wonderful opportunities for music in the shape of the various scenes which were simply montages of Van Gogh's paintings, symphonies of colour needing tonal interpretation. I liked Van Gogh himself, very well played by Kirk Douglas, who looked remarkably like him. From my point of view, the picture was an artistic apotheosis. Shortly afterwards I prepared a concert suite from the score, basing it on and freely developing it from the main dramatic moments. This was recorded by Decca along with my *Mark Hellinger Suite*. A lengthy extract from the *Lust for Life* score may be found on my second Polydor album, which on its front cover reproduces in full colour *The Red Vineyards*, the only picture Vincent's art-dealer brother Theo managed to sell during the painter's lifetime.

At about this time I wrote the *Overture to a Symphony Concert*. I owed a work to my old publisher Kurt Eulenburg who had had a terrible time in the war, first in a concentration camp and then destitute in exile with his family in Switzerland. Somebody had wanted to do my *Variations* and had asked him for the material. He had the score, but no parts, and of course no money to pay a copyist to prepare a new set, so he had copied them all out himself.

On this occasion he asked me for a shorter piece, not more than eight minutes. I suggested an overture. The Hungarian revolution was in progress and at first I thought of a revolutionary piece, but eventually I abandoned the idea and wrote a plain *Overture to a Symphony Concert*. But it seems to me in retrospect that the music is full of conflict and heroism and embodies something of the spirit of my country's fight for its freedom. I must emphasise, though, that this happened subconsciously. I conducted the first performance in Düsseldorf, and György Ligeti, now a leader of the avant-garde, was in the audience. In my dressing room afterwards the only comment he could make was that my piece was very contrapuntal. Not knowing whether I was supposed to say thank you or apologise, I kept silent. When in later years I got to know some of Ligeti's own works, I realised that the idea of contrapuntal activity went as much against the grain of *his* musical nature as his eternal homophonous *pianissimos* went against mine.

My Double Life continued. A friend had sent me a little volume of French folksongs and one of these, *The Vintner's Daughter*, I had arranged as a set of variations for piano. Eugene Ormandy liked the piece and asked me to orchestrate it for the Philadelphia Orchestra. I was glad to do so, and managed to get two weeks off from the studio for the purpose. After the first rehearsal, Ormandy said he would prefer a loud and brilliant ending to the quiet and reflective coda I had written. Well, I tried my best, but apparently when he played both versions with the orchestra nobody liked the loud ending and he had to give in and go back to the quiet one, which is the way it is published and recorded.

This was not my only symphonic work of the period. I had known the cellist Piatigorsky for years. He was an incomparable raconteur and his book *Cellist* is full of these anecdotes, charmingly written, but with little of the flavour of his own telling of them. He ought to have recorded his book in his excellent English swamped by an absurd stage-Russian accent. Now Piatigorsky was a close friend of Heifetz, and one day he telephoned to say he would like to have a talk with me professionally. He had a 'vonderful plan'. I was to write a concerto for him and Heifetz, a double concerto.

I went to my beloved Rapallo with my family and finished the work in my three months, calling it *Sinfonia Concertante*. When I got back I called Piatigorsky and told him the first draft was finished, and I thought we should all try it through. The first movement began with a long passage for the cello alone before the violin entered. Heifetz pulled a face. 'I can't wait as long as that. Give him about four bars and then I'll take over.' The whole of the first movement went on like that. If the

Early manuscript draft of
the slow movement of the
Sinfonia Concertante,
showing the long cello solo
which Heifetz disliked so
much

Piatigorsky (right) rehearsing
for an RCA recording with
Leonard Pennario (piano)
and Heifetz

one had a long solo, the other insisted on a solo of equal length; if the one had a brilliant passage and the other a lyrical tune there was a squabble again, and so on. I made note of the required changes and saw the movement getting longer and longer.

The second movement was a theme and variations. Now it is well known that the solo cello can easily be overpowered when violin and orchestra are playing together, so I gave the long main theme to the cello to establish it. Then the violin joins in and begins the variations. Heifetz hated it. 'Do you expect me to stand there like an idiot all that time?' Piatigorsky would reply, 'Yes, Jascha, we expect you to stand there like an idiot!' But Heifetz was so adamant that I agreed to write something completely different. We didn't even try the last movement.

A month later we met again to try the new slow movement. Piatigorsky said I reminded him of Toscanini. 'But how, Grisha? You've never seen me conduct.' 'No, but your piano playing's just as lousy as his!' As for my new offering, Heifetz pronounced it lacking in inspiration. Then we tried the last movement. Heifetz complained that it wasn't brilliant enough. We tried the revised first movement, with all its modifications now more than twenty minutes long. Finally Heifetz agreed that the original second movement, the variations, was better, provided that *he* could play the theme at the end, very high, with some cello *pizzicati*, very low.

That autumn Heifetz wanted to perform the slow movement alone at one of his concerts with Piatigorsky. The orchestra for that concert consisted only of strings, two oboes and two horns — the orchestra of Mozart's violin concertos. After much argument I agreed to re-score the movement for this tiny combination, although of course many important orchestral colours went missing as a result. Then to my surprise I learnt from one of the players that all the concerts were to be recorded, including my piece. Heifetz had established the custom of giving the concerts without a conductor, which may have looked impressive, but the orchestra was unable to keep together. I was not invited to the recording, and Heifetz forgot to conduct with his bow during Piatigorsky's solo, so that the *pizzicati* cello and basses didn't know precisely when to play. Not a happy experience for anyone, least of all the absent composer.

The actual premiere of the complete concerto took place later in Chicago, conducted by Jean Martinon; Victor Aitay and Frank Miller were the soloists. It was a fine performance, but I realised, sitting there, that the piece was overlong by a good ten minutes. We made cuts for the later performances, but unfortunately too late for the critics, who all complained of the same thing. I applied myself severely to tightening the piece up, and it is now published in its definitive form.

I was still of course under contract to MGM but unfortunately Louis B. Mayer was no longer with the studio. Mayer was not an educated man, but he had a great flair for show business. He built up the tremendous organisation of MGM virtually from scratch, and produced some of the greatest films of any over the decades. Yet he was forced out by the back door, and immediately the quality of the product began to deteriorate. I did three films in 1957, of which only *Something of Value*, about the Mau-mau, was 'something of value'. I did research into Kikuyu music and wrote my own Kikuyu music for an African choir. I have to confess that I also

John Gavin in *A Time to Love and a Time to Die*

wrote my own Kikuyu words — somebody found me a dictionary and I picked words at random. I hoped the Mau-mau would never see the picture, knowing that I could expect no mercy from them if they did.

There was a deadly atmosphere at MGM at this time — a smell of disease and decay and disintegration. People were fired left and right, budgets slashed, pictures lost all semblance of quality. There was a big announcement to the effect that from now on the accent was on youth — new blood, new producers, new directors, new writers. This sounded splendid until one realised that all the new people were sons and nephews of people already there. The papas and uncles had some talent; the sons and nephews had none. When, in early 1958, a request came from Universal to borrow me, I accepted immediately, without even seeing what I was being borrowed for.

The picture was *A Time to Love and a Time to Die* directed by Douglas Sirk, a man of great talent whom, alas, as I have explained, I never met. When I arrived the picture had reached its last cutting stage, and the producer turned it over to me and wished me good luck. That was all. The picture was well done. It was based, of course, on the novel of Erich Maria Remarque (who appeared in the film) and was set in war-time Germany. It fared badly in America, better in Europe where the war had meant a great deal more.

In the meantime I was keeping in touch with Sam Zimbalist who was preparing *Ben-Hur*, though it was still a long way from going into production. Tunberg's script followed the basic outline of Lew Wallace's original novel, but was still far

At MGM, late 1950s: myself, Sidney Franklin (producer of *The Story of Three Loves*), director Richard Thorpe, Rouben Mamoulian, Dallas film and music critic John Rosenfield (who acclaimed my Violin Concerto at its premiere), Sam Zimbalist, producer of *Ben-Hur*

from perfect, and Zimbalist knew it. Other writers worked on it, including S. N. Behrman, Christopher Fry and Gore Vidal, who had just published his book about the emperor Julian. Zimbalist shared all his problems with me, and a major question was who was to direct.

One day he called me over to his office and in the strictest confidence told me they had engaged William Wyler. I congratulated him, describing Wyler as one of Hollywood's finest directors, but gave him one word of warning. Wyler was a famous man. From now on, the picture was not going to be Sam Zimbalist's but William Wyler's, and Zimbalist had better accept that. Now this may not mean much in Europe, where the director is always the man whose name is synonymous with the picture. Not so in Hollywood; here the producer was much more important. He represented the studio, and the studio the money. Only a very few directors are generally known in America — Hitchcock, of course, Wyler, Wilder, John Ford, de Mille — five or six in the whole industry. My warning did not worry Zimbalist. He said the only thing that mattered was to do a great picture.

In spite of a budget of fifteen million dollars the studio was not able to run to the expense of sending me to Rome where the shooting was taking place. They were trying to save money, Zimbalist told me. However, I was needed in advance for two sequences. The more important was that of the rowing of the galley slaves, because the script mentioned four different speeds of rowing. It was obvious I would have to be there to determine the speeds, otherwise when the film was cut I would never be able to match the music to the visual. I was also needed for a party scene, a 'Fertility Dance'. Zimbalist tried to persuade me it could be managed without me,' but I remained unconvinced. Meanwhile the studio of course was very worried that I

172

MGM's 'ace' film cutter Margaret Booth
(left) with Mrs William Wyler at the Dallas
preview of *Ben-Hur*

With William Wyler in Rome

might have a month, a week, to myself, and write another concerto for Heifetz, so
they settled another picture on me. I couldn't complain, because I had the time. *The
World, the Flesh and the Devil* was about the only three people left alive in New York
after some sort of atomic disaster, two men and a woman. It was a picture with a
Message, as so many had to be in those days, but one which failed to communicate
itself either to me or to the American public.

At last I announced to the studio that I was leaving for Italy: not for Rome, for
Rapallo. I had a rented house there and had a piece to write (this was the year of the
Sinfonia Concertante). If MGM wanted me down in Rome, I would come. 'In that
case,' said Zimbalist, 'the studio will pay your expenses.' How generous — the train
journey cost all of twenty dollars, and, believe it or not, I got reimbursed.

My work on the picture in Rome was completed in a fortnight or so. For the
'Fertility Dance' Zimbalist went to France to see the Ballets Africains, a negro
troupe from one of the old French colonies in Africa. We were hoping for
something less European than the dancers in *Quo Vadis*. These young Africans
were perfect, and one day they all arrived with their drums. I worked with them so
as to establish a rhythmic pattern to which the dance could be shot.

Wyler wanted the girls to dance bare-breasted, but the management absurdly
shrank in horror from the idea. It wasn't indecent or erotic, but perfectly natural
and quite in keeping with the spirit of a festivity in ancient Rome. Anyway, he had
to make 'protection shots' with the girls both covered and uncovered, in case the
censor wanted to ruin the scene. Wyler wanted the party to begin with a shot from
the roof of the studio, so as to present a panorama of the whole banquet hall. After
the first run-through Wyler called up to Surtees, the cameraman: 'Well, Bob, what

173

With Wyler and the Ballet Africains

do you see?' 'Tits!' shouted Surtees. Wyler doesn't hear very well, and kept asking for the answer to be repeated. All those who understood English were in fits of laughter. One day I paid a visit to Wyler on the set. He was directing the scene with Messala (Stephen Boyd) after Ben-Hur and his family are taken away by Roman soldiers. I noticed how, while the crowd scenes interested him little, his direction of individual actors was painstaking and full of insight. He asked me: 'Can you express musically what is going on in the mind of a man who for the sake of personal ambition is sacrificing his best friend and his family?' I said I could. He broke for lunch, and told me he would re-shoot the scene in such a way as to give me more scope for a musical interpretation. In the evening I was called to the office of the production manager, who informed me that my presence on the set that day had cost the studio $10,000. Were I to show my face there once more, they would ship me back post-haste to Rapallo.

Zimbalist wasn't looking well and had lost a lot of his pep. He still asked me into his office to discuss matters of concern, always in tones of the greatest secrecy. It

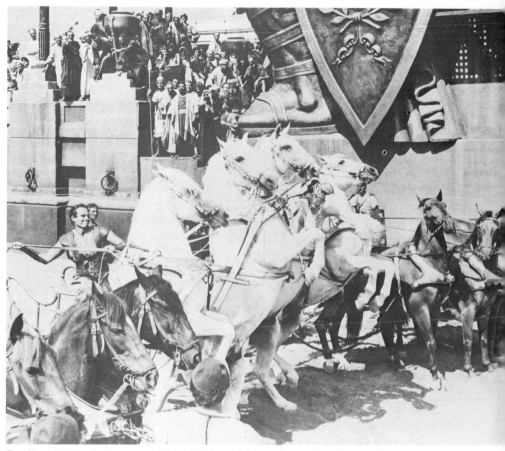

Ben-Hur: the Chariot Race (which both Wyler and I agreed should *not* have music)

turned out he was being hounded by the studio in Hollywood. Wyler's professionalism, dedication and perfectionism led to constant re-takes (like the one described above), and too much money was being spent. The New York head of MGM came to Rome to see what it was being spent on. When he left he said, 'Sam, the whole future of MGM is in your hands. Goodbye.' Well, this goodbye was, unfortunately, a kiss of death. Zimbalist didn't survive the picture. At the end of the summer, when I had finished the *Sinfonia Concertante*, my family and I went home. I was driving along Sunset Boulevard with the radio on — as on that day in 1940 when the fall of France was announced — when I heard the news of Zimbalist's sudden death in Rome. I had lost a loyal friend, a trusted collaborator and a splendid human being.

The moment this tragedy occurred Margaret Booth, the Supervising Editor, was sent to Rome. It was probably she who told Wyler that my presence might be a good idea, because shortly before Christmas 1958 I was told to go there too. I flew for the first time since I took the plane to Paris in 1940.

Ben-Hur: exhorting the orchestra to a climax   *Ben-Hur*: first page of the titles sequence

To begin with, I suggested that I write the marches there and record them there with a large wind band. One Sunday just before Christmas, in a wet, cold Rome empty of tourists, I went up to the Palatine Hill where once the palaces of the Caesars had stood. The whole of Rome stretches before you, with the forum below. I sat there alone, trying to imagine the great scenes on the Via Sacra so long ago. I began to whistle scraps of ideas and to march about excitedly and rhythmically. Two young girls looked aᵗ me in terror and fled, muttering 'Pazzo!' ('madman'); but of my lunacy was born the 'Parade of the Charioteers' which is now played at football matches and university festivities all over America.

On Christmas Eve I decided to go to hear the Midnight Mass at St. Peter's with the famous Vatican choir. I refused all invitations and walked there through a deserted Rome. Bernini's superb square was empty, so I presumed that everybody was already inside St. Peter's. However, the famous doors were closed and no one was to be seen. I was walking disconsolately down the Via della Conciliazione when a car drew up beside me. It was a former pupil of mine and his wife, who had had the same disappointing experience. Later we found out that the Pope celebrates the Midnight Mass in the Sistine Chapel for the cardinals only. Not being cardinals, we went to the American Seminary on the Gianicolo, where the celebrations included Irving Berlin's 'I'm Dreaming of a White Christmas'.

I don't like organised festivities and at home on New Year's Eve I go to bed early. I did the same in Rome. Suddenly a loud crash woke me. Then came another crash, and another, and all the bells of Rome started pealing. I wondered whether World War III had begun. Peering out, I watched in amazement as a laughing family at the window opposite struggled to push out a bath tub to join the toilet bowl and bidet which already lay shattered on the pavement beneath. Apparently it is a Roman New Year's Eve custom to cast out everything that is old in order to make way for the new. For three days Rome looks like a battlefield and I don't advise anybody to go for a walk at midnight on December 31st. They might well start the New Year in hospital.

Early in 1959 everyone went back to Hollywood and Margaret Booth started the cutting. *Ben-Hur* was an enormous picture, twenty-four reels (a reel is about ten minutes long), and to assemble the picture from the thousands of feet of film was a gigantic task which took nearly nine months. I was glad of this time to complete the score. At one point Wyler came back from a skiing holiday and called me to his office to tell me that he had a great musical idea.(I had dreaded this.) His idea was that, as the picture began with the birth of Christ, we should have the well-known Christmas tune 'Adeste Fideles' ('O Come all ye Faithful') to make the public aware that this was the first Christmas. I argued that this was an eighteenth-century tune, completely at variance with the specialised pseudo-archaic style I was trying to evolve for the picture. He told me that didn't matter at all. We argued over this, in amicable terms, for months, but as there was no sign of a change of mind on Wyler's part I at last went to see the new head of the studio, Sol C. Siegel, and threatened to resign if Wyler had his way. Siegel told me to do it *my* way and agreed to back me up.

I had no difficulty conceiving the music stylistically. This time I didn't go to first-century sources, but simply developed the 'Roman' style I had already established in *Quo Vadis* to create an archaic feeling. I had been warned by colleagues in the music department that Wyler was a difficult man, but I didn't find him so. He made some suggestions which I accepted, some which I rejected. We worked well together, though once, in front of the whole orchestra, I offered him my baton, which sent him back to the control room very quickly.

At last we got to the dreaded Nativity scene. We played the simple carol-like music I had written. I could see conflict on Wyler's face, but at the end he came over and said, 'It's very lovely, isn't it?' 'Thank you, Willy,' I replied, and that was the end of that.

The rhythm-track we had laid down in Rome for the rowing of the galley slaves worked perfectly with the music I composed in Hollywood. Wyler had liked the music when we recorded it, but when he heard it married to the picture he objected. All he wanted was the relentless beat of the rowing-master, the hortator, on his wooden block. When we tried it like that he decided it wasn't quite right, and asked for the music to be added, but very low. 'Better,' he said, but now it could be a little louder. The mixer restored the original level. Wyler was delighted and pronounced it perfect.

Wyler never said anything about the music to me at the time, but I had spent about a year and a half on it; I felt I had done my very best and expected some reaction. None came.

All the major studios give a so-called 'sneak preview' out of town, where it is understood that the press will not be present so that changes can still be made if the audience reaction isn't favourable at any point. *Ben-Hur* was shown in Dallas and

Gene Kelly presenting me with my *Ben-Hur* Oscar, my third

was a sensation. There was a standing ovation in the cinema, which is very unusual. People were eager to fill out the questionnaires which had been distributed. Wyler came up to me, embraced me, and said, 'Miki, you've written a great score.' 'But Willy, you've known this music for months and never said a word.' 'Ah,' he replied, 'but my wife's mother is a piano teacher here in Dallas. She knows everything about music. She just told me it was a great score!' Since then I have refused to listen to mother-in-law jokes.

I won my third Oscar for that score, and it is the one I cherish the most. The music of *Ben-Hur* is very close to my heart. The first call of congratulation the morning after the Oscar presentation was from Wyler, and this is a fond memory.

Just before I left for my summer holiday in 1959 the studio asked me to go to Madrid. It seemed that an independent producer, Samuel Bronston, was producing a picture there, and MGM thought I should do the music. Having just done a picture in which Jesus played a supporting role, I was dumbfounded to learn that the new film was *King of Kings*, in which he was the star! But as by this time I had apparently become the musical expounder of the Ancient World *par excellence*, I agreed.

I had never been to Spain, and my family were very excited. We would be there for about two weeks while I did the music for Salome's dance. This was quite a challenge after Richard Strauss. I could hardly hope to surpass his, but I knew that mine at least would be different.

The studio had told me not to try to discuss the dance with Bronston as he wouldn't know anything about it. When we got to Madrid I tried the writer, but he was very evasive and quickly left town. The director was even more vague. When pressed, he told me that the choreographer was his wife. She had once been a dancer with Hermes Pan who had staged many musicals, and, though she had never done any choreography before, felt she could do this. Bronston had found his Salome in Chicago. She was a schoolgirl of about sixteen, a bit plump, who, somewhat surprisingly, had never acted or danced before.

I was almost in tears. Here was a choreographer who had never choreographed and a dancer who had never danced. I finished my piece, about six or seven minutes long, and was practising it on a piano in the basement of the Hilton where we were staying, so as to be able to play it for the lady-choreographer. When I finished there was a huge burst of applause. The kitchen staff had all come in to listen. This was to be my only popular success in Madrid.

Bronston was an independent producer and MGM was afraid that *King of Kings* would prove a rival to *Ben-Hur*; so when they learnt he was running out of money they gladly put up enough to finish the picture, in order that they might have control over its release.

Day after day Margaret Booth and I worked together on the film. What were we to do with this nonsensical biblical goulash? How were all these isolated episodes, some of them as poorly acted as they were directed, going to be shaped into a coherent whole? Finally it was decided to have a narration-over, explaining things

King of Kings: one of the choruses

Composition sketch of the *El Cid* overture

179

Researching the music of the Cid's time with the renowned Spanish scholar Dr Ramon Menendez Pidal

which ought to have been seen in the film but weren't. This narration was to be written by Ray Bradbury, famous for his science-fiction stories. The three of us lunched together repeatedly discussing our problems. We were more or less left alone to save the picture which, to be fair, had its moments, though Salome's dance wasn't one of them. The poor Chicago schoolgirl simply ran about aimlessly from pillar to post making seductive movements. The first preview was so disastrous that Margaret boiled the entire scene down to a couple of minutes, which of course wrecked the music. Anyone interested in hearing it as I composed it should consult the record I made later.

In the scene of Christ's forty days and nights in the desert, an Arab in a burnous approaches Christ, looks at him, and goes away. This, I was told, was the Temptation. I did my best to explain it musically, and in spite of (or rather because of) my disbelief in Schoenberg's twelve-tone system, I wrote the only twelve-tone theme of my career for the Devil. For me twelve-tone music is a stillborn idea and thus naturally and admirably suited to the Devil, the 'Spirit of Negation', the 'Father of Lies'. This was an 'in-joke'; I didn't expect a cinema audience to get the message but thought it might rehabilitate me with the avant-garde. No such luck.

My main problem was to write new music to exactly the same themes and scenes as those in *Ben-Hur* — the Nativity, the Way of the Cross, Golgotha, the Resurrection. It was a tough job, but a young man once told me that as a boy he had been sufficiently moved by the music to familiarise himself with the same events as recounted musically by Bach in the Passions.

The preview was in Scotsdale, Arizona. Catholic priests had been invited and

At work on *El Cid*

were outraged, and the audience wrote abusive comments on their cards. Nevertheless, despite the atmosphere of doom, the next day Bronston, who found my music very *à propos*, invited me to compose the music for *El Cid*. This wasn't an MGM picture, but Bronston arranged matters with the studio — not without some difficulty, since I was wanted for *Mutiny on the Bounty* which was to be a big, important picture. I had read the script of the latter and was appalled by its shallowness, and privately thanked God for Samuel Bronston. He persuaded MGM that as his picture was almost finished I would be able to do his music and still have time to return for *Mutiny on the Bounty*. But I had already decided otherwise.

So I was off to Madrid again, this time for the whole summer. There was research to do, because I knew nothing of Spanish music of the Middle Ages. The historical adviser on the film was the greatest authority on the Cid, Dr Ramon Menendez Pidal, aged ninety-two. It was he who introduced me to the twelfth-century Cantigas of Santa Maria, in one of what must have been at least ten thousand books in his vast and beautiful library. (He knew exactly where these books were; his son, who was only seventy, climbed the ladder to get them down.) I spent a month in intense study of the music of the period. I also studied the Spanish folksongs which Pedrell had gone about collecting in the early years of this century. With these two widely differing sources to draw upon, I was ready to compose the music. As always, I attempted to absorb these raw materials and translate them into my own musical language.

Spain itself influenced the score of *El Cid*, as Rome had influenced *Quo Vadis* and *Ben-Hur*. I couldn't have written such music anywhere else. Where do these

With the family in Madrid at the time of *El Cid*

influences come from? From the air? The food? The architecture? The people? The music one hears? I don't know, but they were definitely there.

A few weeks before my family was due to arrive for the summer, Bronston asked me whether I would like hotel rooms or a house. I chose a house, and he immediately offered to find me the best in Madrid, to pay for it, and to allow me the same weekly living expenses as he himself was getting. It all sounded wonderful.

Then the bombshell burst. He had a favour to ask. The film was an Italian co-production, which meant that in return for the subsidy from the Italian government, a certain number of Italian artists and technicians had to be employed. Originally an Italian composer had been engaged, but Bronston intensely disliked his music and had rejected him in favour of me. Now the Italians were insisting that an Italian composer's name be on the credits. Bronston couldn't afford to lose all the Italian money, so he asked that on the Italian prints an Italian composer's name should appear together with mine. Well, Bronston had been good to me, and now he was in a fix. Eventually I agreed, provided the Italian made no claim for royalties and his credit appeared on the Italian prints only. And so I had a proforma co-composer, but only in Italy!

We found the most heavenly house, which came with cook, maid, butler and gardener. There was a pool, a library and a perfect room for me to work in. The summer went by, and I composed with a kind of exhilaration. I liked the country, I liked the people, and the picture made sense.

My happiness was short-lived. I got a call from MGM who wanted me back for

Charlton Heston as the Cid

Mutiny on the Bounty, which I had forgotten about. I told them I was nowhere near finished, but they said that Bronston's film meant nothing to them, I was to return. Again Bronston worked a miracle and saved me from a fate worse than death.

El Cid was in two parts. I finished the first part (about an hour of music) and we recorded it in Rome, using an orchestra which comprised members of all three of the Roman orchestras. Although the players are quite good, Italian orchestras aren't as quick, efficient or disciplined as English or American ones, and the recording took ten days. We did the dubbing at Shepperton Studios, outside London. Dubbing is the putting together of the different sound-elements of the film — dialogue, effects (plenty of these in the Cid's battle scenes, where the wooden swords used for safety have to be given a metallic sound), and the music. Again and again the sound-effects expert tried to persuade the director to take out music that interfered with her precious clicks and booms. I argued that without the music the excitement was missing. But at the premiere a nasty shock awaited me: scene after scene was music-less. In one scene the music just stopped in mid-bar, presumably so the clinking of a sword could be better heard. I was so angry that I cancelled a publicity tour I had agreed to undertake; I could not talk about music which nobody was going to hear.

Now, twenty years later, I can see that *El Cid* was my last major film score, and my last important film with the exception of *Providence*. Though I did my best with every film which came later, few had real stature. So I must regard 1961 as the climax and watershed of my film career.

183

9: Return to Hungary

Back at MGM they told me they had waited as long as possible for me to finish *El Cid*, but eventually had to give *Mutiny on the Bounty* to someone else. My heart rejoiced. The two pictures came out together. Nobody needs to be told of the success of *El Cid*; *Mutiny on the Bounty* on the other hand was a disaster which nearly finished the studio.

In the spring of 1962 I got a telephone call from a friend in Rome to say that he was producing a film called *Sodom and Gomorrah*, and wanted me to come there to do the music. It was obvious that my contract with MGM wasn't going to be renewed; the studio proposed they give me *Sodom and Gomorrah* and terminate it immediately, as there was nothing more for me to do there. I was glad to go; it wasn't the MGM of the old days. I left without a word of thanks or a goodbye from anybody. My only contact with them after that was when they asked for the repayment of two weeks' salary, as I had had my two weeks' holiday without completing a year. This after fourteen years without a free Sunday! I told my agent to pay it, but never to mention the name of MGM to me again. In Rome I told Esther Williams and her husband Fernando Lamas, and they weren't surprised. Her pictures had made millions for MGM, but when they failed to renew her contract she drove out from the studio and the gateman said to her, 'See you tomorrow, Esther.' 'No you won't,' she answered. 'I'm through.' 'Well, good luck, Esther,' the gateman said. That was the only farewell anyone wished her.

I was happy to be back in Rome once more, that incredibly beautiful city with so many wonderful memories for me. Happy, that is, until I saw *Sodom and Gomorrah*. After the success of *Ben-Hur* everyone was trying to produce colossal ancient-world epics. They were sprouting like mushrooms after rain. But some mushrooms are poisonous.

Sodom and Gomorrah was a super-production costing seven million dollars, with the biblical story decked out with all sorts of absurd and gaudy extras. The director had left already, so we never met. The film was like a parody of the genre: a wretched script, bad acting, some passable battle scenes, some interesting photography; but I was stuck with it, and with close to two hours of music. However, the producer was a friend, the studio was paying me well, and I hoped I might be able to help a bit; but the cards were stacked.

Shortly before the premiere, graffiti appeared everywhere: 'No immoral films in Rome!' There was precious little immorality in the film — there may have been a questionable relationship between the queen and a slave girl, but it was only hinted at. I think these graffiti were a publicity stunt by the studio. If they were, it didn't work. The film was a sad flop, and the studio closed down. However, the record album of my music is again available.

It was this summer, after my family joined me in Rome, that I wrote the *Notturno Ungherese* for the Philadelphia Orchestra and Mr Benjamin, a Southern millionaire who every year commissioned a piece for the orchestra from a composer recommended to him. This year I was the one recommended by Eugene Ormandy. When I met Benjamin he told me he didn't mind what the piece was, as long as it was quiet: he liked to have quiet music in his office while he was working. So once again I was to write background music.

Notturno Ungherese (Hungarian Nocturne) was an attempt to recapture the rare beauty of the nights on our estate in rural Hungary. I think it was Proust who said that art is nothing but a process of recalling one's childhood. This piece was an evocation of my youth.

At the premiere in Philadelphia I sat with Mr Benjamin. Eugene Ormandy conducted. My piece began *pianissimo* and a look of bliss appeared on Benjamin's face. I could see him in his office making gigantic financial deals with this music murmuring in the background. But I cannot remain *pianissimo* for eight minutes. The music gradually builds until, about one minute before the end, it reaches a passionate climax; then it fades gently away again. As the music grew, so did Mr Benjamin's unease, until the climax stirred him to a glare. Then, as the music

With Eugene Ormandy in Philadelphia, 1967

subsided, the angelic smile returned. Afterwards he told me, very kindly, that somehow he could never make composers understand exactly what he wanted.

After fourteen years at MGM it was a strange feeling not to have to hurry back to the studio at the end of the summer. However, with my three Oscars, and with, I suppose, a certain reputation, I expected offers to pour in. Not a bit of it. As biblical films were being abandoned because of the expense, the 'biblical composer' — which was how I was now typecast — wasn't needed. However, in 1963 I got a call from the head of the copyright department at MGM, the Rumanian Rudolf Monta, a dear friend and a very cultured man, one of those few studio people one saw at every concert, opera and art exhibition. It was a joy to be with him. He asked me to do him a favour and write the music for a film being shot in London. My feelings about MGM shocked him, but at last he persuaded me to take the job as a personal favour to him. The film was *The VIPs*, starring Elizabeth Taylor and Richard Burton. Fox's *Cleopatra* had been shooting in Rome while I was there working on *Sodom and Gomorrah*, and the so-called affair between these two had received much vulgar publicity; now MGM was banking on their notoriety to make *The VIPs* a success. (When *Cleopatra* did come out it was anything but a success, in spite of the publicity.)

When I arrived in London at seven o'clock in the morning I was flattered to see a crowd of reporters and photographers at the foot of the gangway. Well, I was a three-time Academy Award winner, and it seemed reasonable that my arrival might be of some interest. Unfortunately they ignored me and rushed towards a group of four long-haired young men, who turned out to be the Beatles. They certainly beat me in popularity.

MGM hadn't changed. The man who met me told me I was expected at the studio in two hours' time, at 9 a.m., to see the picture. I had flown for eleven hours and insisted on going to my hotel to sleep. But in the afternoon I went to the studio and met the producer, Anatole de Grunwald.

After I had seen the picture (or most of it) I asked de Grunwald whether he wanted a flattering Hollywood opinion or an objective London one. He asked for my own, so I told him I felt that there wasn't sufficient explanation as to why Taylor should be leaving a rich and young Burton for a penniless, aging Louis Jourdan. De Grunwald talked with Anthony Asquith, the director, and Terence Rattigan, the writer, and they all tended toward my view: some extra explanatory scenes were needed. But when de Grunwald approached Miss Taylor, her response was that she had accepted a script, agreed to do the picture for one million dollars (in 1963!) and she wouldn't do a single additional scene, not a word more. She was furious that a mere composer like myself should have dared to express an opinion. De Grunwald advised me to stay away from the studio for a while.

This suited me admirably. I spent a week visiting all my favourite museums and picture galleries. There was nothing else to do but spend the money they were paying me, and I started my collection of Roman and Etruscan bronzes at this time.

One day, however, I went out to the studio to visit Margaret Booth, who was again the supervising editor of the picture. I knocked on her office door. No answer. I thought I would leave a message on her desk and opened the door. To my and their great horror I saw there de Grunwald, Asquith, Rattigan and Margaret, sitting with Taylor and Burton and looking at the picture. I mumbled some apology and quickly left. An hour later they called me and apologised. They hadn't dared introduce me because I could easily have had my eyes scratched out if they had mentioned my name!

It was finally decided that all that was needed to finish the picture was one additional scene, which Rattigan then wrote. Miss Taylor was adamant. At last she agreed — provided the studio gave her the mink coat she had worn in the first scene. They did so, and the picture was completed.

Just after we finished dubbing, I was shocked to learn that my old friend Monta, for whom I had consented to do the picture, had died in Hollywood. My last friend at MGM was gone. I was sent to Rome to record a *VIPs* album, and I also recorded four of my symphonic works for RCA Victor, to balance the scales of my Double Life. The picture did well, but wasn't a sensation. Studios never learn that famous stars and massive publicity aren't enough; the pictures themselves must have some quality. The public can't be fooled all the time. When Grace Kelly was at the height of her career and packing them in to two good films, *Green Fire*, in which she also appeared (and which I had to score) was so poor that no one went to see it.

The following summer, 1964, we went to Rome again. For the first time since *To Everything there is a Season*, written at the end of the war, I embarked on the writing of a choral work. Dr Maurice Skones, the director of the excellent Pacific Lutheran University Choir at Tacoma, Washington, asked me to write a piece for them. I chose again a passage from Ecclesiastes, about the vanities of life, and worked on it all summer. Harmonically the choral writing is more advanced than my first motet, something which American and English choirs cope with easily. The aforementioned choir recorded both motets, together with my setting of the 23rd Psalm. Rudy Monta's wife Marguerite had died shortly after him, and on the order of service for her funeral the text of the 23rd Psalm had been printed. I set it for unaccompanied mixed choir and dedicated it to their memory.

I had met the pianist Leonard Pennario through a mutual friend. He had recorded my piano sonata on an album with sonatas by Bartók and Prokofiev; now he asked me for a piano concerto. This intrigued me, because I am not a pianist. Concertos composed by pianists fall naturally under the fingers, but (often because of this) may be deficient in purely musical qualities. Would I be able to write virtuoso piano music? The scale of a concerto is much grander than that of a sonata. I had already made an arrangement of music from *Spellbound* for piano and orchestra, the *Spellbound Concerto* (which Pennario also played and recorded), but a true concerto was something else.

I began in the summer of 1965, again in my beloved Italy. Sad to say, Rapallo had changed greatly since 1953. The charm of this twelfth-century town was being ruined by the modern housing going up around it, and the whole place was now overlooked by a garish modern hotel. It had been so enchanting — Sibelius came here to write his Second Symphony in 1902; Max Beerbohm, Shaw's incomparable Max, lived and died here, and so did Gerhart Hauptmann; now all the charm and beauty was spoiled. I looked round and discovered that Santa Margherita, also in the bay of Rapallo, was still untouched. Quaint sixteenth-century houses painted different colours with *trompe l'oeil* designs encircle the pretty bay, and the council forbids any change without permission. Not even a tree can be cut down. I moved there.

I found that writing for piano went much more slowly for me than writing for strings, which I know intimately, for I had to try out everything painstakingly at the piano. I finished the first movement by September, and for the first time stayed on through the winter because I wanted to finish the piece in Santa Margherita.

Pennario and I met in Rome the following March (1966). He was very enthusiastic, which he always is, because he somehow has a weakness for my music. He gave the first performance with the Los Angeles Philharmonic under Zubin Mehta during their 1966-67 season. Pennario played extremely well; the public got very excited and there was a standing ovation at the end. This was less usual than it is today, when in Los Angeles anything less than a standing ovation is held to imply that the concert wasn't good enough.

The local critic didn't like the piece, which poses the question: does one write for the public, or for the critics? Three thousand people applaud enthusiastically and one journalist makes uncharitable remarks. Which is more important? And how do critics feel able to make a definite judgement after one hearing? As a composer, I would never presume to do such a thing. When my pupils brought their music to me I always made them play it twice, something I learnt from Honegger. There is too much of the unexpected in a first hearing; after a second hearing things begin to fall into place. It is still usual to despise Hanslick for his dislike of Wagner, but Hanslick was a great scholar, a university professor, who for his own aesthetic reasons didn't appreciate Wagner's music. He might have been wrong, but at least it was from a standpoint of knowledge and ability, and after a careful study of Wagner's scores. People should read his criticisms of the four Brahms symphonies written after their first performances; their insight is a marvel.

For a composer, the only thing that matters is communication. I try to express myself, and to communicate with my public. Film composers, and especially Hollywood film composers, are the easiest prey for critics. You can positively sense them waiting to pounce, and once you bear the cinematographic taint nothing you write in any other context is inviolate. My *Theme, Variations and Finale* was once described as 'typical film music': this was a work written in 1933, at which time I knew nothing of films and had written not a note of film music. Admittedly vast quantities of bad music were manufactured in Hollywood during the so-called Golden Age, but no more proportionately than was written and performed in concert during the same period.

Of course, some critics are knowledgeable musicians, but the majority are not. If the audience walks out in droves, the critic will praise the piece to show his appreciation of a work far too esoteric for the common herd. If they love it, he will sneer because their vulgar taste cannot accord with his refinement. Many are poseurs, who know that controversial reviewing makes good 'copy' which is appreciated by editors. Piatigorsky once said, 'Why should we artists read what our inferiors write about us?' Max Reger's answer to a critic who tore his Piano

After a performance of the Piano Concerto in Honolulu; Leonard Pennario is on the right

Concerto to shreds after its premiere is too well-known to be repeated here. Benjamin Britten took the trouble to mail torn-up reviews back to their authors. But why bother? After all, criticisms are written for the public and not for composers or performers.

Once the Los Angeles critic C. Sharpless Hickman informed me that he heard my second string quartet and how much better it was compared to my rather tentative first effort in the medium. I thank him profusely. It was, of course, the same quartet, since at that time I had written only one. On the other hand, the late John Rosenfield of Dallas, about whom Antal Doráti writes lovingly in his memoirs, was in a different category altogether. Before the premiere of my violin concerto with Heifetz, he wrote to me and asked whether I had a recording of it with piano. I had one and sent it. He came to every orchestra rehearsal and then wrote a glowing review, in the headline of which my name was misspelled 'Rósza' (which happens all the time). Next day I received an apology from him for this error, and enclosed with his letter were ten copies with my name correctly spelled, which he had had his paper specially reprint!

André Previn gave my Piano Concerto its second performance, in Houston, again with Pennario as soloist, and after that it was performed in Hawaii and in Philadelphia (where I conducted). The Philadelphia is the most amazing orchestra. They are sensitive and responsive, and play exactly as they are conducted. A good conductor is like a good rider — the horse responds to authority and will never

189

throw you. But with horse or orchestra, a lack of authority, a feeling of indecision, is sensed at once. I remember a bank director in Budapest who was an amateur conductor. He gave a concert for all the notables of the city and during the interval the leader took him aside and said, 'Mr Conductor, the orchestra would like some beer, please, and if we don't get it we will play the second half exactly as you conduct it.' They got the beer.

Countless performances of the concerto took place in the next few years, and apart from Pennario three other pianists have it in their repertoire; its most recent convert is the distinguished English pianist, Eric Parkin, who has also made a record of my solo piano works.

I had worked in the cinema now for thirty years, not for the sake of artistic fulfilment, or from any great interest in the cinema *per se*, but simply because I needed to make a living. I could claim, impressively, that I veered irresistibly towards film music as a natural expressive outlet, that I derived my greatest feelings of satisfaction from opportunities to reinforce and transmit the emotions of Clark Gable, or to enhance the facial features of Lana Turner; but I would be deceiving myself and my readers if I did so. I actually never liked the cinema very much, but for me, as for many other composers, it was a source of income, and once committed to it we did our best. Some of the film works of Shostakovitch and Prokofiev are as good as anything in their concert output, and a few, like *Hamlet* and *Ivan the Terrible*, are among their best works. The same goes for Walton's three great Shakespearian scores — they are vintage Walton, only more direct in expression than his concert works. This directness is a *sine qua non* if film music is to do its job properly. If the music is too complicated, too technical, the public, whose attention is to a far greater extent directed toward the visual image, will never get its message. One must face the fact that music plays a subordinate role in the cinema. I have felt technically restricted sometimes, but had to impose these restrictions on myself in the interests of the drama.

Some know-alls will tell you that film music is by its very nature worthless. Emil Ludwig, the German historian, once asked how it was possible to expect a composer to write a piece of music lasting precisely three minutes eleven seconds. What the composer wanted to express might be best realised in a passage of five or two minutes in duration, but never exactly three minutes eleven seconds. Of course this is nonsense. To me, time in music is like space in painting. When Michelangelo was asked to paint the ceiling of the Sistine Chapel, it wouldn't have done him much good to ask for another ten feet in one direction and another five in the other, because what he had in mind wouldn't fit the space available. It is exactly the same with film music. The discipline of having to compose to a given duration need not affect the quality of the music so composed at all.

So, after thirty years of snatching a month here or two months there in which to concentrate on my concert music, I was at last my own master. I had no contract with anybody, I could choose, I could refuse. I was a free man. Just the same I had no call to feel resentment towards the studios or to denounce the system in its entirety. We were captives, but for the most part happy and well-paid captives. Nevertheless, thirty years was enough. Heifetz, at the height of his solo career, put down his violin, saying, 'Enough.' I felt the same. I was willing to do occasional films, but grinding out scores one after the other, regardless of the quality of the films they were designed to accompany — that became a thing of the past.

The pattern of my life remained the same. I spent the winters in Hollywood and the summers in Italy as before. America has given me much for which I am grateful. I am a loyal citizen and love my adopted country dearly. If I don't confess the same love for the denizens of Celluloid City I have to point out that Hollywood is not America, and for my non-cinematographic music I need the geographical change. I love my little house in Italy, where I am writing these words. I love the village and its people. And I lack the greatest antagonist of any creative person, a telephone. The number of times in Hollywood I have been interrupted at a crucial moment of creation by the telephone are countless. And after the call is done I return to my paper to find the inspiration of the moment gone for ever.

Geographically this part of Italy is important to me too. I have never written any film music here, and can keep the two halves of my Double Life distinct and separate. Here I find the absolute quiet and solitude I need if I am to concentrate. I seldom see people and am completely absorbed in my work. Milhaud and Shostakovitch could compose in the midst of turmoil; not I.

Nor can I work for long periods without a break. In Hollywood I have to discipline myself, for film scores have to be written in next to no time. A film may be years in the writing, years in the preparing, years in the making; yet the music, one of its most important constituents, is almost without exception rushed through in a few weeks. The late Alfred Hitchcock asked me at the time how long it would take to write the music for *Spellbound*. I stipulated six weeks. 'Six weeks!' he thundered. 'I shot the whole picture in that time!' 'Very possibly,' I replied; 'but how long did it take you and Ben Hecht to write the screenplay?' He just grunted. I went on to point out that I could *record* a score in three days, two even; but first it has to be set down on paper, a far more laborious and time-consuming process than most non-musicians realise.

In Santa Margherita I can let the ideas flow freely, and if they don't come of their own accord I don't need to force them. But once I have started a work under these near-ideal conditions, I must persevere with it to the end. I cannot drop a movement and pick it up again six months later as if nothing had happened.

I met the eminent cellist János Starker after a New York performance of Jean Martinon's Cello Concerto. He said, 'Why don't you write a concerto for me? How about it?' This 'How about it?' started my Cello Concerto.

Composers are strange animals, and one never knows what actually triggers the idea for a work. But one thing is certain — we all want to be wanted. It is by no mere chance that the Renaissance produced so many hundreds of masterpieces. The Renaissance was stimulated by people who wanted what it had to offer; or, to be plainer, people who were prepared to pay for it. People talk with disdain about the artist who works for money, but Bach worked for money and so did Haydn. Bach had to produce a cantata every Sunday, and Haydn symphonies, operas and chamber music for his employer. Most big works were commissions — somebody wanted them; and this simple feeling that one is wanted can ignite the imagination.

I believe commissions to be one of the most important factors in the life of a creative artist.

Now I am not a cellist, and the cello is a very peculiar instrument, not at all easy to write for. Again and again we see composers who aren't string players consulting prominent players for advice. Mendelssohn worked with Ferdinand David, Brahms worked with Joachim — and I worked with Starker, as I had with Heifetz.

I finished the first movement of the concerto, and then the second, and then I received The Call. Hollywood was calling, more specifically MGM again. In my euphoria after the premiere of my Piano Concerto I had rashly agreed to write the score to a film the Hungarian producer George Pal was making. I had forgotten all about it but now here it was, a science-fiction movie called *The Power*. I saw myself entering my fifth period, Rózsa the science-fiction expert. By now it was 1968 and I hadn't done a film in four years.

Well, I had promised Pal, and I like to keep my promises; moreover, I was fond of him, for he was an amiable and charming gentleman. Since the main character in the film was a gypsy, and Pal was a Hungarian, he wanted me to use a cimbalom. A cimbalom is a sort of large zither played with hammers, which produces a very distinctive sound, something between a badly-tuned piano and a broken-down harpsichord. I don't like the instrument much, (I don't like *anything* to do with gypsy music), but I didn't object, because it seemed appropriate for the character of the man. I was also told that the picture was important because the main star was engaged to marry the U.S. President's daughter. She was certainly around most of the time, but the marriage was called off and the picture immediately became less 'important'. It wasn't a success and the cimbalom didn't become my second theremin.

After this I returned to Santa Margherita, finished the Cello Concerto, and János Starker and his wife came to visit me. Starker went to work on the piece and suggested several technical changes to make it more cellistic. That winter I orchestrated it and the premiere was fixed for the Berlin Festival the following summer.

I wrote to my old teacher, Hermann Grabner, in Berlin, to say that at last I would be coming to see him, for the first time since 1931. We had corresponded regularly, and I had sent him all my records as they came out (he bought himself a record-player specially in order to be able to play them). He wrote back saying he had changed the date of his vacation so as to be there when I arrived in September. He was excited and looking forward to welcoming me and promised to attend the rehearsals, as he had done for my first violin concerto in 1929. Shortly afterwards I read in the paper that he had died suddenly in Bolzano on his vacation. I reproached myself bitterly. I had been to Germany dozens of times, to all the other major cities, but had never gone to Berlin to see him, the man who had once written to my father: 'If there is one man who has the right to become a composer, it is your son.' My happiness at the success of the Berlin premiere was tempered only by my private awareness of Grabner's absence.

The first American performance took place in Chicago in 1971, again with János Starker; the conductor was Georg Solti, who had previously conducted other works

After a performance of the Cello Concerto with János Starker (left) and conductor Harry Newstone

of mine in Frankfurt and Los Angeles. Meanwhile Mario Castelnuovo-Tedesco had died: in Hollywood we had been friends for years. He fled Italy when Mussolini began to adopt his idol Hitler's racial policies. He was a fine musician, never appreciated by the studios, who composed prolifically in a typical turn-of-the-century romantic-impressionist style. He became a guitar expert, though he couldn't play the instrument, and even published a teaching method for the guitar. He had responded sympathetically to my music from the early days in Hollywood, and he was impressed by *Jungle Book* to the extent of making his own settings of Kipling and dedicating them to me. Later he wrote a little piece on my name 'in the Hungarian style'. In fact it was as much Hungarian as he was Chinese, but a kind gesture just the same.

It is hard to imagine that a composer of this international stature lived in Los Angeles for thirty years and received no official recognition. MGM gave him almost nothing, just odd sequences in other people's films.* Yet he never complained; he was a happy, gentle soul who never pushed himself and found complete fulfilment in his family. He was performed in more important cities than Los Angeles and that was enough for him. He liked to have his friends for dinner, and afterwards we would listen to tapes of his works that had just arrived from Berlin, from Florence, from all over the world. Mario might not have spoken the musical language of the 20th century, but everything he wrote (and he wrote a great deal!) was deeply felt, inspired and masterful. Young performers should study his music; they will discover gems for every instrument and combination.

My agent rang me in Italy to offer me another picture produced by and starring John Wayne. I told him I wasn't interested in Westerns, but he assured me that this wasn't a Western. When I got back I discovered it was a war picture set in Vietnam

---

*For instance, the masterly score for Albert Lewin's *The Picture of Dorian Gray* is almost entirely his (totally uncredited) work.

193

called *The Green Berets* in which the Duke was winning the Vietnam war single-handedly — a typical Wayne film except that the injuns had become the Viet Cong. It was a big success in America, but caused a scandal in Europe where anti-American feeling was running high. There were demonstrations outside cinemas in many countries, and my own reputation barely emerged unscathed. Recently I was reading something about my work by a French writer who actually said: 'In spite of his association with *The Green Berets*, this time Miklós Rózsa has come up with a very good score.' Apparently I am now *persona grata* again.

Then Sherlock Holmes came into my life. Once a year I used to meet Billy Wilder at a Christmas party given by a mutual friend, the screenwriter Walter Reisch. At the party in 1971 he told me that he was going to make a picture about Sherlock Holmes, and that as Holmes was a violinist he was going to use my Concerto. The film was to be in four separate episodes, four separate adventures. I was overjoyed; the script had the wit, the imagination and the charm of Wilder's best films, and I was certain that this was going to be the best of them all.

It was produced in London and good English actors were engaged (Holmes was played by Robert Stephens, Watson by Colin Blakely). I went to London at the start of the production because of a ballet scene and also a back-stage party which needed balalaika music.

The film was very good, but very long — well over three hours, which didn't matter because of the quality of the material (and there was to be an intermission).

With Billy Wilder, recording *Sherlock Holmes*

194

Then came a directive from America: the film had to be shortened to under two hours. If I had been Wilder I would have told them to go to hell, even if it had meant the end of my career. But Wilder acquiesced, and two episodes were dropped completely, while the others were cut and hacked about in an attempt to make one story out of two. The weakest story, about a submarine disguised as the Loch Ness monster, was left intact, but elsewhere all the best bits were eliminated.

As to the music, I enjoyed adapting my Concerto. The first theme of the first movement was used for Holmes' cocaine-addiction, the second movement for the love theme; the turbulent last movement became Loch Ness monster-music. For the scenes shot in the lovely Scottish highlands Wilder wanted Scottish music of some kind. As usual, I did my homework and wrote music based on some Scottish national tunes I had researched. Wilder complained that it was *too* Scottish. The scene itself was a happy one, with Holmes, Watson and the 'Belgian' girl scooting along on bicycles. Then Wilder, perhaps remembering 'Bicycle Built for Two', asked for a waltz, but when he heard it he complained that it was too Viennese. There was only one session left, in two days' time, and he at last allowed me to write something that I considered appropriate. I used the love theme, but with an urgent, pulsating rhythm underneath, and it worked well. The truncated film as you see it today is a sorry travesty of the original and a great disappointment to all involved.

Then I was offered *The Golden Voyage of Sinbad*. I was pleased at the prospect of returning to the fantasy-world of *The Thousand and One Nights*, but this amateurish

As I appear in *The Private Life of Sherlock Holmes*

Robert Stephens, Genevieve Page and Colin Blakely in *Sherlock Holmes*

concoction had none of the qualities of the immortal *Thief of Baghdad*. The only good thing to come out of the film from my point of view was that I made the acquaintance of Ray Harryhausen, the brilliant animator.

For many years my American publishers had asked me for two things, a fanfare for brass and percussion, and some choral pieces shorter than the two motets and my 23rd Psalm. I wrote the fanfare quickly and dedicated it to the American bicentenary in 1976, when it was quite widely performed. As for the choral pieces, there was the usual problem of finding texts to set to music. The publishers tried to interest me in Latin poetry — Horace, Virgil and so on — but to no avail. I find difficulty in responding to a literary text; this is the reason I have never written an opera. However, I eventually came upon some translations by Arthur Waley of old Chinese poetry which took my fancy with their charm and humanity. Three of these I set to music, trying to express the universality of the human condition.

Leonard Pennario often gives chamber music soirées, and the best musicans in Hollywood are invited to play. Piatigorsky was often there with his cello and invariably had the party of forty or fifty guests laughing with his wonderful stories. On one occasion Pennario gathered a group together to play my Quintet op. 2 which dated from my conservatory days. We had had innumerable rehearsals all those years ago, but these artists, after a single run-through, gave the most thrilling performance. The head of a local record company was there and wanted to record the piece. Pennario and I both tried to persuade Piatigorsky to take part in the recording, as he had just played so magnificently, but he begged to be excused — he

196

was no longer well, and feared the strain of recording. But he suggested his pupil Nathaniel Rosen, who played splendidly. Rosen had won in 1978 the coveted Tchaikovsky Competition in Moscow, only the second American ever to do so. Rosen is without doubt Piatigorsky's master-pupil, a reincarnation of the great old man himself.

Along with the Quintet we recorded my Trio, op. 1, of the previous year, 1927. In revising the piece for the recording I had to look at myself as I had been fifty years before — an odd experience. I could see elements of immaturity, of course, moments when I was still feeling my way; but the basic characteristics of my mature style are, in embryonic formations, unmistakably present already.

I can't complain that I have ever been neglected as a composer, but suddenly in the 1970s there was a general resurgence of interest in my music. Much of my important film music was re-recorded or reissued on record, and some of the symphonic works, also, were made newly available. Breitkopf & Härtel published Christopher Palmer's monograph study of my life and work, and to my surprise I found that societies bearing my name were springing up on three continents. I always imagined that societies such as these were formed after the death of the composer, but apparently we are living in a faster or more enlightened age. After the first society was started in Belgium, John Fitzpatrick formed one in the United States, at my suggestion naming it 'Pro Musica Sana'. The society brings out a quarterly newsletter with essays about my works, reviews, news items, letters and so on. The members are very loyal to me, sometimes travelling hundreds of miles if I am conducting somewhere. Another society sprang up in Australia, and there is another New York group. Lastly, an 'Association Miklós Rózsa' was formed in France. Of course, I have nothing to do with the running of these societies, and I don't contribute articles to the journals, but I am flattered that they exist. However, I stipulated from the beginning that they should also write about other composers' works, which they do.

Breitkopf & Härtel asked me for a large orchestral piece, but not a symphony. I suggested a three-movement work which we could call *Tripartita*, and they agreed. I wrote the piece in the summer of 1971 and revised it in the following summer. Breitkopf recommended I approach a fellow Hungarian, István Kertész, to give the first performance, and this was agreed upon. Then, tragically, Kertész was drowned in the Mediterranean. The first performance was given at Gelsenkirchen under Ljubomir Romansky in the autumn of 1973. The recovery of the arts in Germany after the war is astounding. Gelsenkirchen is typical of literally dozens of smallish towns with its own opera company, theatre company and orchestra. There the *Tripartita* was enthusiastically received. André Previn gave the second performance in London, and Antal Doráti the American premieres in Washington and New York.

In the late summer of 1974 I accepted an invitation to return to Hungary to conduct a concert of my works. This was my first visit in forty-three years. At first I was hesitant, but what finally decided me was the fact that my aunt, my mother's sister, was eighty-three and very ill and had expressed a wish to see me before she died.

Back in Budapest after 43 years, August 1974   *Baghdad* in Budapest

I have always loved my native country. It was the over-bearing self-importance of the inhabitants of its capital that drove me out. Had they changed in forty-three years? Did the small-mindedness, the petty rivalry and the conviction that in Hungary everything is better than anywhere else still prevail? Was the old Latin saying: 'Extra Hungariam non est vita; si est vita, non est ita' — ('Outside Hungary there is no life; if there *is* life, it is not the same') — still taken to heart?

I got no answer because I met very few members of my profession. The conductors who had performed my works, Ferencsik of the Philharmonic, Lukács of the Opera and Lehel of the Radio, came to hear me, but I was longing to meet also the composers, my brothers-in-arms, as I was to meet my French colleagues six years later in Paris.

However, many things compensated for this disappointment. The St. Margaret Island where I stayed, and where I had spent three summers with my parents, was even more beautiful than before. I found the statues of Bartók, Kodály, Ady and the other heroes of my youth. At that time they were despised eccentrics; now they are respected classics. A Korda film-festival was in progress, and *The Thief of Baghdad* was in its fifth month. Hungarians think of it almost as a Hungarian film, because of the three Kordas, screenwriter Lajos Biro and myself. There was a special showing of it in my honour. Almost involuntarily I found myself viewing it again with joy, and was struck by its perennial freshness, its timeless quality, its poetic beauty, its unbridled fantasy; one of my commentators has written that the music 'seems part of everyone's ciné-musical past, like a fairy castle glimmering in the distance.' After the performance people stood in line and I signed six hundred and twenty autographs on specially printed cards. They brought me flowers, thanked me with tears in their eyes, and some old ladies kissed my hands, just for coming home. I felt like a returning hero. The same public, too, came to my concert and applauded vociferously. As an encore we gave a short fantasy from the *Thief*, and when Sabu's little tune 'I want to be a Sailor' came up, I heard the audience whistling and singing. My public had taken me to their hearts, but as far as my fellow Hungarian composers were concerned I might as well not have existed.

During my visit the telephone never stopped ringing, and most of those who called wanted something. People naïvely imagine that my long years of association with motion pictures have somehow endowed me with a kind of omnipotence in the industry. Shortly after the war I got a letter from a Hungarian film-cutter living in Paris, who had decided he wanted to become the head of a 'scenario department' in Hollywood; could I arrange it for him? A Hungarian, of course, wouldn't start as a mere scenarist, but only as the *head* of the department. A man descended upon me on this visit, wanting me to take him to Hollywood and make a new Alexander Korda out of him, nothing less. A woman came to tell me about her daughter's stormy life — could I recommend that it be made into a Hollywood film? These people, of course, believe the pulp-magazines and know nothing of the true facts of life in films. The business is as brutal, ruthless and competitive as it could be. Even past achievements count for little: what does count is a recent success, luck, social *savoir-faire*, knowing the right people, some talent, and a thousand other intangibles, which neither I (an innocent onlooker) nor anyone else have the power to manipulate. I always made it plain at the outset to my USC students that the most important lesson of all was one I could not teach them: how to get a job. And of the hundreds of students who passed through my hands — some of them talented — only one made good in a big way: Jerry Goldsmith. This is a reflection, not on the quality of the students, nor (I hope!) on my teaching, but on the unpredictable and irresponsible nature of the movie world.

By this time I was starting to pay the price of a longish life: friends, colleagues and contemporaries began to die. Muir Mathieson and Vincent Korda in England; Bernard (Benny) Herrmann in Hollywood, although for several years he had been resident in London. Herrmann was the most un-Hollywoodian Hollywood composer. He was a born non-conformist and told anyone his unexpurgated opinion about anything, anywhere and any time — no matter what the consequences for his own career might be. He was a splendid musician and a great musico-dramatist with an unmistakable musical personality of his own, much imitated by lesser talents. Hitchcock's many successes were in part attributable to his music, but even this relationship came to grief on account of Herrmann's unbending nature. Our friendship flourished untroubled until his untimely death, and I was one of the few friends with whom he never quarrelled. He knew that I respected his talent and integrity, his refusal to compromise, and I like to think he respected mine. I have related already how he wanted to compose the music for *Julius Caesar*, but never resented the assignment coming to me. In London he invited me to hear his recording of this music, and watched me like a hawk to see my reactions to his interpretation. He was overjoyed when I praised him and thanked him.

My good old friend Piatigorsky died after an operation for lung cancer. Shortly before, he had told me about the brilliance of the viola playing of Pinchas Zukerman, saying that in his opinion Zukerman was now the best viola player in the world. So I began to think of writing a viola concerto to complete my little family of concerti for stringed instruments.

Back in Santa Margherita, in my hermetic isolation from humanity, I began to sketch a few ideas. I was interrupted by a telephone call summoning me to Paris, where I was being asked to write the music for a film called *La Reine Renée* (Queen Renée). I had never heard of the lady, but supposed that it must be an historical film of some sort. My agent in London enlightened me. I had misheard, and what was being said was *Alain Resnais*, the name of the director! The film itself was called *Providence*. I knew Resnais's reputation and had seen *Hiroshima Mon Amour* and *Last Year in Marienbad*, so I was interested.

Sitting alone in the Billancourt studio, I saw the film. It was in English and had splendid actors, but at that stage I understood very little of what it was about. However, I saw many possibilities for interesting music. At the end of the showing Resnais appeared and introduced himself, asking whether I would be interested in writing the music. I said I would and he seemed very pleased. So was I when it turned out he knew *all* my music, not just my film scores.

Resnais and I had long discussions about the music. He knew exactly what he wanted, and told me that there would be forty-two minutes of music in the film. Amazing! Usually by this time the directors are bored to tears with their pictures, and have only the vaguest of suggestions to make. But Resnais had thought it all out carefully and intelligently; stylistically, artistically and dramatically he was completely prepared. He was an artist of the highest calibre.

I made detailed notes as we went through the film reel by reel, because it was so complex and difficult. I needed constant guidance and reassurance from Resnais; week by week I would get him to come and listen to what I had written, and there was never a word of disagreement from him, with one exception. One scene had an explosion in it, and I assumed (under Hollywood's influence) that the music would be expected to explode as well. When I played my 'exploding' music to Resnais he said, 'No synchronisation, please. I don't want any synchronisation.' I couldn't have been more pleased, as I have always been opposed to the idea of music merely duplicating what is being shown on the screen. In my view the music should add a new dimension, should tell the audience something it can't be told in any other way. And I was also pleased to hear Resnais say that in the dubbing there would be no conflict between music and effects; either one or the other would be featured, not both simultaneously. I remembered the long heavy battle scenes in films like *Ivanhoe* and *El Cid*, the millions of notes I had expended in composing music designed to carry the action forward and invest it with all the necessary colour, drama and excitement. Then what happened? In the dubbing the music would be all but annihilated by the tiring 'realism' of effects.

It was good to be working in Paris again. My mind went back some forty years to when I had been there as a young man composing the *Theme, Variations and Finale*, and where I had discovered to my amazement that a reputable composer like Honegger wrote, as I thought, 'foxtrots' for films. The score of *Providence* includes

Dirk Bogarde and Ellen Burstyn in *Providence*

a little piece for piano and strings called *Valse Crépusculaire* (Twilight Waltz) which sounds to me like a nostalgic reminiscence of my youth in *la ville lumière*. I first thought of it walking in the narrow streets of Montparnasse, *à la recherche du temps perdu*.

Resnais asked for 'une musique grise' — grey music — for *Providence*, and I dubbed the score my 'anti *Ben-Hur*', for it had absolutely nothing of the spectacular about it. We recorded it in London with the excellent National Philharmonic Orchestra, and Resnais seemed delighted with everything. During the dubbing he telephoned me from Paris to say that, in his view, one of the shorter, less important dialogue scenes worked better without music than with it. Would I have any objection to my music being taken out in this instance? Of course I had no objection whatever, but what touched me was the fact that this great artist had had the courtesy to ask for my approval *before* making what was a very minor modification to my score. Normally the composer is the last to know, and by the time he does know he is powerless to do anything about it. *Providence* proved a great success in Europe and Great Britain, and my collaboration with Resnais I count among my happiest.

With Resnais recording *Providence*   Receiving honorary doctorate from Wooster

I had had to drop my work on the Viola Concerto for the sake of *Providence,* and when I came to take it up again somehow the spell was broken. This has always been one of the severest penalties my Double Life has imposed upon me. During the composing of the Viola Concerto I had to contend with three major interruptions, and each one meant the discarding of a movement or part of a movement. During one of the periods in which I had had to put the Concerto on one side I even wrote a completely unrelated work, the *Toccata Capricciosa* for unaccompanied cello, which I dedicated to the memory of Piatigorsky. Musicologists tell me that the origins of my music in folksong — which in its pristine state is of course unaccompanied — account for the success of my works for unaccompanied instruments: the Sonata for Two Violins, the Sonatina for Clarinet Solo and my latest, this *Toccata Capricciosa* for cello. The work is not an elegy: rather does it reflect something of Piatigorsky's incomparable vitality, open-heartedness, buoyancy and bravado, qualities which he shared with his teacher, Julius Klengel (to whom my Cello Duo is dedicated), and which are sadly missing in many performing artists today.

Another film which delayed the completion of the Viola Concerto was Larry Cohen's *The Private Files of J. Edgar Hoover,* a dramatised biographical account of the founder of the FBI; it has so far not been released in America but was a great critical success in England. Again I came to London to do the recording, which took place in Anvil Studios at Denham. Forty-year-old memories of the Korda days, *Knight without Armour, The Four Feathers, The Thief of Baghdad,* all came flooding back, especially since around this time all these scores were being revived in the

202

With André Previn (centre) and John Williams, Pittsburgh 1979

form of new recordings. I went to Denham cemetery to pay my respects to the memory of my great collaborator, Lord Vansittart. I found a modest marble slab dedicated to him. There should be a London memorial to this great man, who was almost alone in warning English politicians of the impending German danger.

Another pleasurable experience was *Time after Time*, a semi-tongue-in-cheek fantasy in which H. G. Wells and Jack the Ripper are transported by the Time Machine from late-Victorian London to present-day San Francisco. Music is especially important in fantasy films on account of the dimension of reality it provides. Of this the young writer/director Nicholas Meyer (author of *The Seven Per Cent Solution*) was not only intelligently aware, but not afraid to acknowledge openly the contribution he said my music had made to his picture. He and his producer took a full page in Variety to thank me, a public gesture the like of which had never been made before in all my years in Hollywood. The picture was a big success when it came out, and so was the record album that was released along with it.

In the early summer of 1980 the Academy of Science Fiction, Fantasy and Horror Films gave me their 'Best Music of 1979' award for my score to this film. At the same time Wooster College in the state of Ohio conferred upon me my third honorary doctorate of music. I felt much like Brahms, who said that although awards and public tokens of recognition didn't interest him he liked to have them all the same.

Early in 1978 recognition had come from two relatively unexpected quarters. My music for *Providence* won the César, the French Oscar. I was warmed and touched, remembering again that it was in Paris I had first become aware of film music and conceived the notion that I too might make some mark in that area. It seemed fitting that at the outset of the last period of my creative life I should be so honoured by the very city where, in a sense, part of my life's work had begun.

The other award came from nearer home and was of poignant personal significance. For some time now my mother had been ailing: she was in her ninety-fourth year, and by early February 1978 it was evident that she could not live much longer. As far as was possible in a strange land, she had maintained a totally Hungarian way of life: she never properly learned English, read only Hungarian newspapers, had only Hungarian friends. Therefore, the news that I was to be presented with the Abraham Lincoln Award — bestowed as it was by the American–Hungarian Foundation — delighted her more than if I had been the recipient of a Nobel Prize. I received the award jointly with Dr Halsey Stevens, the distinguished composer and Bartók scholar, and in view of this I decided to talk at the ceremony not about myself but about Bartók in Los Angeles. This created a minor sensation and, when reported to my mother, gladdened the last days of her life. For her, Bartók's name meant her youth, when he played for the students in Professor Thomán's class.

In the spring of 1980 I was invited to open the Angers Festival with three concerts of my works. *En route* for Angers I passed through Paris, where I was treated by my colleagues somewhat as a returning long-lost brother. I felt as much at home there as when I first arrived in 1931, and insisted on staying in the same hotel, the Hotel Vernet in the rue Vernet. Again I found the same Etoile, the same Champs Elysées, the same beautiful, bewitching, ever-young Paris.

The reception at the French Performing Rights Society (SACEM), the innumerable newspaper, magazine, radio and television interviews, and, most important, the extreme kindness shown me by my composer-colleagues and the heart-warming spirit of fraternity in which they received me — for me this was a kind of apotheosis. At the SACEM reception I made a speech (in French, in which I seemed miraculously to have recovered my old fluency) recalling all the great Frenchmen who in one way or another had touched my life, always to the good — Dupré, Roland-Manuel, Honegger, Münch, Monteux, Feyder, Duvivier, Resnais. One composer said to me, 'Any friend of Honegger's is a friend of ours,' and I felt proud to think yes, I *had* been a friend of Honegger's. I remembered too the thrill with which in 1932 I saw the poster announcing my first Paris concert in the Ecole Normale de Musique; when now, in the front hall of the SACEM building, I saw the enormous posters announcing my Angers concert with a picture of myself and with my name in giant letters, I experienced the same thrill, and the intervening forty-eight years fell away as if they had never been. I realised too in that moment that were I twenty-four again and arriving in Paris for the first time, I should do exactly the same now as I did then.

Epilogue (stock-taking)

As I write these final pages of my recollections, I find myself in my early seventies; a good enough time to pause and take stock. What have I achieved in my life, how have I achieved it and has it been worth the achieving? For me a burning question has always been: was I right to devote so much creative energy to the writing of film music? Did I betray my heritage? My view is that I did not, inasmuch as I never lost sight of my *real* profession: that of composer, not of music to order but simply of the music that was in me to write. To this profession I remain always true; the title of this book implies as much, I think.

Yes, I had to come to terms with Hollywood, as did everyone in his own way who wished to contribute creatively to it. Of Hollywood as a community, I have written much; I could have written a great deal more, but these are things which are better left unsaid, at least by me.

What, I find myself wondering, would have become of me had I never been drawn into the cinema? Materially, certainly, I would have been greatly the poorer; and when I look at the careers of many of my Leipzig colleagues — grey, unfulfilled, limited lives lived out for the most part amid humdrum provincial academic surroundings — I feel grateful for the challenges and excitement offered me by my work in a complex, unpredictable, often exasperating but always vital medium.

Whether Hollywood affected in any crucial way the course of my purely musical development is hard for me to say. This much however must be entered to its credit: that it kept my feet firmly on the ground, it kept me in touch with my public. Inasmuch as more people are exposed to music through the cinema than through any other medium I feel it my duty to ensure that any music of mine they may hear shall be of the highest possible quality; it is, if you like, a way of educating people musically. And I do write my music for people, not for computers. I have said already, and in this instance I make no apology for repeating myself, that I believe in music as a form of communication; for me it is more an expression of emotion than an intellectual or cerebral crossword-puzzle. Like Sir Thomas Beecham I have no time for any music which does not stimulate pleasure in life, and, even more importantly, *pride* in life. For this reason I find myself as out of sympathy with the so-called avant-garde of today as I did with the avant-garde of my own youth — Schoenberg and the Second Viennese School. I am an unashamed champion of tonality. Its possibilities were supposed to be exhausted at the turn of the century; yet today, eighty years later, composers are still finding new and vital things to say within its framework. I am a traditionalist, but I believe tradition can be so recreated as to express the artist's own epoch while preserving its relationship with the past. I am old-fashioned enough also to maintain that no art is worthy of the name unless it contains some element of beauty. I have tried always in my own work to express human feelings and assert human values, and to do this I have never felt the slightest need to move outside the orbit of the tonal system. Tonality means line; line means melody; melody means song, and song, and especially folksong, is the essence of music, because it is the natural, spontaneous and primordial expression of human emotion.

There are those who would allege that my music, through its refusal to take cognizance of modish contemporary trends, can play no part in the present-day scheme of things, and is therefore devoid of meaning and value. Well, it may be so; yet my works appear on concert programmes all over the world; my films are constantly being screened in the cinemas and on television; I have festivals devoted to me; I get requests to make records and conduct concerts of my works, to give seminars, lectures, radio and television interviews, to receive academic honours. My fan-clubs flourish, and literally thousands of enthusiastic letters I receive each year testify to the fact that my music brings joy to people, stimulates pleasure in life and pride in life. And as an *apologia pro vita sua* — whether that life be single, double or quadruple — this is the most, and the best, that any creative artist has the right to expect.

Two survivors of the Golden Age: with Lillian Gish, Santa Fe, 1982

Appendix 1: List of concert works

1927	Trio-serenade, for string trio (revised 1974)	Op. 1	B&H
1928	Quintet in F minor, for piano and strings	Op. 2	B&H
1929	Rhapsody, for cello and orchestra	Op. 3	B&H
	Variations on a Hungarian Peasant Song, for violin and piano (also for violin and orch.)	Op. 4	B&H
	North Hungarian Peasant Songs and Dances, for violin and orch. (also for violin and piano)	Op. 5	B&H
1930	Symphony (unpublished)	Op. 6	—
1931	Duo, for violin and piano	Op. 7	B&H
	Duo, for cello and piano	Op. 8	B&H
1932	Variations, for piano solo	Op. 9	Salabert
	Serenade, for small orchestra (revised 1946 as Op. 25)	Op. 10	B&H
	Scherzo, for orchestra (unpublished)	Op. 11	—
	Six Bagatelles, for piano solo	Op. 12	B&H
1933	Theme, Variations and Finale, for orchestra (revised 1943 and 1966)	Op. 13	E
	Sonata, for two violins (revised 1973)	Op. 15	B&H
1935	Ballet, Hungaria	—	—
1938	Three Hungarian Sketches, for orchestra (revised 1958)	Op. 14	E
1940	Two Songs, for contralto and piano (Lord Vansittart)	Op. 16	FM
1942	High Flight — Song, for tenor and piano (John Magee)	—	FM
	The Jungle Book — Suite, for narrator and orchestra	—	BB
	Lullaby from The Jungle Book, for 4-part mixed chorus, *a cappella*	—	BB
1943	Concerto, for string orchestra (revised 1957)	Op. 17	B&H
1946	Lullaby and Madrigal of Spring, for female voices, *a cappella* (Max Krone)	Op. 18	AMP
	Kaleidoscope, for piano solo (also for orchestra)	Op. 19	AMP
	Spellbound Concerto, for piano and orchestra	—	Chappell
	To Everything there is a Season — Motet, for 8-part mixed chorus, with organ ad lib.	Op. 21	B&H
	Hungarian Serenade, for small orchestra	Op. 25	B&H
1948	Sonata, for piano solo	Op. 20	B&H
1950	Quartet no. 1, for strings	Op. 22	B&H
1951	Sonatina, for clarinet solo	Op. 27	BB
	Quo Vadis — Suite, for orchestra	—	UA
1952	The Vintner's Daughter — Variations, for piano solo (also for orchestra)	Op. 23	BB

1953	Concerto, for violin and orchestra	Op. 24	B&H
1957	Overture to a Symphony Concert, for orchestra (revised 1963)	Op. 26	E
1959	Ben-Hur — Suite, for orchestra	—	UA
1961	Twelve Short Choruses from Ben-Hur and King of Kings, for mixed chorus	—	UA
1964	Notturno Ungherese, for orchestra	Op. 28	B&H
1966	Sinfonia Concertante, for violin, cello and orchestra	Op. 29	B&H
	Tema con Variazioni (2nd mvt. of Op. 29), for violin, cello and chamber orchestra	Op. 29a	B&H
1967	The Vanities of Life — Motet, for 4-part mixed chorus, with organ ad lib.	Op. 30	B&H
	Concerto, for piano and orchestra	Op. 31	B&H
1968	Concerto, for cello and orchestra	Op. 32	B&H
1972	Tripartita, for orchestra	Op. 33	B&H
	Psalm 23, for 4-part mixed chorus, with organ ad lib.	Op. 34	BB
	Nostalgia — Two Songs, for soprano or tenor, and piano (Michael Gyarmathy)	—	FM
1975	Festive Flourish, for brass and percussion	—	BB
	Three Chinese Poems, for mixed chorus	Op. 35	BB
1977	Toccata Capricciosa, for cello solo	Op. 36	B&H
1979	Concerto, for viola and orchestra	Op. 37	B&H
1981	Quartet no. 2, for strings	Op. 38	B&H

B&H	Breitkopf & Härtel	FM:	Fentone Music
E:	Eulenburg	UA:	United Artists Music
BB:	Broude Brothers	AMP:	Associated Music Publishers

Appendix II: Filmography

1937	Knight without Armour		The Fugitive)
	Thunder in the City	1940	Four Dark Hours (US: The
	The Squeaker		Green Cockatoo; reissue: Race Gang)
	(US: Murder on Diamond Row)		The Thief of Baghdad
1938	The Divorce of Lady X	1941	That Hamilton Woman (GB:
1939	The Four Feathers		Lady Hamilton)
	The Spy in Black (US: U-Boat 29)		Lydia
	Ten Days in Paris (US: Missing		Sundown
	Ten Days/Spy in the Pantry)	1942	Rudyard Kipling's Jungle Book
	On the Night of the Fire (US:		(GB: The Jungle Book)

	Jacaré (GB: Jacaré—Killer of the Amazon)		The Light Touch
		1952	Ivanhoe
1943	Five Graves to Cairo		Plymouth Adventure
	So Proudly We Hail	1953	Julius Caesar
	Sahara		The Story of Three Loves
	The Woman of the Town		Young Bess
1944	The Hour Before the Dawn		All the Brothers were Valiant
	Double Indemnity		Knights of the Round Table
	Dark Waters	1954	Men of the Fighting Lady (GB:
	The Man in Half Moon Street		Panther Squadron)
1945	A Song to Remember (after		Valley of the Kings
	Chopin)		Seagulls over Sorrento (US: Crest
	Blood on the Sun		of the Wave)
	Lady on a Train		Green Fire
	The Lost Weekend	1955	Moonfleet
	Spellbound		The King's Thief
1946	Because of Him		Diane
	The Killers	1956	Tribute to a Badman
	The Strange Love of Martha Ivers		Bhowani Junction
1947	The Red House		Lust for Life
	Song of Scheherazade (after	1957	Something of Value
	Rimsky-Korsakov)		The Seventh Sin
	The Macomber Affair		Tip on a Dead Jockey
	Time Out of Mind (GB: Illusions)	1958	A Time to Love and a Time to
	The Other Love		Die
	Desert Fury	1959	The World, the Flesh and the
	Brute Force		Devil
1948	The Secret Beyond the Door		Ben-Hur
	A Woman's Vengeance (GB	1961	King of Kings
	reissue: The Gioconda Smile)		El Cid
	A Double Life	1962	Sodom and Gomorrah
	The Naked City	1963	The V.I.P.s
	Kiss the Blood off My Hands	1968	The Power
	(GB: Blood on My Hands)		The Green Berets
	Criss Cross	1970	The Private Life of Sherlock
1949	Command Decision		Holmes
	The Bribe	1973	The Golden Voyage of Sinbad
	Madame Bovary	1977	Providence
	The Red Danube	1978	The Private Files of J. Edgar
	Adam's Rib		Hoover
	East Side, West Side		Fedora
1950	The Asphalt Jungle	1979	The Last Embrace
	Crisis		Time after Time
	The Miniver Story	1980	Eye of the Needle
1951	Quo Vadis	1981	Dead Men don't wear Plaid

Appendix III: Discography (*Concert Music*)

(1) **Concert Works** (compiled by Frank DeWald)

	Label	Works	Performers	Availability/ Remarks
1	Alco 1210	Duo for Cello and Piano, op. 8 Bach: Concerto for Violin, Oboe and Orch.	Alec Compinsky, vc.; Sara Compinsky, pfte.	1951-*c*.1960
2	Vox PLP-7690	*Theme, Variations and Finale*, op. 13a Concerto for Strings, op. 17	London String Orch.; Royal Philharmonic Orch./ Rózsa	1952-*c*.1960
3	Concert Hall G4	*Hungarian Serenade*, op. 25 Lopatnikoff: Diverti- mento for Orch.	La Jolla Musical Arts Festival Orch./Nikolai Sokoloff	1953 Limited edition of 500 copies
4	Music Library 7071	*To Everything There Is a Season*, op. 21 Wilson: *A Thing of Beauty, Finger of God* Ives: *Harvest Home Chorale III*	Columbia University Teachers' College Choir/ Harry Robert Wilson	1955-1973
5	RCA LM-2027	Violin Concerto, op. 24 Spohr: Violin Concerto Tchaikovsky: *Sérénade Mélancolique*	Jascha Heifetz, vl.; Dallas SO/Walter Hendl	1956-1969
6	Capitol 8376	Piano Sonata, op. 20 Bartók: Piano Sonata Prokofiev: Piano Sonata	Leonard Pennario, pfte.	1957-*c*.1960
7	MGM E-3565	Concerto for Strings, op. 17 Rieti: *Dance Variations*	MGM String Orch./ Carlos Surinach	1957-*c*.1960
8	MGM E-3631	*Hungarian Serenade*, op. 25 Kodály: *Summer Evening*	MGM Orch./Arthur Winograd	1958-*c*.1961

Label	Works	Performers	Availability/ Remarks
9 Decca DL-9966	*Theme, Variations, and Finale,* op. 13a *Three Hungarian Sketches,* op. 14 *Concert Overture,* op. 26	Frankenland State SO/Rózsa	1958-1970
10 MGM E-3645 SE 3645	*North Hungarian Peasant Songs and Dances,* op. 5 *The Vintner's Daughter,* op. 23a *Hungarian Serenade,* op. 25	Oliver Colbentson, vl.; Frankenland State SO/ Erich Kloss	1958-1965 Limited circulation
11 West- minster XWN- 18805 WST- 14035	*Variations on a Hungarian Peasant Song,* op. 4 Concerto for Strings, op. 17 *Kaleidoscope,* op. 19a	Dénes Zsigmondy, vl.; Vienna State Opera Orch./ Rózsa	1959-*c.*1962
12 Dot DLP-3304 DLP-25304	*To Everything There is a Season,* op. 21 Wright: *The Psalms of David*	Hollywood Methodist Church Choir/ Norman Söreng Wright	1960-1969
R-1 RCA LM-2767 LSC-2767	(Stereophonic reissue of No. 5 with a different coupling, the *Romantic Fantasy* of Arthur Benjamin)		1964-1977
13 RCA LM-2770 LSC-2770	*Tema con Variazioni,* op. 29a Beethoven: Piano Trio Haydn: Divertimento for Cello and Orch.	Jascha Heifetz, vl.; Gregor Piatigorsky, vc.; chamber orch./Heifetz	1964-
14 RCA LM-2802 LSC-2802	*Theme, Variations, and Finale,* op. 13a *Three Hungarian Sketches,* op. 14 *Concert Overture,* op. 26a *Notturno Ungherese,* op. 28	RCA Italiana Orch./Rózsa	1965-1967
15 Orion ORS-73127	*Variations on a Hungarian Peasant Song* op. 4	Endre Granat, vl.; Erwin Herbst, pfte. Leonard Pennario, pfte.	1973-

Label	Works	Performers	Availability/ Remarks
	North Hungarian Peasant Songs and Dances, op. 5 Duo for Violin and Piano, op. 7		
16 Orion ORS-74137	*Kaleidoscope*, op. 19 Piano Sonata, op. 20 Castelnuovo-Tedesco: *Le Danze del Re David; Cipressi*	Albert Dominguez, pfte.	1974
17 Grossmont FM-74051	Sonatina for Clarinet Solo, op. 27 Various short works by Karg-Elert, Wellesz, Stravinsky, Doran and Sutermeister	Charles MacLeod, cl.	Dates unknown; Limited circulation
18 Orion ORS-75191	String Trio, op. la Quintet, op. 2	Endre Granat, vl.; Milton Thomas, vla.; Nathaniel Rosen, vc.; Sheldon Sanov, vc.; Leonard Pennario, pfte.	1974-
R-2 Ember ECL 9043 (UK)	(Midprice reissue of No. 15)		1976-
R-3 RCA Gold Seal GL-25010 (UK)	(Midprice reissue of No. 14)		1976-
R-4 Citadel CT-6001	(Reissue of No. 10, minus op. 5 and with added narration in op. 23a)		1976-
R-5 West- minster Gold WG-8353	(Budget reissue of No. 11)		1977-
19 Entr'acte ERS-6509	Duo for Cello and Piano, op. 8 Sonata for Two Violins, op. 15a *Toccata Capricciosa*, op. 36	Jeffrey Solow, vc.; Albert Dominguez, pfte.; Endre Granat and Sheldon Sanov, vc.	1978-

	Label	Works	Performers	Availability/Remarks
20	Entr'acte ERS-6512	*To Everything There Is a Season*, op. 21 *The Vanities of Life*, op. 30 The Twenty-third Psalm, op. 34	Choir of the West/ Maurice Skones	1978-
21	Citadel CT-7004	Variations for Piano, op. 9 *Bagatelles* for Piano, op. 12 Sonatina for Clarinet Solo, op. 27 *Valse Crépusculaire* (from *Providence*)	Albert Dominguez, pfte.; Ralph Gari, cl.	1978-
22	Vox SVBX-5109 (3 discs)	String Quartet, op. 22 Quartets by Bloch, Hindemith, Korngold, Stravinsky, Surinach, and Tcherepnin	New World Quartet	1978-
R-6	Varese-Sarabande VC-81058	(Reissue of No. 9)		1978-
23	Unicorn UNS-259 (UK) UNI-72029 (US)	Variations, op. 9 *Bagatelles*, op. 12 Piano Sonata, op. 20 *The Vintner's Daughter* op. 23	Eric Parkin, pfte.	1979

Appendix IV: Discography (Film Music)

(2) **Film Music (Select)** (compiled by Alan Hamer)

1937 Knight without Armour
●Suite (arr. Christopher Palmer)—
Polydor 2383 384
RPO/Rózsa

1939 The Four Feathers
●Sunstroke/River Journey—
RCA ARL 1-0911
Nat.PO/Charles Gerhardt

1940   The Thief of Baghdad
●Suite—RCA LM 2118
Frankenland State SO/Rózsa; narrator:
Leo Genn
Reissue: United Artists 29725
●Highlights—EB Collection No. 8
(Filmmusic Collection)
RPO/Elmer Bernstein
Reissue: Warner Brothers BSK 3183
●The Love of the Princess—RCA ARL
1-0911
Nat.PO/Gerhardt
●Short Suite—Polydor 238332
RPO/Rózsa

1941   That Hamilton Woman
Lady Hamilton (UK)
●Love theme—Polydor 2383 440
(DGG 2584 021—Europe and USA)
RPO/Rózsa
●Love theme—Varese-Sarabande
VCDM 100020
LSO/Morton Gould

1941   Lydia
●Concerto and Four Piano
Improvisations—Citadel CT-7010
Albert Dominguez, pfte.
●Main theme and waltz; Four Piano
Improvisations—Polydor 2383 440
(DGG 2584 021—Europe and USA)
Eric Parkin, pfte.; RPO/Rózsa
●Waltz—MGM E-SE 4112
Rome SO/Rózsa
Reissue: MFP 5232

1942   Jungle Book
●Suite—RCA Victor DM 905, 3 × 12″,
78 rpm
NBC SO/Rózsa; narrator: Sabu
Reissue: Sound Stage 2309 (non-
commercial)
Reissue: Entr'acte ERM 6002
●Suite—RCA LM 2118
Frankenland State SO/Rózsa; narrator:

Leo Genn
Reissue: United Artists 29725
●Song of the Jungle—RCA ARL 1-0911
Nat. PO/Gerhardt
●Suite—Colosseum Colos SM 6662
Nuremberg SO/Klauspeter Seibel;
narrator: Elmar Gunsch

1943   Five Graves to Cairo
●Suite—Polydor 2383 440 (DGG
2584 021—Europe and USA)
RPO/Rózsa

1943   Sahara
●Main Title—RCA ARL 1-0422
Nat. PO/Gerhardt
Reissue: RCA AGL 1-3782

1944   Double Indemnity
●Mrs Dietrichson/The Conspiracy—
RCA ARL 1-0911
Nat. PO/Gerhardt
●Suite—Polydor 2383 384
RPO/Rózsa

1944   Dark Waters
●Soundtrack excerpts—TT-MR-4 (non-
commercial)
Studio Orch./Rózsa

1945   Blood on the Sun
●Soundtrack excerpts—Citadel CT-6031
Studio Orch./Rózsa

1945   The Lost Weekend
Soundtrack excerpts—TT-MR-2 (non-
commercial)
Studio Orch./Rózsa
●Suite—RCA ARL 1-0911
Nat. PO/Gerhardt
●The Walk along Third Avenue and
Love Theme—Polydor 2383 327
(DGG 2584 013—Europe and USA)
RPO/Rózsa

1945   Spellbound
●Eight excerpts from the soundtrack—
ARA A-2, 4 × 10″, 78 rpm
Studio Orch./Rózsa
Reissue: REM LP 1, 10″
Reissue: Archive Album—AEI 3103
●Concerto (orchestral version)—
Capitol L 453, 10″
Frankenland State SO/Kloss
Reissue: Capitol P 456
●Concerto (version for pfte. and orch.)
—Capitol SMK 1036
Leonard Pennario, pfte.; Hollywood
Bowl SO/Rózsa
Reissue: Capitol SP 8598, SP 8494,
SP 8689 (etc.)
●Near-complete, 1957—Warner
Brothers WS-1213
Orch./Ray Heindorf
Reissue: Stanyan SRQ 4021
●Concerto—EMI TWOX 1007
Semprini, pfte.; Ron Goodwin Orch.;
●Concerto—Angel SZ-37757
(EMI-ASD 3862)
Bournemouth SO/Kenneth Alwyn;
Daniel Adni, pfte.
●Paranoia theme and Concerto
(orchestral version)—MGM E-SE-4112
Rome SO/Rózsa
Reissue: MFP 5232
●Dream Sequence/Mountain Lodge—
RCA ARL 1-0911
Nat. PO/Gerhardt

1946   The Strange Love of
Martha Ivers
The Killers
●Theme—Sound Stage 2308 (non-
commercial)
●Soundtrack excerpts—TT-MR-4 (non-
commercial)
Studio Orch./Rózsa
●Two excerpts (in Suite *Background to
Violence*)—Decca 710015
Frankenland State SO/Rózsa

Reissue: MCA 7205
Reissue: Varese-Sarabande VC 81053
●Prelude—Polydor 2383 440
(DGG 2584 021—Europe and USA)
RPO/Rózsa

1947   The Red House
●Suite (four excerpts)—Capitol CB 48,
2 × 10″ 78 rpm
Frankenland State SO/Kloss
Reissue: Capitol L 453, 10″
Reissue: Capitol P 456
●Suite—RCA ARL 1-0911
Nat. PO/Gerhardt

1947   Song of Scheherazade
●Four songs adapted from Rimsky-
Korsakov—Columbia OL OR MK 272,
2 × 10″, 78 rpm. Tenor: Charles
Kullman

1947   Time out of Mind
●New England Symphonette (arr.
Castelnuovo-Tedesco)—Première
Records PR 1201 (non-commercial)
Live broadcast transcription of
Hollywood Bowl concert. Orch./Rózsa
Reissue: TT-MR-4 (non-commercial)

1947   Brute Force
●Soundtrack excerpts—TT-MR-3 (non-
commercial)
●Two excerpts (in Suite *Background to
Violence*)—Decca 710015
Frankenland State SO/Rózsa
Reissue: MCA 7205
Reissue: Varese-Sarabande VC 81053

1948   A Double Life
●Suite—Sound Stage 2308 (non-
commercial)
Live broadcast transcription of
Hollywood Bowl concert. Orch./Rózsa
Reissue: Première Records PR 1201
(non-commercial)

●Fantasy—Polydor 2383 327 (DGG
2584 013—Europe and USA)
RPO/Rózsa

1945   The Naked City
●Pursuit and Epilogue (in Suite
Background to Violence)—TT-MR-3 (non-
commercial)
●Pursuit and Epilogue—Decca 710015
Frankenland State SO/Rózsa
Reissue: MCA 7205
Reissue: Varese-Sarabande VC 81053
●Pursuit and Epilogue—Polydor 2383
327 (DGG 2584 013—Europe and USA)
RPO/Rózsa

1949   Madame Bovary
●Soundtrack excerpts—MGM E-3507
MGM SO/Rózsa
Reissue: MGM Select 2353095
Reissue: MGM MI-1394
●Waltz—MGM E-SE-4112
Rome SO/Rózsa
Reissue: MFP 5232
Reissue: MGM 2SE-10
●Highlights—EB Collection No. 12
(Filmmusic Collection)
RPO/Elmer Bernstein

1949   The Red Danube
●Suite—Polydor 2383 440 (DGG 2584
021—Europe and USA)
RPO/Rózsa

1950   The Asphalt Jungle
●Prologue and Epilogue—Polydor 2383
384
RPO/Rózsa

1950   Crisis
●Revolution March/Village Square—
MGM 10756
V. Gomez, guitar
Reissue: Sound Stage 2308 (non-
commercial)

●Guitar Suite—Citadel CT-7004
Darryl Denning, guitar

1951   Quo Vadis
●Soundtrack excerpts (without
dialogue)—
MGM E-103, 4 × 10″, 78 rpm
RPO/BBC Choir/Rózsa
Reissue: MGM E-103, 10″
●Dramatic highlights (soundtrack:
dialogue and music)—MGM E 134, 2 ×
10″
Reissue: MGM E 3524
●Suite—Capitol L 454
Frankenland State SO/Kloss
Reissue: Capitol P 456
●Three Movements from Suite—Capitol
ST-2837
Capitol SO/Rózsa
Reissue: Angel 36063
●Triumphal March—MGM E-SE-4112
Rome SO/Rózsa
Reissue: MFP 5323
Reissue: MGM 2SE-10
Reissue: MGM Select 2353092
●1978 Re-recording—Decca PFS
4430/LON 21180
RPO/Saltarello Choir/Rózsa

1952   Ivanhoe
●Soundtrack excerpts—MGM 179, 10″
MGM SO/Rózsa
Reissue: MGM 3507
Reissue: MGM Select 2353095
Reissue: MGM MI 1394
●Overture: RCA ARL 1-0911
Nat. PO/Gerhardt

1952   Plymouth Adventure
●Soundtrack excerpts—MGM 179, 10″
MGM SO/Rózsa
Reissue: MGM 3507
Reissue: MGM Select 2353095
Reissue: MGM MI 1394

1953 The Story of Three Loves
●Nocturne/Love Scene—Polydor 2383 327 (DGG 2584 013—Europe and USA)
RPO/Rózsa

1953 Julius Caesar
●Dramatic highlights (soundtrack—music and dialogue)—MGM E-3033
MGM SO/Rózsa
Reissue: MFP 2122
●Suite—Decca PFS-4315
Nat. PO/Bernard Herrmann
Reissue: London 21132
●Overture—RCA ARL 42005
Nat. PO/Gerhardt
●Overture (revised version)—Polydor 2383 440 (DGG 2584 021—Europe and USA)
●Brutus' Soliloquy—DCT DLP 3107
Orch./Elmer Bernstein
Reissue: Contour 2870337

1953 Young Bess
●Highlights—EB Collection No. 5 (Filmmusic Collection)
RPO/Elmer Bernstein
●Suite—Polydor 2383 327 (DGG 2584 013—Europe and USA)
RPO/Rózsa

1953 Knights of the Round Table
●Soundtrack excerpts—Varese-Sarabande STV 81128
LSO/Muir Mathieson
●Scherzo (Hawks-in-Flight)—RCA ARL 1-0911
Nat. PO/Gerhardt
Reissue: RCA RL 42005
●Suite—Polydor 2383 327 (DGG 2584 013—Europe and USA)
RPO/Rózsa

1954 Men of the Fighting Lady
●Blind Flight—Polydor 2383 384
RPO/Rózsa

1954 Green Fire
●Theme—Sound Stage 2308 (non-commercial)
●Theme—Major 139
Orch./Joe Leahy
Reissue: PARLO R-4016

1955 Moonfleet
●Seascape (Prelude)—Polydor 2383 384
RPO/Rózsa

1955 Diane
●Beauty and Grace—MGM E-SE-4112
Rome SO/Rózsa
Reissue: MFP 5232
●Finale—Polydor 2383 327 (DGG 2584 013—Europe and USA)
RPO/Rózsa

1956 Tribute to a Badman
●Suite—Polydor 2383 384
RPO/Rózsa
●Suite—Varese-Sarabande VCDM 1000.20
LSO/Morton Gould

1956 Lust for Life
●Suite—Decca 710015
Frankenland State SO/Rózsa
Reissue: MCA 7205
Reissue: HIGH USR 7474 (non-commercial)
Reissue: Varese-Sarabande VC 81053
●Short Suite ('Summer and Sunflowers')—Polydor 2383 384
RPO/Rózsa

1958 A Time to Love and a Time to Die
●Soundtrack excerpts—Decca DL 8778
Studio orch./Rózsa

Reissue: MCA VIM 7204
Reissue: Varese-Sarabande VC 81075
●Love Scene—Polydor 2383 327
(DGG 2584 013—Europe and USA)
RPO/Rózsa

1959   Ben-Hur
●Suite—Capitol ST-2837
Capitol SO/Rózsa
Reissue: ANGEL S 36063
●Prelude—CBS BPG 62246
Orch./Rózsa
Reissue: Columbia CS 8918
●MGM Deluxe MlEl
Rome SO/Carlo Savina
Reissue: MGM Fold Out SlEl
Reissue: MGM Silver Screen 2353030
Reissue: MGM MMF 1009
●MGM Lion SL 70123
Frankenland State SO/Kloss
●MGM SE 3900 (More Music from)
Frankenland State SO/Kloss
Reissue: MGM Select 2353075
Reissue: Metro MS-503
Reissue: MGM C-857
●Suite (arr. Black)—Decca PFS 4243
(London SP 44173)
Nat. PO/Stanley Black
Reissue: Decca STBA 2
●Suite—EMI TWOX 1034
Ron Goodwin Orch.
1977 Re-recording—Decca PF3 4394
Nat. PO/Rózsa
Reissue: London SPC 21166

1960   King of Kings
●1960 Re-recording—
MGM Deluxe SIE/IE2
Rome SO/Singers of Roman
Basilicas/Rózsa
Reissue: MGM Silver Screen 2353035
●Suite—Capitol ST-2837
Capitol SO/Rózsa
Reissue: Angel 36063

●Devil Scene—Decca PFS 4432
Nat. PO/Stanley Black
●Robert Ryan reads from the New
Testament with incidental music from
1960 Re-recording—MGM E-SKI 3970
●*King of Kings—The Story of Christ in
Song* (twelve short choruses arranged for
SATB [accompaniment ad lib] from the
scores for *Ben-Hur* and *King of Kings*)—
Medallion ML311
The Brigham Young University A
Cappella Choir/Ralph Woodward

1960   El Cid
●1960 Re-recording—MGM E 3977
Graunke SO of Munich/Rózsa
Reissue: MGM Silver Screen 2353046
(+ one extra excerpt)
●Suite—Capitol ST-2837
Capitol SO/Rózsa
Reissue: Angel S 36063

1962   Sodom and Gomorrah
●Soundtrack excerpts—RCA LSO 1076
Rome SO/Rózsa
Reissue: RCA CR-10023 (RVC)
●Other soundtrack excerpts—
Citadel CT-MR-1 (non-commercial)
●Love Theme and Answer to a
Dream—MGM E-SE-4112 Rome
SO/Rózsa
Reissue: MFP 5232

1963   The V.I.P.s
●1963 Re-recording—MGM E-4152
Rome SO/Rózsa

1968   The Power
●Soundtrack excerpts—Citadel
CT-MR-1 (non-commercial)
Studio Orch./Rózsa

1968   The Green Berets
●March Theme—MFP 5171
Orch./Geoff Love

1970　The Private Life of
Sherlock Holmes
● Fantasy—Polydor 2383 440
(DGG 2584 021—Europe and USA)
RPO/Rózsa

1973　The Golden Voyage of Sinbad
● Soundtrack excerpts—United Artists
UAS 29576
Rome SO/Rózsa
Reissue: LA-309-G

1977　Providence
● Soundtrack excerpts—Pathé Marconi
C 066-14406
Reissue: DRG 9502
Nat. PO/Rózsa
● *Valse Crépusculaire*—Citadel CT-7004
Albert Dominguez, pfte.

1977　Fedora
● Soundtrack excerpts—Varese-
Sarabande STV 81108
Graunke SO of Munich/Rózsa

1979　Time after Time
● 1979 Re-recording—Entr'acte
ERS 6517
RPO/Rózsa

1981　Eye of the Needle
● 1981 Re-recording—Varèse Sarabande
STV-81133
Nuremberg SO/Rózsa
Reissue: That's Entertainment,
TER 1010

INDEX
(Figures in italics indicate pages of illustration)

223